THE
NEW POLAND

BERNARD NEWMAN

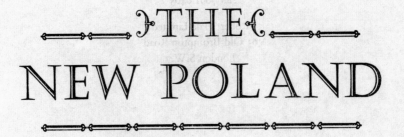

THE
NEW POLAND

*Illustrated
and with maps*

ROBERT HALE · LONDON

© Bernard Newman 1968
First published in Great Britain 1968

SBN 7091 0405 7

Robert Hale Limited
63 Old Brompton Road
London S.W.7

PRINTED IN GREAT BRITAIN
BY EBENEZER BAYLIS AND SON, LTD.
THE TRINITY PRESS, WORCESTER, AND LONDON

CONTENTS

ILLUSTRATIONS

MAPS

PICTURE CREDITS

Colour: Polska Agencia Interpress; black and white, Bernard Newman except the first six which are from official Polish sources.

INTRODUCTION

THE TRUMPETER OF CRACOW

I

EVERY hour, day or night, people in the market square of Cracow gaze upwards to the higher of the two towers of St. Mary's Church. A man with a silver trumpet appears at four windows in turn, facing the four points of the compass. There he begins to sound the alarm. After a couple of bars it stops abruptly—not merely breaking the air of the alarm, but breaking the last note he plays.

In 1241 Poland was ravaged by Tatar invaders. As their army poured into Cracow, a watchman with a trumpet sounded the alarm. He was espied by a Tatar archer, whose arrow pierced his throat. And for hundreds of years the trumpeters of Cracow have sounded the *heynal*, breaking off in the middle of a note—exactly where their predecessor died so long ago.

Today Cracow is a modern city in a country with a Communist government. More than once the suggestion has been made that the old-fashioned *heynal* should be replaced by a chiming clock. The very idea rouses the citizens of Cracow to anger. But at last a compromise was arranged. A conventional chime sounds a few seconds *before* the hour, to be followed by the *heynal* at the hour itself. I asked the trumpeter if he would care to be replaced by a clock: he stared at me in utter incomprehension.

Warsaw was almost completely destroyed by the Nazis, and even when the war ended the remnants of its population were still living in appalling conditions in shacks and cellars. Obviously it would take years to rebuild the city. Where should reconstruction begin?

With the historic Old Town, was the decision. Foreign

architects, especially the Americans, assumed and urged that Warsaw should begin again, and that a completely new concrete city should emerge. No, the people decided. Not only the Old Town first, but the Old Town reconstructed exactly as it was before its destruction. But this would take much longer than concrete buildings. Never mind that: we will put up with our shacks and cellars. Restore the Old Town as it was.

I referred to the towers of the church at Cracow, which is known affectionately to the citizens as Marjacki, Little Mary. The towers are not twins: are not even of the same height. They were built, declares legend, by two brothers. The elder was a hard worker, and his tower rose more rapidly than that of his brother. The latter, jealous, took an iron knife and killed him.

A legend, but it has been told and believed in for centuries. As proof, you may see the knife, hanging on the wall of the Cloth Hall in the market place nearby. And the twin towers are certainly very different.

The most ancient versions of the legend agree as to its origin. They differ in their endings. In one, the murderer committed suicide by jumping from his tower: this is not improbable. In another, the tower of the murdered man completed itself miraculously and beautifully, in a cupola lacking in the tower by its side.

And inside the church is a lovely retable, carved by Wit Stwosz, which we shall see later. Ask almost any Pole about its creator, and he will describe him as a Polish genius of ancient time. (Official accounts do not confirm this. They refer not to the artist but to the triptych as the outstanding work of art in Poland, or even as the outstanding work of Polish art.) But Wit Stwosz is none other than Viet Stoss, the Nuremberg master sculptor of the fifteenth century. True, he did most of his best work in Poland, but he was not a Pole.

A more recent note on Cracow. When Gomulka became the Communist leader of Poland in 1956, he made some decisions which won him popularity. The Polish army was wearing Russian uniforms, and disliked them intensely. Gomulka decided to revert to Polish uniforms.

Cracow, near the mountains, was the headquarters of a Highland brigade. In 1957 I visited the city, and found the streets crowded with excited people: a highland battalion was to make its first ceremonial march in its new uniforms.

The men marched proudly, their khaki cloaks swaying in unison, their billy-cock hats firmly set. And their reception was remarkable. Some people clapped, and others cheered: some smiled and others wept, but many more knelt down in prayer.

Later in the day I had a meal with a senior Polish officer. "This is a happy day," he said. "The troops are celebrating. Listen to them." I heard the sound of hearty singing. German troops sing on the word of command: Polish soldiers sing without any formal order.

"Yes, they are glad to discard the Russian uniforms. Do not misunderstand me. They know that it is essential for Poland to be on terms of close friendship with Russia."

"Tell me this," I said. "Suppose—I don't think it will happen, but suppose the world went to war and a British and American army approached the frontiers of Poland. What would your soldiers do?"

"Oh, that is easy to answer. Most of them would turn round and fight on your side." But he added emphatically: "That is, so long as you did not bring the Germans with you!"

Poland used to be described as "the eastern outpost of Catholicism". This was true, but Poland is not an Eastern country: it belongs to *Central* Europe.

Take a map of Europe, and draw a series of lines across it from end to end—from Iceland to Istanbul, from Gibraltar to the easternmost point in the Urals, from North Cape to Cape Matapan, from Sicily to the Kora Sea, and from Land's End to Astrakhan. Your lines will meet near Warsaw.

This may prove to be significant: for the first time throughout the history of human travel, in these days of aerial transport, the shortest distance between two points is a straight line.

In the main street of Warsaw is a large building, the headquarters of the United Workers', or Communist, Party.

Inside it one day I met a Polish member of Parliament. He looked at me seriously, and suddenly demanded: "What is the difference between Capitalism and Communism?"

It was after lunch, and I did not immediately perceive that the major portion of his lunch must have been liquid. I sat back to consider my answer, but he gave me no time.

"What is the difference between Capitalism and Communism?" he repeated. "I'll tell you. Under Capitalism, man exploits man. Under Communism, it's *vice versa*."

On my 1945 journey I met a famous Russian general, commanding the Soviet armies in Poland.

Elections were due, on the usual Communist single-list model. We were on good terms, and I pulled his leg gently.

"You know, if you had a really free election here, you wouldn't get 20 per cent of the votes."

"You're quite wrong."

"I don't believe I am. I have been round the villages as well as the towns. Twenty per cent."

"You are quite wrong," he said. "We shouldn't get 10 per cent of the votes. But," he added, "come back and look at the country in twenty-five years' time."

In September, 1967, I heard President de Gaulle address the Polish Seym, or parliament. Mr. Gomulka replied. Each man roused enthusiasm only at one point—where he referred to the integrity of the Oder-Neisse frontier.

I found that this question was paramount all over Poland. Britain and U.S.A. had never recognized the frontier—the Yalta agreement declared that the question must await the final peace treaty—which has not yet been signed! But everyone believed that something was going to happen—and they could not be blamed.

In February, 1967, Mr. Kosygin, Prime Minister of the Soviet Union, paid an official visit to Britain. The final joint communiqué contained many platitudes: the two countries would work for peace and *détente* in Europe. They "noted" several promising moves towards international co-operation, and concluded that "the encouragement of such co-operation between all countries of eastern and western Europe on the basis of respect for their sovereign equality and territorial integrity should continue to be a major aim of both Governments."

At his press conference Mr. George Brown had to answer

questions from international journalists about the phrase concerning "territorial integrity". Did this mean that Britain had at last recognized the Oder-Neisse line? He replied, very deliberately, "Yes, in a way."

The phrase was received with joy in Poland but with opposition in Germany. Mr. Brown later explained that what he had in mind was that one day, when a German peace treaty was signed and the wishes of the inhabitants of the area had been considered, the existing line would obviously become the final frontier.

This explanation was largely ignored in Poland, where the newspapers banked on Mr. Brown's "Yes, in a way". What way? Could there be more than one? It seemed that Britain was about to follow France in recognizing the disputed frontier. The Poles ignored the German reactions.

A mixed group of men were wrecked on a desert island. The two Scotsmen founded a Burns Club and the two Welshmen a choir: the two Irishmen began to fight, while the two Englishmen did not speak to each other, as they had not been introduced. And the two Poles founded three political parties.

Ignace Paderewski, the famous pianist who became the first prime minister of the new-born Poland at the end of the First World War, used to tell the story of a cosmopolitan university. One of its professors gave to his students, as the subject for a thesis, "The Elephant".

Later he began to mark their efforts. The English student had headed his essay: "The Elephant—how to hunt him". A Frenchman had chosen the more intriguing title, "The Love Life of the Elephant". A German student preferred: "An introduction to a preliminary study of the gastronomic possibilities of the Elephant". The American wrote on "How to build bigger and better Elephants". The Russian produced the startling title: "The Elephant—does it exist?" And the Polish student headed his thesis: "The Elephant and the Polish question".

The stories and incidents I have quoted have a distinct bearing on the minds of the Polish people today. Tradition means a good deal to them, and is seldom if ever willingly discarded. But despite their intense pride in their land, the Poles *can* compromise.

And their love of tradition does not preclude modern ideas or
keep them from facing a situation which might be unpleasing.
The history of Poland shows that it has only been safe while its
neighbours Russia and Germany were on bad terms. When they
were friends, Poland suffered. The last occasion was in 1939,
when Stalin and Hitler made the pact which precipitated the war.
A nation steeped in history is unlikely to forget this—or the
German conduct in occupied Poland. Six million Poles died—
more than one-fifth of the population: most of them were
murdered. The survivors find this terror difficult to forget. A
Western alliance proved to be useless: Britain and France were
too far away—and today they are very friendly with Germany:
so Poland turned to Russia. Stalin had imposed on the Poles a
very unpopular Communist government; but most Poles, whatever their politics, believe that their alliance with Russia is
essential. How else could their Western frontier on the Oder-
Neisse be maintained?

Yet the Russian alliance is unlikely to be eternal. Paderewski's
story is still topical. There has always been a "Polish question",
there still is, and there is no guarantee that there will not be one
tomorrow. When a country finds itself in a difficult situation, it
is as well to consider how it got there: this may give a hint as to
how the problem can be solved. Every country leans on its
history: Poland especially so. I do not propose to write a detailed
history of the country, which would need a whole volume to
itself. But I will select incidents from the Polish story which have
a direct bearing on conditions in the country today.

I

THE STORY OF POLAND

I

THE history of Poland begins with legend. A valley in Ruthenia had been ravaged by the waters of a flood. When they subsided, an old man called together his three sons. He was old, and must soon die, he said. "But you must live, and find new pastures—the flood was a sign from the gods that this valley is not for us. Go hence, and found new families and tribes."

Russ marched to the east, and built a hut on the banks of the River Volga. Czech travelled to the west, and settled among the rolling hills we now call Bohemia. And Lech journeyed to the north, where he found a broad fertile plain and where the rivers ran gently. On one of the hills he found a nest of white eagles, which was a good omen. So there he made his new home: it became a village and then a town. Its name is Gniezno, which means a "nest". This then was the cradle of the Polish race, and is today the centre of its religion: and the white eagle became the emblem of the Polish nation.

Thus the Slav races occupied central and eastern Europe. The descendants of Lech became a great tribe, their lands stretching from the Carpathians to the Baltic Sea. They had no king: they lived in peasant communities, each with its headman and its council. Sometimes a man of personality and courage would become the leader of a group of villages: and then a leader of leaders would emerge.

The descendants of Lech were at first called Polanes or Polakes —"field dwellers"—and they settled along the banks of the Oder and Vistula. This region was full of wild animals, and the people used their skins as clothing. Herodotus talks of men who could turn themselves at will into wolves. Their settlements were remote from the more advanced corners of Europe, in the west. When

15

England was becoming a kingdom and Charlemagne had founded an empire, Poles and Russians were lagging five hundred years behind the civilization of Western Europe.

One of the men of strong personality who became a local leader was Piast, an honest wheelwright greatly esteemed by his fellows for his wise counsel. When his son was seven years old, friends and relatives gathered for the boy's first hair-cutting, an ancient Slav tradition. Then two strangers arrived, and were welcomed.

The oldest man of the family cut the boy's hair, and the others caught the curls as they fell, and blessed them. The two strangers asked if they might take part: they pressed their fingers on the boy's forehead in the form of a cross, and blessed him in the name of their Lord. The guests thought that the strangers were angels, and did not know that they were priests. Nor did they understand the Sign of the Cross.

A new leader of the tribe was needed, and Piast was elected. If Lech were the founder of the Polish race, Piast was the founder of the Polish nation. This was in 842, when its recorded history begins. And—unique in Europe—Piast was the only national leader who was neither a conqueror nor a warrior, but an honest artisan.

II

Poland still consisted of a group of tribes, but unification was near. It was Piast's grandson who solved the mystery of the two strangers who had blessed his father. His name was Mieszko, and he wandered into the land occupied by his distant relatives, the descendants of Czech. One day he sought hospitality at a castle, and was given more. He returned to Poland with a wife, the lord's daughter—who was a Christian. Now the Sign of the Cross could be explained: and thus Christianity came to Poland.

This proved to be a happy event for the Poles. The Holy Roman Empire had recently been founded—on the ruins of that of Charlemagne—and two of its objectives were the imposition of Christianity on other peoples, and their subjection to the Emperor. Force was the method employed to both ends. But when the Polish leader had accepted Christianity and paid tribute the Emperor no longer had an excuse for ravaging his lands, and

Poland escaped years of terror. Yet there was enough trouble close at hand. The western frontier was reasonably secure, but the Russian tribes began to attack from the east.

And the manner of the coming of Christianity proved to be very important. The Russians were evangelized from Constantinople under the Eastern Orthodox Church. The Poles accepted their religion from Rome, and so were brought into contact with western culture and tradition. Hence Polish thought and manners have been not eastern, but western, for a thousand years.

The son of Mieszko was the first king of Poland to be crowned —in 1025. His capital was at Poznan, and his domains were wide: he gave good government to his people. His grandson, Boleslas the Brave, extended the country's frontiers: they now stretched from Kiev to the Oder, and for a time even moved westwards to the Elbe. So the Oder frontier of today is no modern novelty. And Poland's present Baltic coastline is almost exactly that of the Poland of Boleslas the Brave.

Then, as now, rulers could be very foolish. Charlemagne, who built up a great realm, divided it among his sons. So did Boleslas: and within hours of his death the country was plunged into civil war—thus inviting the aggressions of Teutons from the west, Russians from the east, and Swedes from the north.

The Russians were soon replaced by the Tatars, Mongolian barbarians who subdued southern Russia and swarmed into Central Europe. It was left to the Poles and Czechs to halt them. At the Battle of Lignica (1241), the Poles fought under Henry the Pious—a direct descendant of Piast—and suffered grievous casualties. Yet the Tatars, fought to a standstill, had themselves taken such punishment as to persuade them to retire into Asia.

With enemies on every side, the frontier on the Elbe could not be maintained, and successive kings held it along the Oder. War was almost continuous. Eastern marauders raided southern Poland no fewer than ninety times. One Polish king, Boleslas the Wry-Mouthed, by the time he was fifty, had won forty-seven victories, and after each he returned to quell inevitable strife at home. And Polish diplomacy was feeble. After a victory, a peace treaty would be signed—to be broken by the enemy as soon as it suited him.

Yet another danger threatened. A military Order, the Teutonic Knights of the Cross, had been formed with the blessing of the

2

Pope for service in the Crusades. Some preferred action nearer home, and began to terrorize the Baltic provinces with the aid of lawless mercenaries returning from the Crusades, who would do anything for the chance to loot. The Knights who fought in the name of religion would capture a village, and summon the people to accept the Cross. Those who clung to the old pagan gods were put to the sword: the "converts" became serfs of the Knights. These at last occupied the lands which later became Estonia, Latvia and Lithuania, but their headquarters were still in East Prussia. By an accident of history, their "colonization" by-passed a narrow strip of territory west of the Vistula, which remained Polish.

The local heathen population of East Prussia had the choice of assimilation or extermination: many chose the former, and gave their name to the state which was to emerge and to become paramount in Germany. And the narrow strip of Polish territory west of the Vistula was to become known to the world as the Polish Corridor!

The Knights had been *invited* into Poland. With his country divided by internecine war, and threatened by pagan invaders from north and east, a weak Duke of Moravia requested the aid of the Teutonic Knights. They came, expelled the barbarians and captured their homelands: what is more, they seized the adjacent Polish regions as well. In 1308 they captured the Polish city of Danzig, and massacred all its inhabitants. Then they began to raid into Poland, where the local barons thought of nothing but their own welfare.

But then Casimir the Great became king of Poland. He was an economist, he codified the many and varied laws of his land: he founded the university of Cracow—long before the Germans had any university. "He found a Poland made of wood, and left it made of stone."

There was no middle class in Poland, to stand between the nobility and the peasants, who were little more than serfs. The economy was weak: by tradition, nobles took no part in commerce, and the peasants were not allowed to do so. Casimir had fallen in love with a Jewish girl, which may have liberalized his ideas. He invited Jews as well as Germans into Poland as traders, and the country gained by their activities.

Casimir, who was the last of the twenty Piast kings, left his country to a relative, the king of Hungary. This ruler had an only daughter, Jadwiga. She was persuaded to marry Jagiello, Duke of Lithuania, whose territory stretched from the Baltic to the Black Sea. Thus the two kingdoms were united, and Jagiello became a Christian.

Soon he found it essential to make a firm stand against the marauding Teutonic Knights. The clash came in 1410 on the field of Grünwald, better known as Tannenberg, where the Knights were crushed by the Polish-Lithuanian army. More than once they tried to recover their lost power, but failed. Danzig again became Polish, and East Prussia was held as a fief of Poland!

The Teutonic Order tried by every possible means to liberate its territory from Polish suzerainty. In 1510 Albrecht Hohenzollern—a nephew of the King of Poland—was elected Grand Master. He failed to secure the help of the German princes and the Pope. Then he took the advice of Martin Luther: he dissolved the Order, became a Protestant, and proclaimed himself Duke of Prussia.

But he still paid homage to the Polish king—in the market place of Cracow in 1525. His title was to be "Prince in Prussia", whereas the king was to be "Master and heir of all Prussian territories". The inheritance of the prince might pass only to his descendants and his own brothers, and on the extinction of the Hohenzollern line Prussia was to revert to Poland! He received his insignia from his king: an eagle, akin to that of Poland, but black instead of white.

III

For two hundred years the seven kings of the Jagiellonian dynasty ruled Poland and Lithuania, and they ruled justly. "I am not king of your consciences," one of them told his subjects. "No one may be imprisoned until he is legally convicted," declared another, 250 years *before* the passing of our own Habeas Corpus Act.

Religious wars never touched Poland: at the height of her power her smaller neighbours hastened to seek her protection. A new menace had appeared—the Turks were advancing into Europe. They threatened Vienna: the emperor fled, but sent a dramatic appeal to the Poles: the Pope also asked them to hasten to the aid of Christendom.

John Sobieski was the Polish leader. He gathered an army of 40,000 men. Its pride was the regiment known as the Winged Hussars—3,000 knights in heavy armour, each carrying a lance eight yards long. So heavy was their armour that only the strongest could carry it, and only the strongest horse could carry the man. They were the tanks of their day.

By now the Turks were outside Vienna. Sobieski called for volunteers for a glorious suicide, and 200 Winged Hussars charged furiously into the heart of the Turkish army. Then, taking advantage of the confusion thus produced, the main body of the Poles attacked. They were hopelessly outnumbered, but the charge of the Winged Hussars was irresistible.

The Turks fled in disorder, and never returned. The report of Sobieski to the Pope was modest: "*Venimus, vidimus, Deus vicit.*"

Scots will be interested to note that Sobieski was the great-grandfather of Bonnie Prince Charlie.

Before this the Jagiellonian dynasty had come to an end. Thereafter the kings were elected, and, to put it mildly, were not of outstanding quality. Most were foreign—John Sobieski was the only distinguished Pole among them—and most were feeble or uninterested. The nobles, by whom they were elected, looked for rulers who would relieve them of taxation and other obligations.

Government became a farce. The *liberum veto* applied—one vote against a law, and it was defeated. For generations Poland had known parity with England—the only two parliamentary governments in Europe. But now, at a time of general progress elsewhere, Poland came to a standstill because one member could wreck any Parliamentary proposal.

Sobieski was the last great king of Poland. He was followed by weaklings—no match for the rising power of Russia. Poland was large, fertile and rich. Her knights were unsurpassed and her peasants were sturdy soldiers. All that was needed was determined leadership, and this was not forthcoming. And her neighbours were predatory.

In 1772 they all attacked at the same time. The first "Partition" of Poland was made—a slice of territory going to Russia, to Prussia and to Austria. (The Prussian share of the booty included what was later known as the "Polish Corridor".)

The last days of Poland emphasized the tragedy. Catherine the Great of Russia sent 40,000 men to march on Warsaw. "The future will show whether anybody but me can give Poland a king," she declared.

The unfortunate monarch, Stanislas Augustus Poniatowski, became her puppet: the real ruler of Poland was the Russian ambassador. At the time of the second Partition, in 1793, Poniatowski held out for three days with his parliament, surrounded by Russian soldiers. For three days no food was allowed to pass through the cordon. Then the king fell in a faint. The Russian ambassador put a pen in his hand, and guided it as he signed the act of partition.

By this time the Polish resistance was desperate, and the hour

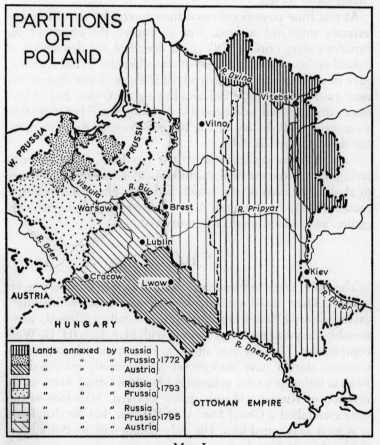

PARTITIONS
OF
POLAND

Lands annexed by Russia ⎫
" " " Prussia ⎬1772
" " " Austria ⎭

" " " Russia ⎫
" " " Prussia ⎬1793

" " " Russia ⎫
" " " Prussia ⎬1795
" " " Austria ⎭

MAP I

produced its leader. Tadeusz Andrzej Bonaventura Kosciuszko had fought for America in the War of Independence. When he returned to Poland, still reeling under the shock of the Second Partition, the peasants rushed to his standard, and though ill-armed and outnumbered, they defeated the Russians at Raclawice. But in a further battle Kosciuszko was seriously wounded and captured, and the Polish resistance collapsed. A Russian massacre at Warsaw, and the war was over.

The Third Partition removed Poland from the map of Europe. The southern provinces were annexed by Austria, the north-western by Prussia, and the remainder—two-thirds of the country—by Russia.

At that time powers esteemed their success by the amount of territory they had secured. But in Europe the effects of the Partitions were critical. Talleyrand described the destruction of Poland as "worse than a crime—it was a blunder". And Rousseau gave its people some pertinent advice: "Poles, if you cannot pre-vent your neighbours from swallowing you, you can at least ensure that they will not succeed in digesting you." For more than a century the Poles lay in the Russian-Prussian-Austrian maw, but they emerged as Poles.

"The Poles never learn until it is too late," was a popular saying. Just before the final Partition the Polish nobles had agreed to abolish the *liberum veto*, which had been one of the principal causes of Poland's weakness. A new unity emerged: a generation earlier, and Poland might have survived.

IV

The Poles were not unaccustomed to defeat: but they never gave in. They joined any international movement which might even indirectly favour their cause: it usually collapsed, disas-trously. They had no better fortune with Napoleon (H. G. Wells commented: "Poland was ablaze with a spirit which surely a Corsican should have understood"). He greatly esteemed the Poles as fighters: 80,000 volunteers joined his Grand Army in the invasion of Russia: and only 3,000 survived. Napoleon at one time established a Grand Duchy of Warsaw, but he abandoned it as soon as it suited him. His only lasting gift to Poland was the legal Code Napoleon.

In 1830, 1846 and 1853 the Poles revolted against Russia. This was quite hopeless: the Russians had arms, the Poles had not, and the defeat was followed by savage reprisals.

Thousands of Poles had taken refuge abroad, where they formed patriotic organizations and committees, badgered the politicians of their adopted country, or fought on revolutionary barricades. They aroused a wide sentimental support, but no action.

Inside Poland the situation was desperate. The Russians were incompetent but oppressive: nor did the Poles make their own lot any easier. A czar would propose some minor liberal act—an extension of local government, or the Polonization of a university —the Polish reply would be a demand for more, and an armed revolt to attempt to secure it.

The clash was complete. Eastern Europe had two utterly opposing ideas. Even before the French Revolution, the Poles had adopted their own ideals of liberty: events in France encouraged them. But every attempt to gain their freedom was shattered by dissensions in the Polish ranks. And revolutionary ideas of human liberty were anathema to the reactionary czars and the Russian landowners.

A great citadel was built on the outskirts of Warsaw—not to protect the city, but to over-awe it. Many Polish leaders were publicly hanged from meat-hooks under savage conditions. Anyone who has any doubts as to Polish suspicions of Russia in our own time has only to read the history of the 150 years of Russian occupation.

The Prussians ruled differently. Their régime was efficient, but stern. Use of the Polish language was declared illegal: Polish towns which had borne their names for a thousand years were now given Germanized variants. Education was in German: the attempts at denationalization were thorough, and insurrections against authority were impossible in an efficient police state.

When Bismarck established a fund to settle Germans on the Polish lands, the Poles took up the challenge. They contributed their savings so that their own peasants could acquire land. Moreover, the Prussians were Protestants: the Poles Catholics, so that religious clashes augmented nationalist squabbles.

In Austrian Poland the situation was easier. There was a moderate measure of self-government. Polish was the language of the schools—and in the universities of Cracow and Lwow. The aim of the Russians and Germans was to liquidate Polish intellectuals: that of the Austrians to use them.

A liberal spirit gradually pervaded Europe. The small states in the Balkans won their freedom from Turkish oppressors. The position in Poland was more complicated, and more than one Pole realized that the chances of success were very small. A European war was imminent, with Germany fighting Russia. Yet, for the Polish cause to benefit, both Germany *and* Russia would have to be defeated. This was surely impossible. But one Polish leader refused to admit this. Even before the war began he had outlined his plans, and, fantastic as it then seemed, he saw them carried to fruition. His name was Josef Pilsudski.

V

First however we must glance at the internal conditions during the period prior to the Partitions.

The growth of democratic ideas was slow. For centuries power had lain with the nobles, and these were numerous.

When Boleslas the Brave (or Great) was attacked on all sides by foreign foes, he needed warriors. So he conferred noble rank on "whomsoever possessed a horse and bore arms". This was the beginning of the Polish *Szlachta*, or gentry. Hitherto the nobility had consisted of the great landowners, ranging from the relatives of the king to peasants who by hard work and foresight had greatly augmented their holdings. Some of the nobles lived in princely fashion—with a town house, a country castle, and a retinue of gentlemen to lead the peasants in war. The Radziwill family, one of the greatest in the land, had 20,000 retainers.

The Polish lord kept open house, and his hospitality was famous. His peasants were virtually serfs, but he used to look upon himself as the head of a huge family—in times of distress, his serfs came to him for help. His bounty formed the welfare state of his day.

The second class of Polish society was not so wealthy but far more numerous than the first: the *Szlachta*. The omnibus creation of Boleslas the Great was assured of a constant supply of recruits. When a gentleman died, all his sons became gentlemen—there was no rule of primogeniture. Picture this over a few generations, and it will be seen that many of the *Szlachta* were humble folks, in effect free peasants. Yet all had equal privileges—including that of electing a king. "We are all equal among ourselves. The lord is a rich gentleman, and the gentleman a poor lord." Poland might well be called "a republic of nobles". When its population was five million, the *Szlachta* numbered 200,000—so that the proportion of the Poles who had the right to vote was considerably higher than that of the English.

Obviously the election of a king gave the opportunity for hard bargaining: one privilege granted by a king was that the *Szlachta* might appoint others to their own ranks.

This was indeed a peculiar form of "democratic nobility". But a privileged class is inevitably ultra-conservative and reactionary, suspicious of reform and progress.

The lot of the peasant could well be pitiful. Some of the nobles were generous to their "family". Others, less humane, treated the peasants as cattle. They were tied to the land: only one son of his family might emigrate to a town. The peasant's holding was let on share-cropping terms, which included so many days' labour in the lord's fields. He could only seek justice in the court over which his own lord presided. The potential abuses of such a system are obvious.

Most of the greatest men in Polish history emerged from the ranks of the minor *Szlachta*—natural leaders with skill in battle, or highly cultured. Most of the teachers and priests—often united in the same man—were of the poorer gentry class.

Poland lacked that middle class which was to prove so valuable elsewhere. The cities were disenfranchized. In earlier reigns German artisans and traders, followed by Jews, had settled in Poland. The jealous *Szlachta* saw in them an opportunity for the heavy taxation which they themselves escaped.

Considering the long submergence of the Polish peasant, his modern development is remarkable. In recent years he has become the backbone of the new Poland. He is a good worker, usually of high intelligence, and of great courage. He has deserved the success which is now recognized as his due.

A synopsis of important influences on modern Polish problems might be useful.

1. There is little or nothing new in the frontier problems.
2. For hundreds of years the Polish western frontier ran along the River Oder. The frontier with Russia was much farther east than that of today. And the "Polish Corridor" was fundamentally Polish. (These points will be dealt with in detail later.)
3. Poland is a Roman Catholic country, and for centuries was the eastern outpost of Christendom.
4. Poland is a country of modest size and power between two giants. *Poland has known peace only when Germany and Russia have been enemies:* whenever they were friendly they combined to despoil Poland.
5. The "republic of nobles" was a strange form of democracy— but it was more democratic than most other contemporary systems of government.
6. The Poles have been their own worst enemies, and have contributed more than once to their country's "martyrdom": their courage has been outstanding not only in battle against what appeared to be hopeless odds, but in their amazing recovery from the consequences of defeat.

POLAND REBORN

I

As Josef Pilsudski had realized, Poland could only be restored to the map of Europe if both Germany *and* Russia were defeated.

On 6th August, 1914, he invaded Russia—with an army of 600 men! Legally he was an ally of Austria, but his equipment was grotesque: his rifles were fifty years old and his cavalry had no horses! But his army grew, and it played its part in defeating the Russians. When the Germans and Austrians captured Warsaw, they proclaimed an independent country—the Polish territory which they had conquered from Russia. Their aim was to secure recruits for their own armies. But Pilsudski was determined to form a *Polish* army. He gathered recruits from the German and Austrian forces, and Poles in the Russian army deserted to him by the thousand.

But the Germans grew suspicious, disbanded his force, and flung him into jail. Nonetheless a Polish Legion was formed in France, and this rendered yeoman service to the Allies.

While the ardent Pilsudski languished in jail, one of his compatriots was active. The famous pianist Ignace Paderewski was a Pole: in the U.S.A. he had chanced to make the acquaintance of Colonel House, President Wilson's intimate. Paderewski skilfully used House's influence on the American president, and the thirteenth of the Fourteen Points which the latter promulgated as the basis of peace in 1917 explicitly demanded the re-creation of an independent Poland.

Despite the strict censorship, this news spread like wildfire across the country—there were, of course, millions of Polish emigrants in the U.S.A. And well before the end of 1918 there were obvious signs of the coming collapse of the Central Powers. The Austrian forces were now little more than a rabble: the Poles seized their arms, and drove them out. The German surrender led to the disarmament of their forces in Poland. And before that Russia had collapsed in revolution. Pilsudski's dream had come true.

But in the moment of victory fresh dangers threatened. There were endless debates about the character of the new Poland—already under attack from the Ukrainians in the east. Then Paderewski was persuaded to undertake the formation of a non-party government, a task in which his international prestige was immensely valuable.

The western frontiers were soon settled. In the main, they followed the lines existing in 1775, before the Partitions began. There were German protests about the misnamed "Polish Corridor", which in fact was historical and ethnic Polish territory. But the defeated Germany could do nothing.

A more serious threat developed in the east, where the Bolsheviks were disposing of the White armies which opposed their seizure of power. Poland seemed about to be invaded, and Pilsudski struck first. In spite of initial successes, his ill-equipped forces could scarcely hope for success against the growing Russian armies.

He then made a pact with the Ukrainians—the two branches of the Slav races are quite close. The Russians were alarmed—the loss of Ukrainian wheatfields would be a major disaster.

The world over there were socialists and others whose sympathies lay with Russia, and to these the fact that Polish armies were on Russian soil suggested Polish aggression. The Russians struck back, with great force, and the Poles reeled back into their own country.

The Russians followed up their success. Their march was proclaimed as the beginning of world revolution. "Our way to world-wide conflagration passes over the corpse of Poland," declared the Russian commander.

Pilsudski rallied the Poles to his cause The Western allies could do little to help. France sent a military mission, but this was virtually useless, and British dockers refused to load munitions to be shipped to Polish ports!

The Russians advanced almost to the gates of Warsaw, but though the Poles were outnumbered, they were fighting for life and liberty. In the face of their determined resistance, the Russians broke: their discipline was poor, and their defeat degenerated into a rout.

But the eastern frontier of Poland still had to be established.

II

While the Polish-Russian conflict raged in Poland, the individual Western powers strove for a cease-fire. The British drew up a provisional boundary—later it was called after Lord Curzon, the Foreign Secretary. The Curzon Line never purported to be a definitive frontier, but was intended as a mark of demarcation between the two armies—an attempt to stop a war. Both of these were invited to halt ten kilometres short of the Line. Russia, then confident of victory, marched on.

Now, following their defeat, the Bolshevik leaders signed the Treaty of Riga—the official *Great Soviet Encyclopaedia* claimed it as a victory. The leader of the Russian delegation at Riga claimed that the frontier there established was only a temporary expedient, as the whole world would shortly fall within the Communist fold. Lenin, on the other hand, believed that the Curzon Line was "unfair" to the Poles, and had offered a frontier actually farther east than the Line.

But the agreed frontier held a danger which the Poles should have recognized. They themselves had been more than troublesome when the Russians ruled them: and now they were to rule large numbers of Russians. The population between the Curzon Line and the Riga frontier was very mixed.

Poles	3,914,000
Ukrainians	4,365,000
Bielo-Russians	1,284,000
Russians	102,000
Lithuanians	76,000
Jews	899,000
Others	128,000

On the whole the Poles were most numerous in the north and south of the region. Yet a city like Lwow was overwhelmingly Polish, while the surrounding countryside was largely Ukrainian.

Polish Ukraine consisted of two provinces. Eastern Galicia had never been part of Russia—it was under Austrian rule from 1772

MAP II. RACES IN POLAND

to 1918. Volhynia, to the east, had been seized by Russia in 1772. Its capital, Lwow, was the home of a famous *Polish* university.

This latter province did not settle down easily under Polish rule after 1918. There were "incidents"—true, they appear trivial in retrospect. The Ukrainians were allowed to publish their own newspapers and they sent members to parliament: their aim was not union with Russia but an independent Ukraine. Hitler seized on the trouble-making potentialities of the situation when he established his Ukrainian Bureau: its purpose was to foment trouble between Poland and Russia: in this he succeeded.

At the centre of the eastern provinces were the Pripet Marshes. Here the population was mixed, but mainly of Bielo-Russian ancestry—people who had long been isolated from the centres of power. Life was very primitive in the marshland villages, for long apart from what is commonly called civilization. I found little political or national consciousness when I visited the Pripet Marshes between the wars. "Are you Polish or Russian?" I would ask a local peasant. "I am from here," would be his reply.

The situation in the north was akin to that in the south. Just as Lwow was Polish in the midst of an Ukrainian countryside, so Vilno and its neighbourhood were Polish: but the rural population was mixed with Lithuanians. Vilno (Vilna, Wilno, Vilnius— all the same place) had moreover been the Lithuanian capital at the time when the country was large and powerful.

When it united with Poland its people were backward pagans. Polish priests and administrators arrived: Polish schools were established. Thus the character of Vilno changed. If a Lithuanian youth wanted education, he had to learn Polish to get it. The process of voluntary or involuntary Polonization was rapid. By 1772, when the city and region were seized by the Russians, Vilno was Polish. The surrounding region became an ethnic tangle, the Russians inter-marrying with Poles and Lithuanians.

At the end of the war in 1918 confusion was confounded. The Lithuanians as well as the Poles had recovered their independence, and they naturally claimed their ancient capital, Vilno. Then the town was seized by the Bolsheviks. Defeated by the Poles, they had to retreat from Vilno in disorder—and in doing so they handed Vilno back to the Lithuanians.

In August, 1920, an agreement was signed at Suvalki between Poland and Lithuania. This should have settled the town's fate. But *two days* later the agreement was broken! The Poles seized Vilno.

It was claimed that the raid was the work of a "rebel" general, Zeligowski, whose men hailed from Vilno, and who were determined that it should be Polish. But the affair was supported by Pilsudski—who clung tightly to his acquisition. These were the days of the *fait accompli*, usually accepted meekly by the rest of the world. Lithuania naturally protested loudly against the capture of Vilno—and then legalized such methods by its own seizure of Memel from the defeated Germans.

For nearly twenty years the quarrel between Poland and

Lithuania continued: the disputed frontier was closed. When I crossed it in 1934 I needed months of diplomatic preparation and a military exercise to get me over the frontier—I was only the fourteenth person to pass in twelve years.

Here was an insoluble problem. The Lithuanians wanted their ancient capital: the Poles wanted a Polish city. What compromise could possibly satisfy both?

Not until 1938 were diplomatic relations resumed. Then the threat of Hitler was too obvious, and was aimed against Poland and Lithuania alike. An uneasy truce began. Given a few years of peace, and a real friendship might have developed. But Hitler's calculations were not in years but in weeks.

III

Ardent patriots have for long talked about "racial frontiers". There is no such thing. An European frontier is theoretically supposed to follow a line where one race ends and another begins. This is impossible: there is no such line anywhere.

Others prefer the "natural" frontier. All satiated countries claim that their boundaries are "natural". A range of mountains, or a mighty river—here, we are told, is the perfect geographical division, a real boundary. But this again is untrue.

The sample usually quoted is the line of the Pyrenees, stretching conveniently from Atlantic to Mediterranean, and separating Frenchmen from Spaniards. This is a complete fallacy. The frontier zigzags haphazardly along the range, dipping in turn into France and Spain: and far from separating peoples, the Pyrenees form the backbone of two races which are neither French nor Spanish—the Basques in the West and the Catalans in the East—the Pyrenees, in fact, unites racial interests rather than divides them.

A river is even less effective as a frontier. When the invading tribes of older days found green pastures on one side of a river valley, they did not halt, but occupied the other bank as well. No European river has the slightest claim to be called a boundary between two races. The Poles did not settle on one side of a river —they occupied the whole of the Vistula valley. A river never forms a real frontier, it is rather a line along which a racial body might grow.

Nor is a "historic" frontier any better. It might have been formed as a result of battle, or because of the land holdings of a local lord, or of the marriage of his son or daughter. The frontiers of Poland—as of most other countries—have changed many times during its history. It was *quite impossible* to draw any line in Eastern Europe and to say: "All the people to the west of this line are Poles, and all those to the east are Russians." A frontier is a compromise—it has to be a compromise.

Discussing this and similar problems before the last war, I suggested exchanges of population. A compromise boundary should be agreed, and then Polish families living in Russia should be transferred west of the line, and *vice versa*. It would be distressing to the families involved, and they would need to be treated very generously.

My suggestion attracted some attention in Western Europe, but none farther east. Poland was ruled by a right-wing group, fervently nationalistic, and burning to avenge two centuries of wrong. Russia was ruled by a left-wing group determined to spread its creed among its neighbours and ultimately far beyond them. Both were hopelessly old-fashioned in their outlook as regards territory: the more land you held, the stronger and richer you were. But if your territory be inhabited by unfriendly minorities, you are in fact not stronger and richer, but weaker and poorer.

The exchange of populations was begun by Hitler, under appalling conditions: and then Hitler was outdone by Stalin. And the resultant frontiers are still unsatisfactory.

Nationalism can be a virtue or a vice. Patriotism may call out the best in a man, but it can also restrict his outlook with the determination never to see another point of view. It was obvious from the beginning, for example, that the problem of Vilno might not be solved but could be alleviated by compromise. Yet that demands approval from both sides.

In 1934 I went to visit Pilsudski at his country home at Pikiliczki, near Vilno. He was generally regarded as a tough dictator, which was not quite correct. He was patriotic and resolute, and impatient with weaklings. But—and this is very important—by race he was not Polish but Lithuanian. So he was greatly disturbed by the quarrel between the two countries.

My first impression contradicted popular imaginings. His little estate abounded with wild life. He proposed to walk me round; on the hall table was a pile of stale bread, with which he filled his pockets. I also filled mine: evidently the refreshments of an iron dictator were tough. But the bread was not for ourselves: as we walked, Pilsudski fed the birds. This is not quite the conventional portrait of a military dictator.

I led the conversation to the obvious subject: Vilno. About the city itself he was firm: Vilno was Polish. But its countryside was different: he was quite prepared to amend the hastily-drawn frontier so as to transfer dozens of Lithuanian villages. This, for the time, was a liberal decision. But when I reached Kaunas and passed on the idea to the Lithuanians, I got no response whatsoever.

"Politics is the art of the possible." When it is obviously impossible to grant to both sides their wishes in full, obviously there must be compromise; otherwise there is no prospect of peace. Pilsudski's idea of a more accurate ethnic frontier would not have solved the problem of Vilno, but at least it would have ameliorated the situation. As it was, the dispute aroused such hatred that the prospect of the revival of a close relationship between Poland and Lithuania was not even considered.

Pilsudski did well for his country, but today official outlook condemns him—primarily because he fought against the Soviet Union. "He came from the most primitive corner of Poland," said a Polish leader. "He resembled an Eastern potentate rather than a Western statesman. His cabinet consisted of Yes-men. He treated the peasants as if they were serfs. His foreign policy was sound, but at home—he had no idea of economy or organization.

"He built up a strong army—but it was hopelessly old-fashioned. He had the finest cavalry corps in the world—in the age of tanks. So, of course, Poland was easily beaten in 1939.

"Pilsudski kept Sikorski away from high office. Sikorski was a Western intellectual, so Pilsudski did not like him.

"He was hard even to his own friends. During the Partitions Poles might become army officers in Austria and Russia, but not in Germany. Pilsudski's Legion was staffed by Polish officers from the Austrian army. But after he came to power he dismissed them, as they made it clear that they were dissatisfied with his home policies.

"Pilsudski never cared for popularity. He was always alone—

even his ministers were not partners but subordinates. He was a man with a single limited outlook. So today he receives no honour."

All this could be true: but it is fairly obvious that without a man like Pilsudski the reborn Poland would have dissolved in a welter of civil strife.

He had always insisted that he was no dictator. If he had desired such a position, he pointed out with truth, he could have seized it immediately Poland was reborn. "I do not believe that Poland can be governed by the stick. I don't like the stick," he declared. "But it is necessary that the Chief of State should have the right to make quick decisions on important questions. We live in a legislative chaos. We have a legacy of confusing laws from three states. While we argue about them, the world goes by. It won't do. A great effort of honesty is needed after the demoralization of the war years and the centuries of slavery. I know neither the Right nor the Left—only Poland."

In his death he received one of the strangest testimonials a leader ever had: the "king" of the Warsaw underworld issued an order that nothing was to be stolen during the funeral! And, in spite of the huge crowds which gathered to pay their last respects, engaging the full attention of the police in their control, not so much as a handkerchief was stolen.

Like all masterful men, Pilsudski made enemies as well as friends. The ranks of his opponents included not merely place-seeking politicians whose scheming was marred by his bluntness, but conscientious democrats who saw in his autocracy the very negation of those ideals for which they had striven and for which, they claimed, Poland was reborn. At the time of his death they were right: ten years earlier they were wrong.

IV

The frontiers of the revived Poland in the east were disputed, and no one had the will to compromise. What of those in the west?

There they generally followed those of the Poland forcefully disrupted in 1772—and they included the "Corridor"—which was Polish: 89·9 per cent of its inhabitants were Poles.

This was not new. The Teutonic Knights had passed it over

when acquiring East Prussia. Official German maps, both old ones and others dated as recently as 1909, show the "Corridor" as inhabited by Poles. The Germans forgot this in the arguments of 1919. They claimed that the Kashubians, the tribe occupying the "Corridor", were not really Poles, but Germans! But the Kashubians spoke a Polish dialect, had always regarded themselves as Poles, and had always been treated as Poles even by the Germans!

The last but one of President Wilson's Fourteen Points read: "An independent Polish State shall be erected, which shall include all territory with an indisputedly Polish population, to which a free and safe access to the sea shall be given, and whose economic and territorial integrity will be assured by international treaties."

The "Corridor", then, had an indisputable Polish population. It is significant that the title "Polish Corridor" was invented by a German propagandist, thereby implying that it was an artificial creation. But it was a historic Polish province, seized by the Prussians in 1772, and after nearly 150 years still inhabited by Poles.

It is only fair to the Germans to mention another Polish claim—to a section of East Prussia. In its west lived about 70,000 Poles, with 300,000 Masurians in the south. The Masurians were like the Kashubians, a people of Polish stock. But when a plebiscite was held in 1920, the voting favoured Germany. True, the region had been subject to a continuous and intense process of Germanization. But the Masurians themselves had another explanation. The plebiscite was held just as it appeared that the Poles would be crushed by the Bolshevik invasion. In effect, therefore, the Masurian choice seemed to be not between Germany and Poland, but between Germany and Russia. So their region remained in Germany.

The Thirteenth Point assured Poland of "a free and safe access to the sea". But the narrow seaboard, without a port, could scarcely be claimed to provide this, as the statesmen at the Paris peace conference admitted. The River Vistula was the main artery of Poland, and it entered the sea at Danzig.

The city had been German or Polish at different times until 1772, when the Prussians seized it. At the First World War its population was German, with a Polish minority. The peace-makers hesitated, therefore, to hand it over to Poland: they decided that it should become a Free City, with local self-government, but within the Polish economic zone.

This plan could have worked, but the Danzigers never intended it to do so. German dockers even claimed the right to decide which cargoes should use the port! The Polish reply was to build Gdynia, along the coast.

We in Britain can scarcely comprehend the Polish outlook on the sea. In 1934 I went to a cinema in Cracow. The newsreel showed a picture of little waves breaking on a sandy shore: and the caption read: "Waves breaking on the Polish coast". The whole audience was engulfed in a maze of emotional fervour, and tears mingled with their cheers.

("It is the same today," said a French journalist resident in Warsaw. "The news on television is followed by a magazine programme—which *always* includes at least one item about the sea. If no launching of a ship is available, the programme may feature a man taking his dog for a walk along the Polish shore.")

The Germanism of the Danzigers was deeply rooted, and once Hitler achieved power the situation was alarming. The people of Danzig had their chance. Had they loyally accepted their status as a Free City, they might have prospered. They chose instead the narrow path of nationalist irredentism, and their actions precipitated the Second World War. In this they suffered bitterly: and they could scarcely complain when they were not given a second chance.

V

The Polish "Corridor" and Danzig affected German pride, but Silesia touched the German pocket. It is, and was then, a very prosperous mining and industrial region.

A thousand years ago it was called Starapolska, or Old Poland. Then it was acquired by the Bohemians: then the Austrians. Next Frederick II of Prussia seized it by force. "I take what I want. Then I can always find clever lawyers to prove that it is mine," he said, cynically.

A process of Germanization followed—but Upper Silesia remained Polish in its countryside: the Germans often held a majority in the towns.

The powers at Paris in 1919 decided on a plebiscite. Fervent leaders on both sides endeavoured to influence the voting by force. The result was a surprise. The Germans admitted that 56 per cent of the population was Polish, but only 40 per cent voted for incorporation in Poland. The Germans won the towns, the Poles the villages. The League of Nations decided on the division of the territory.

It is not easy to divide a region which has been developed as one economic unit. Poland was allotted only one-third of the territory, but this included nearly three-quarters of the mines and factories of Upper Silesia.

The Germans did not pretend to accept the situation. Because of their much superior propaganda, the world heard much more of the woes of the 263,701 Germans in Poland than of the 625,596 Poles left in Germany. It did not need a Hitler to arouse the Germans to anger over the loss of part of an industrial province. But Upper Silesia meant more to Hitler than all the rest of Germany's border problems.

VI

Again we can summarize:

1. By 1920 the frontiers of the reborn Poland had been fixed. They did not include all the Poles who would have liked to belong to their homeland. On the other hand, nearly one-third of the population of Poland consisted of minorities—a dangerous weakness.

2. A perfect frontier was impossible. But, especially in the east, the Poles had acquired territory not justified on ethnic grounds—surely more important than historic reasons.

3. It is dangerous to have a frontier problem. It is doubly dangerous to have *two*. The Poles were not alone in believing that there could be no alliance between Fascist Germany and Communist Russia: they were wrong.

4. All parties concerned refused to consider an exchange of border populations, the one method which, over the years, could have alleviated frontier squabbles.

5. Lenin was much more far-sighted than Stalin.

6. The old-time passion for the ownership of territory is as dangerous as ever it was: or more so. It is much more important to have a contented and happy population.

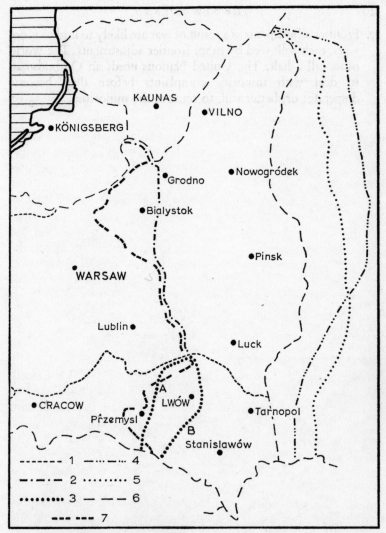

MAP III. THE CURZON LINE—AND OTHERS

1. Frontiers before 1914. 2. Demarcation Line of 8th December, 1919; subsequently adopted by the Supreme Council on 10th July, 1920, as a basis for a Russian-Polish armistice, i.e. the Curzon Line. 3. Two lines of demarcation considered at the Peace Conference as between Poland and Eastern Galicia. Line A was suggested in the event of the whole of Eastern Galicia being ceded to Poland: Line B should an independent Ukraine be established. 4. Frontier suggested by Lenin on 29th January, 1920. 6. The "Riga" frontier. 7. The Ribbentrop-Molotov line of 28th September, 1939.

7. Frontier adjustments as a result of war are likely to lead to more wars, each followed by more frontier adjustments. The world must call a halt. The United Nations needs an Ombudsman to deal with minority complaints before they become desperate: or, better still, to remove the minorities.

3

PILSUDSKI'S POLAND

I

HERE we may well take a glance at Pilsudski's Poland and see how it fared in the period between the wars.

The Poland of 1920 might reasonably be compared to a baby suffering from a poisoned appendix, with an abscess pressing on its windpipe, with every sign of malnutrition, with disfiguring excrescences of irritating boils and pimples, and with two wicked and unscrupulous uncles hovering in the background disputing its inheritance. True, the infant had some friendly aunts, but they lived a long way away. The outlook was not exactly promising, yet it must be recalled that weakly children often survive to become great.

Certainly Poland, of all the reborn or reconstructed states of Europe, had by far the most problems. The outstanding feature of most of them was that they should not have been problems at all. With any infusion of tolerance and confidence, the weakly infant would already have passed into sturdy manhood—actually its growth before the two wicked uncles joined efforts in an attempt at strangulation was remarkable.

Yet many of Poland's early troubles were of her own making. Conservatives and Socialists had worked and fought for the country's freedom: but once this was attained they began to quarrel between themselves—and *among* themselves. In earlier days the absurd *liberum veto* was mistaken for an expression of democracy. The new Poland had not yet learned its lesson. A constitution was formulated, based on that of France. That country has many qualities, but stability of government is not among them. So it was with Poland. Then, when Poland regained its freedom, and when unity of purpose was vital, representatives of more than twenty different parties were elected to the first Polish parliament.

The result can be imagined: all talk and no action: and this at a time when there was so much to do. Much of the country had been devastated by war. There were three disparate codes of laws—and three currencies, all sliding towards bankruptcy.

It took ten years to clear up the legal chaos. A couple married by civil licence in German Poland found they were living in sin if they moved to Warsaw. A completely new currency was moreover established.

Of overwhelming importance was the question of the ownership of land. Peasant Europe has followed a course almost identical in every country, the only difference in lying the pace of the change. For centuries the Polish peasants had been downtrodden, without rights, much less privileges, almost serfs. Their freedom came to them suddenly, and to a peasant freedom means only one thing—the ownership of land; everything else pales into insignificance beside the ultimate goal. The freedom granted by the czars to the Polish peasant was almost meaningless—they still continued to work for their old masters. Nor were their physical conditions bettered, since labour was in ample supply and wages could be artificially kept down to the lowest level.

In the reborn Poland many of the great estates still survived, although, as we have seen, there were considerable stretches where small farms dominated the countryside—in some districts tilled by people of peasant stock, in others by impoverished descendants of noble families. The prime question, as in all eastern and south-eastern countries, was the division of the great estates. Ideas differed very considerably. There were men of the extreme Left who wished to confiscate the great holdings and divide them up individually between the families who had worked on them for so many generations. Other parties, while agreeing that the estates should be expropriated, were in favour of giving the owners reasonable compensation. Politicians representing the landowners, naturally enough, opposed the whole idea of expropriation. Despite the strong representation of the Left in the first parliament, the traditional influence of the landlords was so strong that for some years the only possible solution—a part parcellation of the estates, either with or without compensation—was adopted. In the meantime, however, the problem was tackled by natural devices outside government control.

For the landlords of Poland in the early days after the War

found themselves in no enviable position. They had their land and great houses, but nothing else—whether their liquid wealth had been held in Germany, Austria, or Russia, it was now almost worthless. If they wished to live and to maintain their houses, there was only one solution to the problem—that of the hibernating bear in winter which lives on its own flesh. So the great magnates began to sell portions of their land to maintain the rest. The peasants were comparatively better placed, despite the devastation which had stricken Poland. The landlords had placed their great wealth on deposit at the bank, and had now lost it all: the peasant hid his scanty savings in a stocking, and, when fleeing before invaders or threatened with the devastation of fire, he could carry his portable wealth with him. In the first three years after 1919 over two hundred thousand Polish peasants became proprietors of their own holdings without government aid or influence. In later years the problem was tackled more decisively.

The rebuilding of Poland from the devastation of war was a colossal task. Over half a million dwelling-houses had been destroyed, with a million other buildings. The very necessities of life had been stripped from the country by the occupying Germans. The livestock had been killed off at a fantastic rate by the invaders; the ebb and flow of battle had compelled neglect of the soil.

Communications were in chaos. Railways had been built by the partitionary Powers, based on St. Petersburg, Vienna, and Berlin. Most of the lines had been planned by reasons of strategy rather than economic need, and there was no direct railway communication between some of the largest Polish cities. To add to the confusion, the gauge of the railways of the Russian portion was wider than the rest! Roads, especially in eastern Poland, were almost rudimentary. Bridges were inadequate even before the War—to get a vehicle across the Vistula might entail a journey of a hundred miles—and now many of them were in ruins.

The first requirement of the new state was capital for development. It was not forthcoming. The defeated nations were bankrupt, the victors sorely strained. To set Poland on its feet would have needed colossal credits.

One feature of Poland's financial stabilization is well worth recording. Polish migrants from all over the world flocked "home" to help, bringing their precious savings. Without them the economic life of the reborn state must have foundered: the emigrants' American and Canadian dollars kept Poland alive through the difficult first years of independence. There came the day when a stable Poland might have borrowed freely from the financial Powers: instead she only borrowed their brains, and British and American banking experts helped to make her currency into one of the most stable in Europe.

The problem of education was bravely tackled. In Russian Poland it had been neglected for generations: textbooks in Polish had been forbidden, and there were no places in the schools for three-quarters of the children. And now most of the primitive schools had been destroyed! New buildings were erected, to work double shifts—one batch of children in the morning and another in the afternoon. There was a serious lack of teachers, which could not immediately be made good.

Few countries have ever experienced such confusion. Those which approached it sought a solution in civil war or dictatorship. Poland made the second choice—a dictatorship, but modified by Polish ideas.

II

At first Pilsudski was supported by the Polish workers. Then his influence seemed to wane. He introduced new personalities to the political scene: some were successful, others not—a scathing cartoonist showed him throwing his colleagues into a lake to see if they could swim.

He retired from political life—and the chaos in Poland became worse. There was a strong movement favouring his return. He did return—not as dictator, but as Minister of War. This might be described as "driving from the back seat". He appreciated that the temperament of the Poles made them utterly unsuited to a dictatorship on the Fascist model. Poland is a land of individualists, and Pilsudski resisted as strongly as anybody else the suggestion that they should be formed into a communal horde. He accepted as his function a guiding hand to the new and untried parliamentary machine. If it worked, so much the better; if it failed, then he was always there to keep it going until it got running again.

His first self-imposed task was the breaking up of the political cliques which had done so much harm to Poland—many of their members, as we have seen, were politicians in the days of the partitions, and, though their loyalty to Poland was above suspicion, might be considered as having retained too large a share of alien influence, and had failed to reorientate their outlook to the utterly changed conditions. Pilsudski began to build up what he called a non-party bloc which should only be concerned with the welfare of Poland and should never allow political slogans to compromise its allegiance. Had he been a dictator in the accepted sense, he could have created such a party in an hour; instead, he took four years.

It must be admitted that his methods were not pretty—some of them, in fact, suggested electoral standards of more "advanced" Central European nations. On more than one occasion Pilsudski silenced potential opponents by imprisoning them temporarily at the moment of an election. Although the morality of his tactical devices was open to question, they lacked the venom of totalitarian methods. The peasant leader, Witos, was imprisoned during the 1930 election, but his name was not removed from the list of candidates, and he was in fact elected.

Pilsudski's non-party bloc was "Sanacja", or Sanitary—better translated as "setting one's house in order", and at last it commanded an elected majority in parliament.

He was no economist, and the world depression of the 1930s staggered Poland, but in an agricultural country at least there is no fear of starvation. On the other hand, Poland's exports fell drastically, and unfortunate peasants who depended upon foreign markets for their produce found themselves on the verge of bankruptcy. This meant automatically that the local industries were hard hit, since no one had money to spend. The situation was bravely tackled. What is more, my impression was that the character of the crisis was better understood in Poland than in any country of western Europe. With it went the realization that the phase was bound to pass; the nation made up its mind that it could endure some lean years; and it did. Orthodox economists gave Poland high praise because she weathered the storm without going off the gold standard. This, however, was actually a serious fault in policy, for it led to an abrupt decline in the export trade. Further, impelled by reasons of national pride, the zloty had been "pegged" at a figure far too high.

The economic life of Poland was badly handled, and strange

expedients were adopted to sustain it. The British General Strike of 1926 gave Poland an opportunity which was immediately seized—for unfortunately the doctrine of the brotherhood of man is by no means universally accepted even in labour circles, and the British miner's despair was his Polish colleague's opportunity. The Scandinavian markets, cut off from their normal British supplies of coal, had to secure them elsewhere, and Poland promptly offered supplies on economical terms; economical for Scandinavia, that is to say, but not for Poland. British coal from Northumberland could be shipped cheaply; Poland's coal had to be carried three hundred miles by train before it could reach the advantage of cheap sea transport. Yet rail rates were deliberately lowered so that the export trade of coal might be fostered; which means, in effect, that a considerable bounty was offered in respect of every ton of coal which was exported. Because of this, even after the dispute in the British mining industry had been settled, Poland was able to maintain a considerable share in the Scandinavian market; and a few years later the proud British industry had the humiliation of being forced to make an accommodation with its new rival, agreeing to give her a proportionate share of the Scandinavian market.

The absurdity of the scheme, from a clearly economic point of view, is that Poland's own consumption of coal is ridiculously small; the home price had to be kept high in order that the export trade could be subsidized. This absurd policy applied also to even more important things. Poland, for example, had a considerable production of sugar beet; so that sugar should be available for sale in world markets at competitive prices, it was necessary to maintain the home price at an inordinately high level. Consequently the poorest people were unable to afford sugar. This meant in turn that the price of sugar for home consumption must go up again, so that the subsidy on exports could be maintained. It was admittedly absurd when an Englishman could buy Polish sugar in London considerably cheaper than could a Pole in Warsaw.

Although taken as a whole Polish economy survived the storm of depression remarkably well, the poorer people were hard hit. A reduction in the annual income of an Englishman or Frenchman of five pounds is not a tremendously serious matter, but to a Polish peasant it is a dreadful blow. He can always feed himself, but his purchasing power depends entirely upon world prices for agricultural produce. As these fell, so the purchasing power of the Polish peasant fell: in turn he was unable to buy manufactured goods, and Polish, British, French, and German workmen were thrown out of work. So the vicious circle continued. In spite of that, the Polish peasants tightened their belts and carried on. The sales of farms during the critical years never rose above the average—this is a certain sign of confidence in rural Europe.

We in Britain have an ordered life, and a change of government alters it but little. We tend to be suspicious of "strong man" governments abroad: too often their blatant nationalism has led to war: or, at least, to the death of democracy.

Pilsudski was not a strong man of this type. He used to explain how, when the Russians threatened Warsaw, he retired to a lonely room to make his fateful decisions, and shared Napoleon's thoughts under the same circumstances—comparing himself to a weak young woman on her bed, nerving herself for the ordeal of labour. Yet under his rough skin and hard tone was a deep sensitiveness. He died in May, 1935.

III

Pilsudski's successor was a serious-minded man. Edward Rydz was the son of a peasant, and was born in south-eastern Poland. Orphaned in his childhood, he became a devout student, with a talent for drawing and painting. Some of his contemporaries, indeed, considered him slightly too serious. At the age of eleven he organized a society to combat the habit of smoking by school-boys, and any tobacco found in the school was forcibly confiscated and given to the local home for the aged!

It was while he was a student at Cracow that he came under the influence of Pilsudski, and was one of the earliest recruits for his legions. Before the start of the First World War he had advanced to the command of a battalion, and fought gallantly in the battles of the Polish Legion. On the arrest and imprisonment of Pilsudski, the task of Rydz was to sustain the organization of the disbanded legionaries, to keep the military spirit of Poland alive so that its army would be ready at the critical moment. In this, at least, he succeeded.

By this time his name had taken the double form which is now familiar. In the pre-1914 days, when Polish patriots were necessarily secret plotters, a pseudonym was essential, particularly when operating in Russian Poland. Rydz took as his pseudonym Smigly, and retained both names.

He fought against the Russians when they invaded Poland, but he held aloof from politics—until he was involved after Pilsudski's death. Smigly-Rydz was no genius, and never pretended to be. He was an honest man of average ability—he might have passed as an English country gentleman. It was soon revealed that he was out of his depth in international affairs, for as soon as events had advanced beyond the stage for which Pilsudski had immediately prepared, then the Polish directors began to make vital mistakes.

Pilsudski's policy had been simple. His first instinct was to fling himself into the arms of the League of Nations, whose progenitor had done so much to re-establish Poland. But his severely practical outlook soon discerned that, in spite of brave words, none of the great Powers was disposed to trust her destiny to the League.

He made an alliance with France, the country with which Poland had for long been culturally and emotionally associated. Then he found that the French seemed to be treating him not as a partner but rather as an employee. The alliance cooled: but the French were staggered when Pilsudski made a Ten Year Peace Pact with Hitler. His reasoning was not new: "if you can't beat 'em, join 'em". The French had overlooked one significant fact: the day after Hitler became German Chancellor, Pilsudski proposed a Franco-Polish invasion of Germany at the first sign of German rearmament. France rejected the idea, and so Pilsudski turned elsewhere. But he trusted Hitler not quite as far as he could see him.

Events of 1939 were interesting rather than important. Smigly-Rydz and Beck thought that they were covered by the clauses of the Ten Year Peace Pact: so they were—on paper. The Czech crisis which culminated at Munich, and the seizure of Czechoslovakia in March, 1939, showed how far Hitler's word—or even his signature—could be trusted.

Polish opinion rallied strongly. There had been heated arguments—even a frontier dispute—with Czechoslovakia, but after all its peoples were fellow-Slavs, distant cousins. Who would be the next Nazi victim? The answer was disquietingly obvious.

But even before this, Colonel Beck, the Polish Foreign Minister, had had discussions with Hitler and Ribbentrop. They demanded the return of Danzig to Germany, and better transport facilities across the "Corridor". For these "adjustments" they were prepared to pay. Ribbentrop proposed that Germany and Poland should make a united attack on Russia, and Poland should then be compensated for the loss of Danzig by a slice of the Ukraine!

Beck and Smigly-Rydz refused downright, as they did when Ribbentrop's proposal was repeated. This refusal to join in the attack on Russia inevitably meant that Poland would be the victim of Nazi attack.

Czechoslovakia satisfactorily disposed of, Hitler presented an ultimatum to Lithuania for the cession of the port and territory of Memel, and two days later his forces occupied them both. Yet another two days, and he demanded the return of Danzig, with a motor road and railway across the "Corridor".

Poland declined. Someone had to be the first to say "No" to Hitler, and Britain and France had given her a guarantee, which became a firm alliance.

The effect in Poland was electric. Firm in their courage, the Poles read the events in Czechoslovakia in their true light, and saw only too clearly that Poland must be the next intended victim. Determined to fight whatever the odds, they now found themselves reinforced by the two powerful democracies of western Europe. All doubts were instantly resolved. If there were any Poles who despaired of the ability of their country to hold Germany at bay, their determination and hopes were rekindled by the news. Alas, the Poles did not know that their distant Western allies had no means of implementing their guarantees.

Hitler denounced his pact with Poland—and his naval pact with Britain. German troops poured into Danzig, disguised as "tourists". Frontier incidents began. Hitler did not even trouble to invent fresh "atrocities". He used the Czech ones all over again, merely changing the dates.

When Britain and France made an obvious approach towards Russia, the Poles were not eager for Russian help. The last time the Russians had entered Poland they had stayed for nearly a hundred and fifty years. The suspicions engendered by the

4

Soviet invasion of 1920 had by no means been allayed. So Ribbentrop, failing to get satisfaction from Beck, got it from Molotov, who was much more pliable.

And so the Second World War began.

4

HITLER'S POLAND

I

THE aggressor has every initial advantage. He selects the time and place of the attack, and deploys his forces accordingly.

The German onslaught proved what leading Poles had long suspected—that their frontiers were incapable of defence. In 1919 they had pleaded with the victors that East Prussia should be demilitarized: now it provided the basis for an outflanking movement.

The new German armoured divisions later defeated the combined French and British armies. The Poles could scarcely be expected to arrest their progress. They fought gallantly, with touches of their ancient emotional heroism, as when their cavalry actually charged German tanks. But their country was hopelessly defeated in the air, and in modern war control of the air is decisive. Nazi air raids so disrupted communications that hundreds of thousands of Polish reservists never reached the battle area. On the advice of Britain and France, the Polish government had not ordered an earlier mobilization, lest it should annoy Hitler!

The Poles made a fighting and orderly retreat; there was always the hope that the invaders would outrun their supplies. Then the Poles would gain a breathing space, and prepare for a counter-attack: they recalled the apparently hopeless situation in 1920, when the Russians had been halted at the gates of Warsaw. But miracles seldom repeat themselves. While the Poles resisted the ferocious German onslaught, on 17th September a Russian army of a million and a half men crossed the eastern frontier. From that moment the end of Poland was merely a question of time.

Old diplomatists would be puzzled by modern usages. At the moment the Soviet troops invaded Poland, Russia made a declaration of neutrality!

A few minutes before the invasion began, a note was handed to the Polish Ambassador in Moscow. It declared that the Polish state had ceased to exist, so Russia was sending troops to "protect" the populations of western Ukraine and Bielo-Russia.[1]

The Polish patrols could only offer a token resistance: such was the confusion that some of them believed that the Russians had come as friends!

The Polish command, which had not been inspired throughout, cracked under the strain. Marshal Smigly-Rydz took refuge in Roumania, thereby incurring the odium of his people. By Polish tradition, he should have died with his army: nobody could ever imagine Pilsudski withdrawing because he had lost a battle!

The Nazi armies were not Hitler's only weapon. The greater part of the German residents in Poland now revealed themselves as traitors or "Fifth Columnists". Thousands had been armed, and they now waged a guerrilla war in the rear of the Polish forces. Many acted as guides to the Germans, or indicated objectives for air attacks, or fed or sustained the Nazi troops. Many more acted as saboteurs, wrecking Polish communications. The war was over before it began.

II

"Beat the Poles, drive them to be sick of life. They must be exterminated. If the dismembered Poland under the heel of the

---

[1] The Pact of non-aggression between Russia and Poland amply covered the situation. It read:

Article 1. The two Contracting Parties, recording the fact that they have renounced war as an instrument of policy in their future relations, reciprocally undertake to refrain from taking any aggressive action or invading the territory of the other Party, either alone or in conjunction with other Powers.

Article 2. Should one of the Contracting Parties be attacked by a third State or by a group of other States, the other Contracting Party undertakes not to give aid or assistance, either directly or indirectly, to the aggressor State during the whole period of the conflict.

Pacts and treaties have been freely advocated as panacea in the new Europe, often by countries whose primary impulse is war-weariness. We must not expect them to be enthusiastically received, especially in the small countries. In 1939 the peace of Europe was amply covered by a multitude of pacts, but at the moment of crisis very few nations honoured their signatures.

Prussian official be a menace for all-powerful Germany, may it not be said that a freed Poland would re-establish by her very existence the balance of power necessary for the existence of Europe? Beat the Poles, drive them to be sick of life."

This sounds like one of the stirring periods of an address by Hitler or Goebbels. Actually it is a quotation from a speech by Bismarck. There was little new or original in the Nazi philosophy.

Consider, for example, the declaration of the Prussian minister Hammerstein, in 1904. "The Polish problem will cease to worry us only when there are no more Poles, but only Polish-speaking Prussians. In my opinion our patience is still too great. It is not an adversary worthy of us: our business is to command and theirs to obey."

Shortly before the invasion of Poland, Hitler addressed his generals. He told them that Poland must be punished severely. The Polish upper and educated classes, especially the clergy, must be exterminated. He would not ask the generals to do this work—it would be entrusted to the S.S. All he asked of the generals was that they should not interfere.

Hitler extended the term "intelligentzia" to include anyone out of the ordinary—even outstanding sportsmen. After a casual beginning, in which local Nazi officials were allowed freedom for any repressive action, the repression was organized. Concentration camps were set up all over the country, and travelling extermination centres also came into use.

Conditions of everyday life were made quite clear from the first moment. Poles of both sexes were ordered peremptorily to leave the pavements when German officers and non-commissioned officers passed. They were also obliged to bare their heads when a German approached. In the western provinces the use of Polish was forbidden in public—the Gauleiter at Bydgoszcz naïvely remarked in one of his manifestoes: "In some shops the Poles had the audacity to speak Polish even after the city had been occupied by the Germans."

Hitler blatantly proclaimed his policy. "What will the new social order consist of? A part of it will be the new class of lords ... below there will be the new middle status, the basic of party comrades ... and still lower ... the great mass of nameless eternal subjects ... The lowest social stratum, situated much lower than the nameless subjects, is made up of foreign labourers coming from countries conquered by us, and whom without hesitation we may call the modern slaves."

Western Poland was incorporated into the Reich. Immediately the deportation of the Poles began: most were concentrated in the "Governor-Generalship", a rump Poland established south and east of Warsaw: later, the fiction that there was still a Poland on the map was abandoned, and Hitler's policy was fully implemented.

The execution squads were kept busy. The slightest suggestion of opposition to the invaders was punished by the shooting of hostages. Wholesale deportations began: the aim was to reduce the Polish population at all costs.

The methods by which this objective was achieved are important. Comfortable people who have escaped the direct impacts of war complain that they have heard enough of horrors: this plaint is usually a sign of selfish outlook or uneasy conscience. We can never understand the Polish attitude to the Germans today unless we try to appreciate the conditions of the German occupation.

A German poster, issued early in the war, is very revealing of the Nazi mentality.

In order to curb the insolent behaviour of a part of the Polish population I decree as follows:

1. The Polish inhabitants of both sexes are obliged to make way before the representatives of German authority in so far as the latter can be recognized through their uniforms or armlets on their sleeves. The streets belong to the victors and not to the vanquished.

2. The Polish inhabitants of male sex are obliged to show their respect to all representatives of the State, the party, and the military forces by uncovering their heads.

3. The Poles are forbidden to employ the German form of greeting by raising their hands.

4. In the shops and at the market stands all representatives of German authority, members of their families, and all German nationals must be served first before the vanquished.

5. The wearing of Polish school uniforms, of caps with Polish badges, etc., as well as the wearing of uniforms or badges by Polish railway and postal officials, is prohibited.

6. It is forbidden particularly to the young people to forgather in streets and at street corners.

7. Anyone accosting a German woman or girl will receive exemplary punishment.

8. Polish women who accost Germans will be confined in brothels.

9. All vehicles and bicycles must be equipped with red rear-lights. Non-compliance will be punished and the bicycle confiscated.

10. Instructions issued by members of the National Motor Car Corps or Auxiliary Traffic Police must be strictly observed.

All Poles who have not yet grasped that they are the vanquished while we are the victors, and who will not comply with the above decree, will be punished with all severity of the law.

Only a German authoritarian mind could issue a series of regulations mingling threats of death with directions about red rear-lights; and only a German official would fail to see the humour of paragraph 3!

The economy of Poland was completely ruined, the currency left in chaos, the natural wealth exploited, the factories devastated, and the communications destroyed. Not even in the fierce medieval days was repression so complete and so inexorable.

Winston Churchill put it with his usual dramatic fire: "Every week Hitler's firing parties are busy in a dozen lands. Monday he shoots Dutchmen; Tuesday, Norwegians; Wednesday, French or Belgians stand against the wall; Thursday it is the Czechs who must suffer, and now there are the Serbs and Greeks to fill his repulsive bill of executions. But always, all the days, there are the Poles."

III

The official estimate of the number of Polish dead is 6,028,000. Of these, 3,000,000 were Jews, and only about 30,000 Jews survived the Nazi terror.

Before the war, Jews formed 10 per cent of the Polish population. In Warsaw and Cracow they numbered 30 per cent, in Vilno and Lwow 40 per cent, and in Pinsk 80 per cent.

We have seen that Polish kings, exercising that toleration which was a tradition of their country, invited Jewish traders to settle in Poland centuries ago. In the early stages of the immigration the Jews brought unquestioned advantages to the land of their adoption, for they had business capacity, enterprise and capital, all of which (except the last) were sadly lacking among the native population. In exchange for their services as merchants, they were allowed to settle in the towns, and to some extent—especially from the cultural and religious points of view—were allotted a liberal measure of self-government.

By no means all the Jews were descendants of those who were invited to settle by the Polish monarchs; here, indeed, lies the ground of one of the Polish complaints. In Czarist days Jews were forbidden to settle in Russia proper, but were banished to the "Pale", the ring of subject states about the western border of Russia. As Poland was by far the largest of the countries of the Pale, she received a tremendous influx of Russian Jews: thus, today, many of the Jewish families of Poland have been settled there no more than half a century. The influence of these Russian Jews had not been at all happy. The psychological basis of their disturbing influence is readily comprehensible. The only government they had ever known was an oppressor.

This concentration of the Jews contributed automatically to the spread of anti-Semitism in Polish districts. "Outsiders" are never welcomed by people who are themselves never far from the verge of poverty, and the outsiders were of a different race and culture. Further, by Russian restrictions and peasant opposition it was almost impossible for the Jew to buy land. Thus, even if it had not been his natural bent, he must have gravitated naturally towards commerce. There is, of course, nothing new in anti-Semitism, which cannot be controlled by government regulation.

German traders settling in Poland might be assimilated in time. The Jews were not: they were always obstinately Jews. The fact that they maintained themselves as a race apart automatically led to many misunderstandings. For example, the Czar in 1915 ordered that the Poles should evacuate their land before the German advance. But the order did not apply to the Jews, who remained behind and did comparatively well. This led, naturally enough, to the suspicion that the Jews were pro-German: it is idle to argue whether the accusation was true or not—most Poles believed it to be true.

The problem of the Jews in Poland was intensified by the rise of the Zionist doctrine. The insistent claim that the Jews were a nation played right into the hands of their potential opponents. "You claim that you are not Poles but Jews," they said in effect; "very well then, what are you doing in Poland? Get out: go to your own country—wherever you imagine that may be."

It was the Zionist doctrine which impelled the Jews of Poland in the first days of the reborn state to put forward claims for a separate Jewish parliament, demanding in fact a state within a state. The Poles rejected this demand as impracticable and no one would quarrel with their decision, for the Jews were freely scattered throughout the country and it was obviously impossible that one law should apply to a man living on one side of the street and another to the man who lived opposite.

The reborn Poland found the greater part of its commercial life in Jewish hands, the distributive trade almost entirely so. But in the new Poland the old snobbish views about participation in industry and commerce had completely disappeared, and the Poles naturally wished to control their own affairs. Polish firms— sometimes with government backing—drove the Jews from the trading field; even in the rural districts the Jewish trader was driven out of business by the new Co-operative Societies. The "poor Jew" had become one of the thorniest problems of the greater question of the Jews of Poland. In the immediate post-war years there were many unfortunate incidents, where peasants attacked the men who held their mortgages: later there were occasional minor outbursts in the towns by irresponsible hotheads who imagined themselves to be budding Hitlers. With the revival of learning in Poland, fostered by the new opportunities, it was discovered that an overwhelming proportion of the professional life of Poland was in Jewish hands. In older days peasants could not become lawyers, teachers, or doctors, and gentry had no such ambitions. Today sons of peasants and sons of magnates study side by side at the magnificent universities, and naturally looked for a place in the professional, cultural, or administrative life of their country. They could only find such places at the expense of the Jews.

Not all the Jews of Poland were poor, for much of the Polish trade was in Jewish hands. Among the intelligentzia and commercial families there was much inter-marriage between Jews and Christians: an increasing number of Jews spoke Polish not as their second language but as their first. But the Jewish proportion of the Polish population was far too high a number for rapid assimilation.

Hitler decided to solve the problem by a simple method: the extermination of the Jews.

Within a few days of the defeat of Poland a ready-prepared programme of restrictions was put into force. Jews had to wear distinguishing marks on their clothing: their businesses were confiscated: their wives or daughters were raped or herded into brothels for the delight of the Nazi soldiers. There had been residential ghettoes in many Polish cities, but Jews had of course been able to live where they wished. Now they were all interned in ghettoes within high walls. In Warsaw 450,000 people were crowded into a small area, living ten or more to a room.

Young, strong Jews were sterilized before being sent to forced labour camps. The food allowed to the ghetto population was a starvation diet. In April, 1943, the Jews of the Warsaw ghetto revolted.

This was quite hopeless, and they knew it: but for nearly a month they kept up the fight. Then the survivors were massacred, and the ghetto was completely destroyed. When I saw it immediately after the war it consisted of acres of broken masonry, devoid of life: except for rats, which fattened on the corpses among the ruins.

Even before this the preparations for Hitler's "Final Solution" had begun. The Jews were herded into death camps. Some were "allowed" to work until they dropped: then, with their weaker friends, they faced execution in gas or steam rooms.

I do not need to dwell upon such horrors of it all. These were described in detail at the Nuremberg trials; and later we shall see Oswiecym, or Auschwitz, the largest of the camps—but by no means the only one. Yet I should emphasize the inhumanity of the Nazi rule in order that we may try to understand the feelings of Jews and Poles for the Germans today.

The Jews suffered worst of all, but the treatment of the Poles was shocking enough. Consider the statistics. 644,000 Poles were killed in battle, air raids, or other military operations: four-fifths of these were civilians. 3,577,000 Poles and Polish Jews died in death camps, mass executions, or the wiping out of the ghettoes: 1,286,000 died in prisons or labour camps—mostly from starvation or brutal treatment. Another 521,000 died outside the camps of wounds, starvation or hard labour. Excluding the military casualties, about five and a half million died during the Nazi terror. Of these, three million were Jews.

This is not the end of the tragic story. 590,000 people were totally disabled, and the excess of TB cases above the normal was 1,140,000. Seventy-nine per cent of the casualties occurred in the towns—which housed a minority of the population, but were of course more susceptible to mass murder. 2,480,000 Poles were deported to Germany or other occupied countries for forced labour, and a further 2,478,000 were compulsorily expelled from their homes for resettlement in areas designated by the Germans. The total number of Poles killed in action or murdered amounted to the fantastic figure of 220 per thousand of the population—the British figure was 8, the American 1·4. To complete the biological picture, it is estimated that the number of births during the occupation was at least 1,200,000 less than normal, and the general mortality rate had increased from 13 to 18 per thousand.

The economy of Poland was completely ruined, and its currency rendered worthless. It was amazing that any of the Poles survived: they were half-starved—their daily food ration amounted only to 500 calories, against the British war-time figure of 2,900 calories.

But the terror only encouraged the Polish resistance. The Home Army was formed: at first consisting of small groups of guerrilla fighters, it developed into a disciplined force, working under the direction from London of the Polish government in exile—and in constant communication with this. It had a real effect on the military situation, but every action provoked German reprisals. The Home Army would attack a German convoy in a country lane. The Nazis would seize all the men, women and children of the nearest village, and "execute" them.

In one respect Hitler completely failed in Poland. He was unable to find Polish quislings, despite his offers of generous bribes. The realization that the spirit of the nation could not be broken helped to demoralize the Nazi army of occupation.

On 22nd June, 1941, the Germans attacked Russia: their pact had served its purpose, and had kept Russia quiet while the Germans overran western Poland and western Europe: now it could be swept aside.

With the aggressor always holding the inevitable advantages, the Russians suffered a series of defeats and began a classic retreat almost to the gates of Moscow. Now the whole of Poland was under German domination.

The Nazi occupation now intensified its terror. Mass executions were continuous, and other types of barbarity were beyond description. It is small wonder that, a generation later, the Polish hatred and distrust of the Germans has not been assuaged. This is directed against the Communists of East Germany as well as against the Socialists, Liberals and Conservatives of the West.

5

BOUNDARIES

I

THE Russian stab in the back at the time of the Nazi onslaught
seriously distressed the Poles—and not merely because it completed their defeat. A Polish friend put it simply at the time:
The Western Allies will drive the Germans out of Poland. But
the Russians never give up territory which they have occupied—
it will need another war to get them out.

But now in 1941 the friends of 1939 were at war with each
other: the German attack on Russia transformed the situation.
Poles and Russians were now fighting a common enemy.

The Polish government-in-exile had a considerable force at its
command—of Poles who had escaped from Poland, as well as
emigrants who had returned from overseas to fight for their
own land. Their contribution to the Allied effort was considerable. For example, one-tenth of all the German aircraft shot
down during the Battle of Britain were the victims of Polish
airmen.

The Polish leader, General Sikorski, hurried to Moscow and
made a statesmanlike pact with Stalin. A Polish army should be
formed to serve beside the Russians. The Soviet-German Pact of
September, 1939, which partitioned Poland, was declared null
and void.

But Sikorski was to find that Stalin's word was worthless. His
pact with Hitler was null and void, he said: but he still claimed
the frontier which it had allotted to Russia. All the Poles living
east of that line must fight in the *Russian* army!

Here was a situation which Nazi propaganda exploited to the
full. But worse was to follow. The formation of the new Polish
army was hampered by the lack of officers. Sikorski asked Stalin
time and again for the return of the nine thousand officers who

had been taken prisoner by the Russians, and of whom nothing had been heard since April, 1940.

And now the advancing Germans announced in April, 1943, that the bodies of these officers had been found in a mass grave at Katyn, near Smolensk, but produced evidence to show that they had been murdered by the Russians.

Even I had known weeks earlier that the officers were dead, for the grave had been discovered by local peasants, and disquieting rumours had flooded Poland. Now again the Germans had a magnificent opportunity for propaganda. They exposed the bodies, and ran special trains for all parts of Poland carrying representative Poles, to whom they exhibited "proofs" of the Russian guilt.

The Polish government in London behaved correctly: it asked the Russians for more information. Eighteen months passed without this being elicited; it followed the example of the British when their prisoners were shackled, and appealed to the International Red Cross.

Stalin, who had previously admitted the "mistake" in a private conversation, now took a different line. He treated the Red Cross inquiry as an insult. The Poles might have expected this, but they had been spurred to action by the underground Home Army in Poland, which reported that the people were incensed at the news. Their government held ample proof that the murder of the officers was a "mistake" of the Russians, not of the Germans, but for the moment it might have been politic to accept the Russian disclaimer.

Stalin acted promptly. Realizing that any investigation would reveal the Russian guilt, he at once suspended diplomatic relations with Poland. He was already seeking an excuse for this, for he was ready to establish his own Polish government.

He had always insisted that Russia's neighbours must have "friendly" governments. This sounded reasonable enough, but by "friendly", Stalin meant "subservient". He had long organized a group of Polish communists in Russia ready for use when required.

His outlook was old fashioned: victory implied an increase of territory. The exiled Polish government in London refused to accept the frontier Stalin had agreed with Hitler in 1939. So he had decided to set up what he called a "friendly" government.

The Communist Party had been banned by Pilsudski as Russian agent. It went underground, however—until it was dissolved by the Comintern *on Stalin's orders* in 1937—because its members leaned to Trotsky rather than to Stalin!

The Union of Polish Patriots was formed in Moscow: when the Russians began to drive the Nazis out of Poland this Union was installed on Polish soil at Lublin as the National Liberation Committee. Soon Stalin declared it to be the Provisional Government of Poland.

There was already a Polish government-in-exile in London, led by a peasant representative, Mikolajczyk. If he had agreed to accept the Stalin-Hitler frontier, the "provisional government" would have disappeared overnight. But he was in close touch with his homeland, and he knew that Polish opinion was overwhelmingly against any surrender of territory.

Though the Russians had a claim to frontier rectification on ethnic grounds, this did not apply to what was virtually the whole of the eastern half of Poland. Stalin, however, was not one to change his mind.

He wanted more territory, and, especially, to take over all the territory peopled by the Ukrainians.

There have always been those in the Ukraine who yearned for independence: even today there are many who would like local home-rule. During the war nationalist ideas had stirred—and Hitler took advantage of them. He already had used his Ukrainian Bureau for subversive purposes.

In the first stages of the Nazi attack on Russia, the Germans captured very many Russian prisoners. Among them was a general, of Ukrainian stock, Vlassov. He may have been originally an Ukrainian Nationalist: certainly he was furious with Stalin for what he believed to be the wanton and incompetent way in which his army had been delivered to the Germans—who now saw how he could be used.

They suggested that he should form a new army from the Russian prisoners-of-war: say, 80,000 men. Vlassov recruited this number within a few days, and later his force neared half a million. The Germans did not trust it to act against Russia: but many a British soldier will recall his astonishment when he discovered that the "German" prisoners he had captured were Russians!

Another task was found for Vlassov's troops. Official Polish documents record that some of the most horrible atrocities were carried out by the S.S., Gestapo, Volksdeutsche (citizens of German stock) and by "Ukrainians in the service of the Germans". These were colloquially known by the name of Vlassovites. "The Ukrainians, incited by the Germans, often even outstripped the Germans in acts of terror."[1]

Thus Stalin's seizure of Eastern Poland apparently had a double objective—revenge not only on the Poles for their victory in 1920, and their continuous suspicion of the Soviet Union, but also on the Ukrainians. The "Vlassovites" who fell into his hands might have been pitied had not so many of them been involved in the mass murders of Poles and Jews.

Though nobody mentions it in public these days—the government, anxious for Russian friendship, would be annoyed—we have not heard the last of Katyn. But no one in Poland has forgotten. When the Poles rose in revolution in October, 1956, the crowds spontaneously began to shout "Katyn! Katyn!"

II

The Polish government in London, through its "shadow cabinet" in Poland, organized the efforts of the Home Army, which continually harassed the Nazis. Later, the Communists raised their own partisan groups, but these were small compared with the organized units of the Home Army.

The time came for this to make a supreme effort. The tide of battle had turned, and by the end of July, 1944, the advancing Russians had reached the bank of the Vistula opposite Warsaw. For weeks the Kosciuszko radio, the Russian radio operated for the Lublin committee, had been exhorting the Poles, and especially the people of Warsaw, to strike against the Nazis. The Russian army was driving the Germans out of Eastern Poland, and had reached the Vistula south of Warsaw. Then, on 29th July, 1944, their guns were heard in Warsaw itself, and the Nazis admitted that they had retreated to Praga, just across the river. On that day the Poles heard a stirring call to arms from the Russian Kosciuszko radio. "People of Warsaw, the time for the last battle

[1] *Poland under Nazi Occupation*. Polonia, 1961.

Castle Square, Warsaw, with the Column of King Sigismumid III:
(*above*) as it was in 1939 and (*below*) as it was in 1945. It has now been
restored to its pre-war appearance

Stare Miasto—the Old Town Market Square—in Warsaw as it was in 1945. The restored square is shown facing page 96

Polish patriots hanged by the Nazis in a Warsaw street

has come! Deal a death-blow to the beast of Prussian militarism! The hour of deeds has struck for Warsaw! Fight in the streets, in the factories, in the houses!" (There is an echo of Churchill in the Russian phrases.) And the following day: "The Russian armies approach Praga. They come to bring you liberation. People of Warsaw, to your arms! Attack the Germans! Help the Red Army across the Vistula! The million inhabitants of Warsaw must become a million soldiers who will destroy the German tyrants!"

Previous appeals had gone unheeded—as early as 1941 the Russians had urged the Poles to make a mass rising—which would inevitably have failed and led to a massacre. The Home Army had hitherto restricted themselves to guerrilla tactics, awaiting the day when it could attack in force. Now, it seemed, that day had come.

At the same time the Polish prime minister arrived in Moscow. The Poles, especially the Home Army, were encouraged. He would doubtless work out a satisfactory arrangement with the Russians.

The Home Army was pathetically weak in weapons. Yet its first efforts were successful until the German armour and guns rolled into Warsaw. General Bor-Komorowski, the Polish commander, appealed to the Allies for aid. To his consternation, the Russians refused this on the grounds that the rising was an internal affair, undertaken without the approval of the Polish command!

Actually, Stalin was aggrieved that the rising was not led by the Communist "People's Army": this was a comparatively weak organization—some of whose members fought gallantly beside the Home Army.

The fact was that the Russians had outrun their supplies, and the northern wing of their army had sustained a defeat and been driven back to the north of Warsaw. But Stalin never admitted defeats, and preferred to put the blame on the Poles.

His next move was indeed a shock. Churchill and Roosevelt were scarcely interested in rival ideologies: they would support anybody who fought against Hitler. As the Russians had refused or were unable to supply the Warsaw insurgents, British and Polish airmen made the precarious flight to drop supplies in Warsaw. And the Russians refused to allow the aircraft of their allies to land at Russian airfields in Eastern Poland to refuel! It was as well that Stalin did not hear some of the acid comments on allies in the R.A.F. camps: dozens of our aircraft and crews were lost for lack of this elementary courtesy.

After a month, however, the Russians changed their minds and attempted to send aid to Warsaw—too little and too late. Earlier it might have been possible. (One Polish unit, serving with the Russian army, crossed the Vistula and joined the Home Army.) But now it was useless. The Polish fighters had been broken up into a number of separate detachments. On the sixty-third day of this remarkable battle the remnants of the insurgents had to surrender.

(Polish historians of today have to write with care. The professional instinct is to record the whole truth, but this might incur Russian displeasure. A Polish official publication[1] thus describes the outbreak of the revolt.

> On 1st August, 1944, when the Soviet offensive drove the Germans to the left bank of the Vistula, the Headquarters of the Home Army issued an order to start an uprising in Warsaw. Militarily the uprising was directed against the German army, but politically it was aimed against the Committee of National Liberation and against the Soviet Union, with whom plans for the uprising had not been agreed. It was obvious that, following the exhaustive Spring offensive of 1944, the Soviet army could not attempt to cross the Vistula in the summer of that year. Thus the insurgents, who in this situation had to rely on their own resources, were forced to capitulate after 63 days of heroic fighting.

This account is somewhat self-contradictory, and ignores such events as the call to arms. And its suggestion that the Russians were too exhausted to cross the river is contradicted by the fact that they already crossed the Vistula farther south: and that a Polish unit accomplished the feat during the battle. The writer is however correct in his differentiation between the military and political objectives: at the moment, however, the defeat of the Nazis was far more important than the imposition of a Communist government on Poland.)

The Russian propaganda had been contradictory. While

[1] *Poland, 1944–1964.* Polonia Publishing House.

condemning the revolt, their Kosciuszko radio station was broadcasting: "We see in the present rising a manifestation of the fighting spirit of the democratic camp, and the Warsaw fighting is to us as sacred as any act of combat against the enemy."

The rising ended in a Nazi massacre, and Warsaw was destroyed. (Later, a Nazi documentary film was captured, and it may be seen at the Historical Museum in Warsaw. It shows German soldiers deliberately and systematically wrecking blocks of buildings with explosives and flame throwers, on Hitler's express order, to destroy Warsaw completely. He was obeyed to the extent of 85 per cent. And, what was worse, a massacre followed: well over a hundred thousand people perished in the Nazi reprisals.)

The Union of Polish Patriots made the usual right-about-turn. It had attacked the Home Army for making the rising—and then, when it was beaten, condemned it for surrendering!

The rising need not have happened. The Teheran Conference had ended. Stalin had declared that he was determined to create and maintain a "strong and independent democratic Poland". The Polish leaders knew that the Russian definition of words like "independent" and "democratic" differed completely from those in the West. They had to face the fact that British and American declarations were pious hopes, and no more: their Western friends had submitted weakly to Stalin's demands. The power lay with the Russians.

They sent a courier to explain the situation to Bor-Komorowski. However, his units were already on the move, and any attempt to cancel the rising would have exposed them to the Nazi fury. So the fight began.

Heroism is a Polish characteristic—I have heard it called a Polish "illness". Battles against hopeless odds are frequent in Polish history: the Poles have lived heroically. The Battle of Warsaw has more than any other affected the Polish temperament, and has subdued the ardent and romantic spirit which for long was predominant. Their pride in the gallantry and sacrifice of the Home Army is undiminished, as is their resentment of the Russian attitude. The name of the Russian general who withheld his aid at the critical period of the battle is worth remembering: it was Rokossowski. We shall meet him again.

III

Mikolajczyk, the peasant leader, continued his efforts to reach an agreement with Russia. At a critical moment, however, the Poles reverted to their ancient weakness, and began to quarrel among themselves.

One can understand the difficult situation of the prime minister of a government-in-exile when asked to surrender national territory! Mikolajczyk protested vehemently against the Allied agreement that Russia should acquire the eastern half of Poland. He did however secure guarantees for the western frontier on the Oder; but, having unwillingly accepted Stalin's boundary in the east, could not carry his colleagues with him, and resigned. His successor was Arciszewski, a Socialist leader, a friend of Lenin, who was however anti-Communist. From this point Stalin pursued his own path without hindrance. Churchill commented that if only the Polish government had accepted the Curzon Line at the outset there need never have been a Lublin Committee (i.e. a rival Communist government).

Arciszewski and his friends pinned their faith to the Atlantic Charter, which everybody had signed—but nobody honoured.

Mikolajczyk was an intelligent man. He saw that Stalin was immovable on the subject of frontiers, so he concentrated on securing a free and independent Poland—much more important than the actual extent of the country. On other issues he was prepared to compromise: he was prepared to include Communists in his government, and to negotiate a defensive alliance with Russia.

But the outlook of Arciszewski was much more popular in Poland, where old suspicions of Russia had been confirmed during the Warsaw rising. Nothing would have altered the situation. Stalin would consider no plan but his own. He referred Mikolajczyk to his puppet Polish government, now installed at Lublin as the National Liberation Committee, and later designated it as the Provisional Government of Poland.

Its members were Russian nominees, most of them Communists, and all of them quite unknown in Poland. Many of their ideas were fantastic. One of them appealed to Poles fighting in the British zones to turn against their leaders! But the Provisional Government was supported by the Red Army.

This was now sweeping the Germans out of Poland, where the confusion was complete. The position was well summarized by a far-sighted Labour member of parliament: "It is melancholy to think that after more than five years of fighting in a war which we entered to defend the independence of Poland, we should be debating whether Poland is to be a state at all."

The quarrel prolonged the war. By September, 1944, many of the German generals recognized that it was lost, but the Nazi leaders decided to fight on. The Allies were so divided over Poland, they believed, that the quarrel had to come into the open. They might possibly be able to persuade Russia to cease hostilities and make an alliance with Germany: or to persuade Britain and America to make a *volte face*. Meantime, thousands more British, American and Russian soldiers had to die.

It was in this uneasy atmosphere of mistrust that Churchill, Stalin and Roosevelt met at Yalta in the Crimea. In his record of events[1] Churchill revealed his uneasiness. He favoured Stalin's territorial claims; but he also realized that Stalin's ideas about a "free" and "independent" Poland were very different from his own. He agreed to the movement of the Polish western frontier to the River Oder, but was uneasy about its southern continuation along the Neisse. Apparently maps were not used in the general discussion—an amazing omission, for there are two rivers Neisse! He indeed admitted that the distinction between the Eastern and Western Neisse "did not emerge as clearly as it should have done".

I was told by someone present at Yalta that this describes the confusion very mildly. In the earlier stages of the discussions, and in the absence of maps, Churchill and Roosevelt supposed that Stalin was proposing the Eastern Neisse as the Polish frontier. He was not: this subject will be dealt with later.

The Yalta declaration on Poland read:

> We came to the Crimea Conference resolved to settle our differences about Poland.
>
> We discussed fully all aspects of the question. We reaffirmed our common desire to see established a strong, free, independent and democratic Poland.
>
> As a result of our discussion, we have agreed on the conditions in which a new Polish Provisional Government of National Unity

[1] *Triumph and Tragedy.* Cassell, 1954.

may be formed in such a manner as to command recognition by the three major Powers. The agreement reached is as follows:

A new situation has been created in Poland as a result of her complete liberation by the Red Army.

This calls for the establishment of a Polish Provisional Government which can be more broadly based than was possible before the recent liberation of Western Poland.

The Provisional Government which is now functioning in Poland should, therefore, be reorganized on a broader democratic basis with the inclusion of democratic leaders from Poland itself and from Poles abroad.

This new Government should then be called the Polish Provisional Government of National Unity.

M. Molotov (Russia), Mr. Harriman (U.S.A.), and Sir A. Clark Kerr (Great Britain) are authorized as a commission to consult in the first instance in Moscow with members of the present Provisional Government and with other Polish democratic leaders from within Poland and from abroad, with a view to reorganization of the present Government along the above lines.

This Polish Provisional Government of National Unity shall be pledged to the holding of free and unfettered elections as soon as possible on basis of universal suffrage and secret ballot.

In these elections all democratic and anti-Nazi parties shall have the right to take part and to put forward candidates.

When a Polish Provisional Government of National Unity has been properly formed in conformity with the above, the Government of the U.S.S.R., which now maintains diplomatic relations with the present Provisional Government of Poland, and the Government of the United Kingdom, and the Government of the U.S. will establish diplomatic relations with the new Polish Provisional Government of National Unity, and will exchange ambassadors, by whose reports the respective Governments will be kept informed about the situation in Poland.

The three heads of Government consider that the eastern frontier of Poland should follow the Curzon Line with digressions from it in some regions of five to eight kilometres ($3\frac{1}{8}$ to five miles) in favour of Poland.

They recognize that Poland must receive substantial accessions of territory in the north and west.

They feel that the opinion of the new Polish Provisional Government of National Unity should be sought in due course on the extent of these accessions, and that the final delimitations of the western frontier of Poland should thereafter await the Peace Conference.

The Poles recognized the declaration for what it was—a complete surrender to Stalin. He had his own way on Poland's frontiers, both east and west. The latter was agreed by all, except for the boundary along the Western or Lusatian Neisse. The Poles were however allowed to take over the territory involved, with the proviso that the final delimitations should await the Peace Conference.

Much more serious were the decisions on internal politics. For all practical purposes power was handed over to the Russian satellite government. The Russians interpreted its reorganization as the inclusion of one or two non-Communist Poles: the British and Americans demanded a more representative basis. Most of the Poles looked to the exiled government as the legitimate authority.

But this was not the end of the tragedy. The London government had a "shadow cabinet" in Poland, and during the war this had rendered sterling service with the Resistance.

The British and American governments began to press exiled Poles to return to the homeland, and to come to terms with the Russian-sponsored government; and it was learned with satisfaction that the Polish "shadow cabinet" had been invited to meet the Russians in conference.

They at once disappeared. Weeks later Molotov announced that they had been arrested on charges of "diversionary activities against the Red Army". And these were the men who had been opposing Hitler ever since Molotov had signed his pact with the Nazis.

Three of the Poles were later released—I met one of them. The others have never been heard of since. Almost certainly they are dead. It would scarcely be politic to mention them in the Poland of today!

The "free and unfettered" elections proved to be a farce: the Russians nominated their own government. This did however include Mikolajczyk and a few of his colleagues. When I visited Poland after the war, I found that the democratic ministers were almost prisoners. Mikolajczyk had long been a neighbour of mine in Harrow, so I called on him early when I returned to Poland during the summer of 1945. He had been allocated a Communist secretary who was virtually a bodyguard—or a spy. I tried for an hour to get rid of this fellow: then at last I succeeded—for two minutes. Mikolajczyk used these minutes to the full—I did not need to ask questions. He was trying his utmost to collaborate with the Communists for the good of Poland, but I was not surprised when a year later he relinquished the task as hopeless. Had he stayed, he would certainly have been "liquidated".

The Yalta agreement was the culmination of the Polish tragedy. The only people not consulted on its terms were the Poles; as when the Munich Agreement carved up Czechoslovakia, the people most concerned were ignored.

IV

The war provided much that is not forgotten in Poland today.

1. The Polish love of Russia, never very pronounced, was not intensified by the stab in the back of 17th September.
2. We can scarcely be surprised that German minorities are no longer welcome in Poland. The treachery of their predecessors is remembered only too well.
3. The Katyn massacre still rankles bitterly in Poland. Numerically, it included only a fraction of the Nazi murders, but its effects were far-reaching: the Poles were desperately anxious to attack the Nazis, but the formation of their new army was seriously delayed for the lack of the 9,000 officers. (Stalin, in an unguarded moment, referred to their execution as "a mistake" —which could well be true.)
4. Similarly, the Russian conduct during the Warsaw rising aroused a resentment which has not yet subsided.
5. The Communist government of Poland has many practical achievements to its credit, but it has had great difficulty in living down the fact that it was not chosen by the Poles, but was imposed from abroad.
6. Few Poles realize the difficulties of Churchill and Roosevelt at Yalta. If they had stubbornly opposed Stalin on the Polish issue, he might once again have made a pact with Hitler. To the Poles Yalta was a betrayal: how could they ever trust their Western allies again?

V

The new government of Poland faced fantastic difficulties. The devastation of the country was almost complete, and the human casualties were shocking. And the war was still raging.

Further, the members of the government were quite unknown to the Polish people. More than once the headman of a village would take me aside and ask if I could tell him who was this man Bierut, who called himself President of Poland: he had never previously heard of him.

Bierut—his real name was Krasnodebski: it was common in Polish underground politics to take a pseudonym—was a printer by trade: he had served in the Russian army in the First World War, got caught up in the revolutionary wave, and remained in Moscow—as a Russian citizen. Stalin used him as a political agent, and as such he was parachuted behind the German lines to organize a Communist rival to the Home Army. He could not be blamed for his complete failure. He was short and sturdy, and very intelligent. He discussed Polish affairs with me very frankly, but I judged him to be a very hard man and a ruthless Stalinist.

The prime minister of the day was Edward Osobka-Morowski. He was a Socialist—in theory—and had been included to preserve the fiction that the government was a genuine coalition. Actually, "fellow traveller" is the mildest description which could be applied to him. He was promptly dropped as soon as he had served his purpose.

Of the other ministers I met, Hilary Minc was a well-educated and intellectual man, with a first-class brain: but, like his chief, hard and ruthless—even with his colleagues.

All the leaders I met are now dead or disgraced—save one. I wrote in 1945:[1]

A man well worth watching is the Deputy Prime Minister, Wladyslaw Gomulka. He is a fervent Communist, without fear or favour—a man of ruthless energy and drive. Genuinely convinced of the righteousness of his cause, he is determined to see Poland become a Communist republic; his faith is such that it is not influenced by the fact that most people in the country do *not* want a Communist Poland. He showed his courage in underground activity during the war, and does not lack it now. He has the reputation of being a man who would risk everything to achieve his purpose. He dislikes his fellow Deputy Prime Minister, Mikolajczyk, intensely, and it is typical of his outlook that his most bitter charge was that Mikolajczyk planned to reintroduce Western Democracy into Poland!

[1] In *Russia's Neighbour—the New Poland*. Gollancz, 1946.

For all his Communism, Gomulka is careful to emphasize that he is a Pole and not a Russian puppet. The future of Poland may resolve itself in a tussle between Gomulka and Mikolajczyk, two able men of strong personality. Theirs is a real clash of ideas—one-party dictatorship and democratic government, Communism and Social Democracy.

Four years later I seemed a very incompetent prophet. Gomulka, a *Polish* Communist, refused to condemn the stand of Tito against Stalin. He was expelled from the party and jailed—to be hurriedly recalled in the critical days of 1956.

The political situation in 1945 was of a type which has now become familiar. The Communist Party knew exactly what it wanted, and followed Lenin's advice, to achieve power un-hampered by ethical considerations. For propaganda purposes other parties were allowed to exist—but the Communists pro-vided them with their leaders.

Suppose at the end of the war the Russians had found them-selves in control of Britain. Following the precedent in Poland, they would have said: "Now, we know that Communism is not strong in Britain, and we want you to retain your own methods of government. Since you prefer two or three parties to the centralized régime, you shall have them. The Labour and Conservative Parties shall continue. However, we shall have to make a few changes in their leadership. We propose to replace Mr. Attlee and Mr. Churchill by Mr. Harry Pollitt and Mr. William Gallacher. Later, when the parties have been reorganized, we shall appeal to Mr. Attlee and Mr. Churchill to return to the ranks, in junior positions, from patriotic motives, for the sake of British unity at a critical hour."

The Communist Party was disguised under the name of the Polish Workers' Party (Polska Partia Robotnicza, or P.P.R.). This was a wise precaution, for to the Poles "Communist" means "Russian".

Associated with it were the Polish Socialist Party (P.P.S.)—which actually supplied the Prime Minister, Edward Osobka-Morowski—the Democratic Party (P.S.D.), and the Peasants' Party (P.S.L.). Later the Socialist Party became the victim of a shotgun wedding with the Communists.

Socialism and State ownership were no novelties to the Poles. Pilsudski had been a Socialist in his youth: and when the Polish leader he had developed industry by establishing State enterprises. And he had begun a policy of breaking up the large estates into peasant farms.

So the first steps made by the Communist-dominated government was little more than extensions of old policies: nationalization of factories and expropriation of estates. Then Poland began to follow Russian patterns slavishly.

The confusion became even more fantastic. The government began to introduce Communism during a time of chaos, when some Poles were returning home from all corners of the world, and others were being expelled from eastern Poland and settled in the west. The economy had completely collapsed: money was worthless. Great areas—and whole towns—were utterly devastated: hundreds of thousands of Poles were searching for their families, and tens of thousands lay dead beneath the ruins. The replacement of photographs of Pilsudski by those of Bierut seemed but a trivial incident at such a time.

On his return from Yalta, Winston Churchill had asked significant questions about Poland. "Will the new government be properly constituted with fair representation of the Polish people? . . . Will the elections be free and unfettered? Will candidates of all democratic parties be able to present themselves to the electors and to conduct their campaigns? . . . The home of the Poles is settled. Are they to be masters in their own house? Is their sovereignty and independence to be untrammelled, or are they to become a mere protectorate of the Soviet, forced against their will to adopt the Communist or Totalitarian system?"

Mr. Churchill declared his faith in the sincerity of Russian intentions. He posed his queries to the British House of Commons, but everyone knew that they could not be answered in London or Washington, or even in Warsaw, but only in Moscow. By 1945 the answer was already apparent.

6

THE THIRD POLAND

I

WHEN the Russian armies did at last cross the Vistula and capture Warsaw, *fifteen people* crawled out of the ruins!

The Home Army casualties during the rising totalled 15,000 dead. The number subsequently massacred by the Nazis exceeded 150,000. Of the pre-war population of a million and a half, more than 100,000 were now in Praga, a suburb on the right bank of the Vistula: another 100,000 had sought refuge in the countryside. Now they began to stream back—to a dead city.

The German plan for Poland had been worked out well in advance. The eastern section of the country was incorporated into the Reich. It had a population of ten million, of whom 600,000 were Germans. The policy was to rid these regions of the Poles— by expulsion, forced labour, murder, or in appropriate cases, by Germanization. The evacuated regions were settled by Germans moved from the Baltic States and Roumania. The rest of Poland became the "General Government", with 12 million Poles and 96,000 Germans.

The Nazis had also applied the Pabst Plan, the basis of which was drawn up in 1939. It was a methodical operation to wipe the city of Warsaw off the map.

German engineers blew up street after street, house by house. The city had already suffered grievous blows, but this was organized destruction. Eleven thousand three hundred buildings were razed to the ground, and 14,270 battered into ruins—in all, 85 per cent of the buildings. Ninety per cent of the city was demolished: the Nazis took a special delight in destroying historic buildings.

The war was still raging and little could be done at once. Warsaw was still a ruin when I visited it a few weeks after the war ended: but it was no longer a dead city.

A trifling incident suggested the agony of its people. The British Embassy staff had arrived, and a friend asked me to take his little dog for a walk. The people I met gazed at us in curiosity and affection, and I often had to stop, as so many wished to stoop and pat the dog. A little thing can draw attention to a big one; and I realized that in the whole of Warsaw I had not seen even one dog or cat. They had all been killed and eaten years earlier.

The city was one huge heap of rubble, and the people improvising shacks or living in cellars. In no civilized country would a dog be assigned to such quarters. The population had now risen to 400,000—most of them across the river in Praga, where, compared with that of Warsaw proper, the destruction was only desultory.

Transport was primitive. The government had allocated a few lorries to serve as buses, but more people travelled by peasant cart, with planks stretched from side to side. "Taxis" consisted of tricycles, each pushing an object like a crude bath-chair.

When I needed to travel by train, a few routes had been cleared, but the rolling stock had been mostly destroyed. The few passenger coaches packed twenty into a compartment, and more on the roof. I found it more convenient to travel on a coal train. For a small present to the guard, I might ride third-class on the lumpy coal: for a larger bribe, first-class on the slack.

I heard a commotion in the street outside my lodging (a barracks): I rushed out. Some people were cheering: others—men as well as women—unashamedly weeping: some knelt and prayed. The cause of the excitement was a tram car, new and bedecked with flowers, being towed through the streets—the first since the great destruction. The chatter of conversation was happy and excited, like that of children at a party. This tram was the swallow which heralds the summer. Normal life was about to return: this was a sign of hope—and while man has hope he needs little else to give him happiness. Despair was already banished from the city. Physically it was a hulk: spiritedly it was vividly alive.

Notices everywhere announced that the clearance of such-and-such a street would begin next week. "Come and claim your dead," it advised. No one could even guess how many tens of thousands of bodies lay buried in the rubble.

The situation demanded stern measures. Every man, from dustman to cabinet minister, was paid 300 zloty a week: in addition—and far more valuable—he got two free meals a day. If the Black Market was fantastic, another was pathetic, as people stood offering for sale personal treasures which they had rescued from the ruins of their homes—a vast Caledonian Market. I met an old friend, a university professor, and his wife. His only "suit" was a pair of cotton overalls: his wife was scarcely decent—her frock was so patched that no further repairs were possible: great slits revealed that she wore no underwear. But they were happy.

Two hundred people, on the average, were killed every week by falling masonry. Others died more dramatically. Russian discipline had snapped with the end of the war, and looting was common. It was often accompanied by shooting: anyone who resisted might die. I saw two Russians looting a shop under the very eyes of a Polish policeman. "But what can I do?" he complained bitterly.

Even the greeting of the day reflected the years of terror. A man meeting an old friend would exclaim: "So you are alive!"

The ordeal of the Polish villages was not as terrible as that of the towns. Nevertheless, a common sight in 1945 was a burnt out village—of the thatched cottages, only brick chimney stacks survived. These villages had supported the Home Army—or were adjudged by the Nazis to have done so.

Where a village was intact, its fields were spoiled. There had been no seed for crops: most of the men were either dead or in forced labour camps, and weeds waist-high filled what once was fertile ground. The rearing of cattle and sheep had been an important part of Polish agriculture. The Nazis had helped themselves freely, to feed their armies.

And now the peasants had another complaint. In the Russian zone of Germany a herd of 500 cattle would be collected. Half a dozen Russian "displaced persons" would be ordered to work their passage home by driving the cattle to Kiev. They had to get their food for the journey as best they could, occasionally making a deal with a farmer, who would provide bread and vodka in exchange for a cow.

But when they neared their own country they might be twenty cows short, so they would loot twenty from neighbouring farms. Poland did not lose, but her peasants in the east did: nor did they disguise their anger. A new word appeared in the Polish language: "Our cow was Russianed".

Such comparatively trivial matters strained Polish–Russian relations. Here was a land ruled by a Communist-dominated government: yet in one day in Poland I heard more anti-Russian comment than I would hear in a week in England. And the commentators were not feudal magnates, but workers and peasants.

Yet, with all its background of tragedy and the immense difficulties of the day, the Poles were facing the future bravely. Their recovery from the devastation of the war was remarkable. They got little help from Russia and none from the West. When the Marshall Plan was promulgated, the Russians refused to allow them to share in its benefits. The Poles deserve great credit for the "Polish miracle" of survival and recovery: so do their government.

II

A hurried stocktaking suggested that the new Poland might have gained by her change of frontiers. But not in territory. In the east she lost 69,860 square miles: in the west she obtained 38,986 from Germany.

Her population, too, was reduced—from 35 million to 25 million; largely due to the appalling casualties of the war. But now it was a Polish Poland, virtually free from large numbers of troublesome minorities.

Industrially, her losses in the east were more than compensated by gains in the west. Her mineral resources in Silesia were important.

There were agricultural gains, too. The Oder–Neisse territories were by no means the most fertile of the German provinces, but at least they were better than those which Poland lost to Russia. And they had been more efficiently worked.

Soviet experts calculated that Poland had lost investments worth 3,500 million dollars in the east, but gained 9,500 million in the west. The Polish government was too polite to challenge these figures, or to comment on the industrial equipment removed by the Russians before the New Territories were handed over to the Poles.

On the whole, however, there were real prospects of higher living standards throughout Poland—in time.

Her most urgent need was for capital. The Americans were

deeply interested in Poland, but not in a Russian satellite. The Russians undertook to "settle the reparation claims of Poland from its own share of German reparations". This proved to be a pious hope, and little more. "You have the mines of Silesia and the farms of Pomerania—those are your reparations," said the Russians. But earlier they had declared that these assets were compensation for the loss of Polish eastern provinces.

The new government faced the problem of reconstruction boldly: it was an obvious priority. But in other respects it relapsed into usual Communist practice, as shaped by Stalin. It pleased the peasants by its programme of land reform, as begun by Pilsudski: all surviving big estates were converted into peasant farms. No sooner was this completed, however, than it alienated their goodwill by confiscating their farms and forcing the owners into collectives, and jailing objectors. It likewise seized all the industrial plants.

These actions would not have mattered so much if they had been accomplished efficiently. But the vital post of chairman of a collective was usually allocated to a Communist official—who could mouth clichés but knew nothing of farming. (The farms were not called collectives, by the way—that would have savoured too much of Russia. Their official title was "co-operative farms".) And the industrial enterprises soon got bogged down in a morass of bureaucracy.

On my next visit to Poland I found the situation changed. The eagerness of the reconstruction drive was spent: now each was thinking of his own welfare. There was endless grumbling about low wages and high prices; of incompetence and bungling in high places.

The democrats in the government had served their purpose and were discarded. Poland was completely under Stalinist rule, which did not promise happiness. But at my next visit, in 1958, the situation had once more changed—a partial return to earlier optimism. Stalin was dead, and had been denigrated—one might also say "debunked"—by Khrushchev. This led direct to the Poznan riots and a minor revolution.

The economic discontent in Poland had kept on rising and was now universal. This was by no means all: the Poles had long protested against being fed on lies. Professor Oscar Lange, a member of the Central Committee of the party and a well-known

The Black Virgin of Czestochowa

Quay in Gdynia, port on the Baltic Sea

The Westaplatte at Gdansk, scene of the start of the Second World War

economist, declared that the much-vaunted six-year plan, far from raising the standard of living, had actually failed: and that the use of compulsion was "leading to the disintegration of the national economy". Whereas government figures "proved" that wages had increased by 26 per cent, in actual fact their purchasing power had been decreased!

Not all the trouble was economic. The Polish mind was never made captive. A Russian-dominated government had been forced on the country, supported by Russian arms: physical revolt was impossible, but Soviet conduct scarcely tended to change age-old Polish prejudices against Russia. Stalin persistently promised "free and unfettered elections", disclaimed any intention to interfere in Poland's internal affairs, and declared that the Poles would live under a parliamentary system "which would be like the Belgian or Dutch". He dismissed as "stupid" the rumour that he proposed to Sovietize Poland. Such were his words, but the Poles were more affected by his deeds—which were the exact converse. He had to proceed rather slowly because at first there were not enough Polish fellow travellers to go round, but gradually and ruthlessly he imposed a Communist police state. The democratic parties were destroyed or absorbed; elections were rigged. Russia was proclaimed to be the friend and protector of Poland—a claim which even the Polish Communists scarcely pretended to believe.

The first protests were made by the Polish intellectuals. The "thaw" which followed the death of Stalin led to a vacillatory relaxation of the censorship. Communist leaders began to admit "mistakes". At least the wholesale Stalinist massacre of opponents had never been applied to Poland. The local O.G.P.U. or M.V.D. had been remarkably tame. People were not afraid of their rulers.

The Russian leaders had little idea of the hatred they had inherited or provoked. They required Poland to maintain a large army, but—wisely, perhaps—did not trust it. So in 1950 they sent Marshal Rokossowski to take command. He had been born in Poland when this was a Russian province, but had lived in Russia since 1917, and spoke Polish with a strong Russian accent. His appointment was incredibly inept, for he was the Russian commander who had held his armies back while tens of thousands of Poles had died during the Warsaw rising. And now he brought with him dozens of senior Russian officers to command the Polish forces. The insult was intolerable to a nation so proud.

6

Then an incident, trifling by our standards, brought the discontent to a head. The poet Adam Wazyk wrote his "Poem for Adults", which Poles correctly interpreted as an attack on the Communist Party. Its effects were fantastic, and were not confined to intellectual circles.

Poznan is the home of a famous trade fair, and here business men from many lands had gathered in June, 1956. It is also the home of the Cegielski engineering works. Its workers had believed in government clichés that the works now belonged to them, but they had long complained that they could not live on their wages. Increases were promised, but these never materialized. Many of the men were skilled workers—supposed to be especially well paid—and 36 per cent of them were Communists—or, at least, members of the United Workers' Party.

There comes a time when patience comes to an end. Russian control—poor economic conditions—no prospects—all these combined to mature a serious discontent. The Communists always argue that in their countries workers cannot strike, as they would be striking against themselves. "Rubbish!" said the Cegielski Communists, as their friends poured into the streets on 28th June, 1956. "We want to eat, too!"

The strikers began to march towards the centre of the city. They were stern and silent—an English girl, married to a Pole, described the march as "the most terrifying thing I ever saw—*because* the men were silent".

The procession gathered in strength: thousands of workers from other factories rushed to join it, with women from shops and schools—and passers-by in the streets. Soon there were 50,000 people on the march. Since the population of Poznan was only 400,000, after allowing for old people and children the proportion of participants was amazingly high. Crude improvised posters appeared: "We want bread!" "Lower prices and higher wages!"

"We gathered in the square in front of the Town Hall," continued the girl. "A man from the local Party headquarters tried to harangue us, but we shouted him down. The crowd got bigger every minute, as word passed round the city. Now there were other banners—scrawled on calico and nailed to wooden supports: 'We want freedom!'"

Like the strike of the East Berlin workers three years earlier, what began as an economic protest rapidly developed into a political revolt.

The mob marched to the jail, and released the prisoners. Then they attacked the Security Police, but when tanks arrived, the rising was crushed.

The government was gravely concerned. The uniformed police had proved completely unreliable, and hundreds of soldiers had refused to obey orders. Yet the worst feature of all, from the government's point of view, was that Communist workers had marched with the rest.

Marshal Bulganin claimed that "foreign imperialist circles" had fomented the trouble, and this was the theme of the Russian propaganda. But this time it was *not* taken up by its Polish satellite. Ochab admitted that not "imperialist agents" but the "soullessness of authorities and bureaucrats" was to blame. And when the Russians lectured him severely on his departure from the "party line", he firmly maintained his standpoint.

Other Communist leaders agreed with him. The reprisals for the rising were very moderate: trials were legal and held in public; of the thousands who had marched, only forty were arraigned. Their sentences were lenient, and they were soon released. In Stalin's day they and many others would have been shot.

But other consequences were much more important. A serious split became apparent in the Communist hierarchy itself. There was one group of Stalinist reactionaries, headed by Zenon Nowak and Marshal Rokossowski, who became known as the Natolin group, from the name of a villa near Warsaw which formed their headquarters. But there were other Communist leaders who admitted the Party's faults and agreed that contact with the masses had been lost.

And there was Wladyslaw Gomulka, whom I had picked out in 1945 as the most efficient of the new Communist leaders.

He was not one of the band-wagoners who had joined the party when it achieved power. He had been a Communist since his youth. He was several times imprisoned by the Pilsudski régime and its successor—which actually saved his life, for when Stalin "liquidated" the Polish Communist Party Gomulka was safe in a Polish jail!

He had organized a small Resistance group during the war—a

Communist group, independent of the Home Army. After the war he became First Secretary of the Communist Party and Minister for the Western Territories. Here, starting from less than nothing, he showed leadership and administrative ability in creating order out of chaos. He also showed his courage—in vehement protests against the organized Russian looting in the newly-occupied provinces. Need I add that the Russian commander there was Marshal Rokossowski.

Gomulka was a Pole, and he wanted not a Russian province but a Communist Poland. His phrase "the Polish road to Socialism" was first coined not in 1956 but in 1945.

When Tito made his stand against Stalin's imperialism in 1948, the Communist sycophants obediently condemned the Yugoslav leader—whom they had hitherto held in great honour. Gomulka refused: Tito's ideals of independent Communism were not far removed from his own. So he was deprived of his posts and expelled from the party. In 1951 he and his more prominent followers were arrested and jailed—needless to say, without trial. During the "thaw" he was released—at Christmas, 1954—but he was kept under house arrest.

Probably his harsh treatment by the Communists increased his popularity in the country. A martyr always commands sympathy. The Natolin group approached him and were spurned. But he was quite ready to talk to the party's other wing.

III

Gomulka and his friends were released. Public opinion was quite clear: the maximum of liberty without provoking Russian intervention. The Poznan rising helped to bring the struggle to a head. (It had been followed by dramatic events in Budapest—the Hungarian outbreak was fervently supported by the Poles.)

The Natolin group was preparing to seize power by force: Russian troops were advancing on Warsaw: a list was prepared of 700 men—including Gomulka—who were to be arrested. The revelation of the plot stimulated opposition to the Stalinists. A militia of workers and students was formed: Poland trembled on the verge of civil war.

Then (October, 1956) Khrushchev arrived in Warsaw with a powerful staff. He had never met Gomulka, and he furiously demanded that the Stalinists should remain in power, threatening the use of force.

Then Gomulka declared that he would broadcast the Russian threat, and with it the news that Russian forces were advancing on Warsaw! Khrushchev tried to save his face by two revised demands—that Poland must retain a Communist government, and be faithful to the Warsaw Pact. But nobody had ever denied the necessity of this. Gomulka wanted a Polish Poland, on friendly terms with Russia, and no more.

More than once Khrushchev threatened to solve the problem by force. But in the evening Gomulka came right out into the open. He declared that the Polish army would not fight against its own people—and challenged Rokossowski to deny this. Rokossowski had to admit that he could not rely on the Polish forces—which seemed to stagger Khrushchev. Gomulka followed up his advantage by saying that the Polish Security Corps commanded all the approaches to Warsaw, with orders to fight if attacked. As Khrushchev could not depend on the Polish army, he would have to bring the Russian forces into action—it would be war between Russia and Poland!

The baffled Russian leaders went home: Gomulka had won, and was the hero of the hour. But far too much was expected of him. He would liberalize the régime, it was thought: but he had promised Khrushchev that the country should still be ruled by a Communist junta.

Nevertheless, he spoke very frankly about Communist failings. The productivity of labour had fallen by 12 per cent since 1949 and by 36 per cent since 1938. As he pointed out, acidly, it was far lower than it was in countries which did not enjoy the advantages of Socialism. There had been much incompetence and waste: and the national budget had not been balanced for years.

When he came to agriculture, his words struck the Stalinists hard. He roundly condemned their policy of forced collectivization against the wishes of the peasants, and proved his point with some startling figures. Individual peasants laboured under every disadvantage—they were always last in the queue for seeds, fertilizers, the use of machinery, credits, subsidies, and all other facilities. Yet the annual value of agricultural output per hectare on the individual farms was 621 zloty. That on the collectives was 517 zloty—and on the State farms no more than 393 zloty!

This was a fantastic rebuttal of the Communist claims. Gomulka demanded that the people should be told "the *whole* truth". He showed no fear of the critical spirit which had spread over Poland: "A reviving and healthy current has stirred the Party masses, the working classes and the entire community. People have started to straighten their shoulders. Silent, enslaved minds have begun to shake off the poisonous fumes of deceit, falsehood, duplicity. The creative and living word has begun to oust the cliché. . . . The criticism of the past has come in a broad wave. It is the criticism of violence, distortions and errors which affected every single sector of life. . . . Above all the working people have demanded that the whole truth should be told to them openly, and without any half-truths."

It was an unrivalled and damning indictment of Communist ineptitude. He went on to outline a more liberal policy—inducements for workers, realistic management, and voluntary collectives. All "unhealthy"—i.e. non-paying—collectives should be disbanded.

His words were revolutionary, and had a joyful reception throughout Poland, many of its people feeling that the process of liberalization, once inaugurated, could not be halted.

And certainly the Stalinists were thwarted. Elections were needed in the Central Committee, to decide on its Politbureau. Gomulka and his friends topped the poll, with more than 70 votes out of 75. And Marshal Rokossowski was at the bottom, with only 23!

But Gomulka had much to do. In the excitement of his stand against the Russians, many Poles *had* expected too much, and now students and workers in many towns took matters—and radio stations—into their own hands. Gomulka had to restrain such exuberance, for he knew that one step too far might provoke Russian intervention. The moment of excitement was over: he urged everyone to go back to work, and, he added, significantly, there must be no incidents.

He spoke in Warsaw to a crowd of half a million. The battle in Budapest had begun the previous day, and the Poles seethed with anger. Yet the more thoughtful among them realized that precisely the same thing could happen in Warsaw, and they still retained bitter memories of the battle in 1944. But a group of young people began to shout: "Rokossowski, go home!" and the cry was taken up by the crowd. Then another chant, more sinister, began: "Katyn! Katyn!" Gomulka pacified them: but Rokossowski *did* go home, and never returned to Poland.

Then Gomulka went to Moscow. Apparently Khrushchev had taken a personal liking to him, and recognized his loyalty to Russia. He even admitted that Russia had been "milking" Poland by paying over-low prices for imports, and promised to make amends. When Gomulka returned to Warsaw, a huge crowd greeted him. His speech was brief and simple: "Comrades! The discrepancy in words and deeds, which frequently occurred in Polish-Soviet relations in the past, has now been liquidated."

The Poles, long adepts at reading between the lines, knew precisely what he meant: maybe a good many of them read more into his statement than he had intended.

IV

Nevertheless, Gomulka's first actions promised well. While he scorned Western forms of democracy, he agreed that the single-list election was not an election at all. Some freedom of choice was to be allowed—say, ten candidates for six seats—but the Communist Party would still choose the candidates!

All kinds of organizations, from factories to poets' clubs, began to nominate candidates. It is certain that popular hopes ran far beyond Gomulka's ideas—indeed, far beyond the bounds of possibility. More than 60,000 candidates were suggested! Gomulka was able to refer sarcastically to the first election after 1918, when representatives of twenty-seven different parties were returned: they did nothing but talk, and this led to the Pilsudski dictatorship.

The 60,000 names were whittled down to 722—and there were 459 seats. About half the candidates were Communists, a quarter came from the Peasant Party, one-tenth from the Democrats, while nearly a hundred were non-party men—among them some avowed Catholic representatives.

Some of the details of the poll were intriguing. Gomulka headed the list in his own constituency, but was followed closely by an independent and a Catholic. The other three Communist candidates were at the bottom of the poll! The Stalinists were hopelessly defeated.

MAP IV. THE NEW POLAND

In all, the United Workers' Party secured a bare majority. At least, some people imagined, the Seym would no longer be a chorus of yes-men. But the Peasant Party and Democratic Party were both Communist controlled.

Maybe the peasants expressed an even more definite opinion on Gomulka's ideas. When he announced that collective farms might dissolve themselves, the number rapidly decreased from 12,000 to 1,750.

Gomulka became more cautious with experience—he was determined not to upset Russia. His prestige began to fall: but he could not possibly have done one-tenth of what the mass of the people wanted or expected him to do.

I paid a brief visit to Poland in 1966. What I heard and saw prompted a lengthy visit the following year, if only to bring myself up to date. So we will now break away from our historic record, and wander around the Poland of today, with special reference to its Western and Northern provinces.

My information was gained in many different ways. I interviewed ministers and local officials—and talked to a wide variety of people: workers, peasants, technicians, schoolchildren. Conversation was never a problem in Poland. The Poles are a talkative people, and no Big Brother could ever hope to silence them. I spent many evenings in local clubs, where conversation was always lively. In a country where the one idea is alleged to be paramount, I collected a surprising variety of opinions.

7

POLISH MIRACLE

I

THE highlight of our portrait of modern Poland must of course be Warsaw.

Whatever you think of the Communist government of Poland, you must at least give it credit for the way in which it dealt with the reconstruction of the country. Of all the cities in Europe, Warsaw was the most damaged. Its people were patient: life in shacks and cellars was at least preferable to life under the Nazis.

There are still plenty of reminders of Hitler's terror. In every street in the centre of the city your attention is attracted by flowers on the pavement, at the foot of the wall. On this is a stone plaque announcing that on this spot 37, or 54, or some such number of Poles, were killed by Nazi bullets.

It was all so simple. A small boy would throw a stone at a German soldier. A dozen hostages would at once be collected at random, and shot. On one occasion forty boy scouts were the victims.

Just after the war was over I secured a German picture of one of these "executions". Six men were lying dead in the gutter: six more faced the Nazi rifles. I was able to trace some of these men. One was a schoolmaster, who set the example to his fellows—he stood erect bravely, with pride rather than fear as he neared the doom which had always threatened him. Another was weeping bitterly. His wife was having a baby: he had dashed out of the house to get help, but had run into the arms of the Nazi revenge patrol.

The reconstruction of old Warsaw was remarkable. I have a picture which I took before the war of the market square, and I cannot tell it apart from one I took recently. But in 1945 it was a shambles.

It had been the centre of the Warsaw rising, and was later handed over to the Nazi *vernichtungskommando*, or annihilation corps. This did its worst. This old district was the first to be rebuilt. The houses are tall, dignified, and decorated: they moreover indicated their former owner's rank—a prince might have a frontage of four windows, a lord three, and a burgher two.

Each of these houses has its story. Number 29 saw a royal romance. King Sigismund Augustus mourned the death of his lovely wife so deeply that his courtiers feared for his mind. They consulted Pan Twardowski, well known as a seer in his day— we shall meet him at Cracow. Twardowski, who claimed to practise magic, persuaded the king that the ghost of his dead wife would appear. But instead of the ghost, the "magician" arranged for the daughter of the house, Baria Giza, to deputize. She was beautiful and charming: the king fell in love with the "ghost", and regained his happiness.

Next door is the Wincaria Fukiera, which for four centuries has supplied the citizens of Warsaw with wine. And close at hand is the Krododyl, one of the city's night spots. It is eminently respectable: here there is nothing approaching strip-tease. In its cellar there is a small dance floor, and a band. I was persuaded to dance, which must have been the funniest item in the evening's entertainment.

On another side of the square several houses have been taken over for the vastly interesting Warsaw Historical Museum. Others form the Adam Mickiewicz Museum, with mementoes of Poland's great poet and patriot.

When the citizens of Warsaw voted to reconstruct the old town first of all, they included the Cathedral of St. John, only a step from the Market Place. Such fragments as remained when the war ended were incorporated into the rebuilt cathedral, but this looks very new. Its interior is not very impressive, but it has some tombs of distinguished Poles.

Most interesting is a side chapel with a figure of Christ on which hair used to grow—or so it was claimed. On a certain day every year the hair was cut by a virgin of Warsaw. But after one cutting the hair ceased to grow—from which it was assumed that the young lady who had cut it was not a virgin. This incident, needless to say, led to endless argument.

The cathedral attracts large congregations, but in interest it can scarcely compare with the nearby church of St. Martin, serving a Franciscan convent. The Stations of the Cross were carved by nuns, and are unusual.

Warsaw has always been famous for its churches, and the first Communist government was highly displeased when the people voted to give them priority in rebuilding—and used them when they were completed. The Communist revenge was cunning. They had built the modern Marszalkowska Street: but its termination would have been dominated by the massive St. Saviour's church, with its two high and delicate towers. So the government built a big block of shops and offices in the middle of Marszalkowska, which disintegrated into two narrow roads on either side of the building. The commanding view of St. Saviour's was completely spoiled.

"Of course, that was in 1952," Polish friends explained. "It would be different now. Gomulka would never do a thing like that!"

Beyond the Market Place are the battlements, rebuilt from the fragments which survived the war. Next comes the New Town—which only dates from the fifteenth century! Thanks to donations from Polish-Americans, some of its churches were restored. One house has two plaques: one records that here the leaders of the Warsaw rising were shot: the other that the house was the birthplace of Marie Sklodowska, better known to the world by her married name, Madame Curie.

The New Town has its own market place. Beyond this is a place which few Poles can pass without emotion. The Racynski Palace was designated and clearly marked as a hospital during the Warsaw rising. But the Nazis fired it with incendiary bombs, and staff and wounded were burned to death.

Churches also suffered in battle. The cathedral was the scene of bitter fighting during the rising: so was the church of the Holy Cross, which contains the heart of Chopin, sealed in one of its pillars.

Chopin was in fact born at Zelazowa Wola, thirty miles outside Warsaw. His home has been preserved—a lovely old house—and every Sunday during the summer recitals of his work are given by famous pianists. Others are given by his monument in Warsaw's Lazcenki Park. It very effectively depicts the youthful Chopin listening to the music of the wind in the trees.

Most of the historic houses of Warsaw have been reconstructed in meticulous detail—except the royal palace, which is no longer required. Immediately beyond the limits of the Old Town modern buildings begin—high blocks of flats, in which apparently no originality is possible. Like ours, they all resemble children's boxes of bricks. One group culminates in the new Opera House, one of the finest in Europe.

Yet architecturally Warsaw is dominated by the grandiose Palace of Science and Culture, which purported to be the gift of the Soviet Union—or of Stalin himself. It contains two theatres, three cinemas, a congress hall and a swimming pool: its high tower commands a grand panorama of Warsaw. Yet, despite its utility, it is by no means popular. It does not "fit". It was built in Stalin's "wedding cake" style which has disfigured Moscow, and strongly resembles Wrigley's chewing gum factory in Chicago.

In front of it is the busy Marszalkowska Street, where the traffic is dense: it leads to the Saxon Gardens, a pleasant little park. And just outside it is a tiny building, trivial in size compared with the Palace of Science and Culture, but far greater is its meaning to the Poles: just three arches of a colonnade of the old Saxon palace—all that survived the war: it houses the tomb of Poland's Unknown Warrior.

When the Poles decided to give special honour to one of their unknown dead, after the First World War, they faced a difficulty. Whence should the body be chosen? During the war, Poles had fought in the armies of Russia, Germany and Austria. Were they fighting for the freedom of Poland? It was finally decided to select the body of the Unknown Warrior from the defenders of Lwow, the first battle of the new Poland.

When the Ukrainians strove to capture Lwow in 1919, the young men of the city were no longer there. Many had been killed, the others scattered, so Lwow had to be defended by old men and boys. And, as it is an old Polish tradition that women should stand by their men in war, the defenders also included women and girls. Hundreds of these were killed during the bitter struggle.

Hence an intriguing possibility: the body of Poland's Unknown Warrior *might* be that of a woman!

Inside the memorial are listed the battles in which Polish soldiers fought in two world wars. But the government imposed by Stalin on Poland accepted his own viewpoint: he despised those Poles who had fought in the West. The memorial therefore recorded only those actions in which Poles had fought under Russian command.

This churlish attitude was applied to the survivors. Many Poles returning home after the war were treated almost as criminals; they had great difficulty in finding work, although there was so much to do—and although many of them were skilled workers.

This outlook changed with the rise of Gomulka. The memorial now contains such names as Monte Cassino and the Battle of Britain. But the earlier attitude did Poland much harm. Today Polish ex-soldiers would be welcomed home, where their skills are in demand. But most have already settled down in Britain or U.S.A. They had heard of the sorry fate of their comrades who returned home, and had no wish to share it.

II

Not enough has been heard of the "Polish Miracle". It saw its greatest triumph in Warsaw, which rose like the traditional phoenix from the ashes.

The old city has been restored, and the new city has been extended far beyond its previous limits. The suburb of Praga, across the Vistula, is almost a city in its own right, one mass of huge blocks of flats. The slums of Warsaw have disappeared, casualties of the war. They included the Ghetto, once a maze of narrow and insanitary streets.

Some of the new building has been too hurried. A friend declared that when he came back from a holiday he could not recognize his own suburb. For twenty years Warsaw has been a vast builder's yard, and there are many piles of debris still to be cleared away. But the city is alive again: even in 1945, in all its misery, I was confident that Warsaw would not die: it refused to die.

It is a young city—in its people as well as its buildings. Only 30 per cent of the population consists of pre-war inhabitants: the rest are newcomers, mostly from the villages. Their manners might be uncouth, but they brought the vitality of youth with them.

The city is lively and bustling: the shops are crowded. In the morning and evening the crowds hastening to or from work overstrain the public transport. I do not remember paying even one fare on a Warsaw bus. Each was so crowded that the conductor could not get to me, nor I to him.

There are great factories, and even greater offices—for Warsaw is the centre of the political and economic life of Poland, with a régime that depends on bureaucracy. On both banks of the Vistula there is intense activity—that of men in a hurry.

There are, however, more than factories and offices. Warsaw is the cultural capital of Poland. Its theatre and cinema are known beyond its frontiers: so is its music, including the Chopin piano competitions and the "Warsaw Autumn" of international contemporary music. And there is jazz for those who like it.

The Opera House at Warsaw has been rebuilt, and is now one of the most up to date in Europe. Its foyers are delightful, its stage large, with all modern appliances. We saw *Halka*, a Polish opera by Stanislaw Monciuszko, bright and tuneful, introducing traditional Polish dances. It was well sung and magnificently staged. Opera can never pay its way—the essential costs are too great—and the Communist countries are much more generous in supporting it than we are. No expense is spared to achieve good results. The Warsaw chorus, for example, is double the size of any I ever saw in England.

The theme of the opera was based on an old Polish folk-tale from the region of the Podhale mountains. A young noble seduces a village girl, but turns to marry the Governor's daughter. The village girl pleads with him, but then, appearing dramatically at his wedding, forgives him. But she has killed her child and now at the last moment she kills herself. It was one of those cheerful stories in which opera delights.

The comments of one of my neighbours were not limited to music or beautiful costumes or staging. "Don't you see, it is a social satire on older days. Then the local lord always put the village girls in the family way."

"What—all of them?"

"Of course. It's well known. That's how the peasants were treated in those days. Ruled by force."

This theory surely suggested a remarkable degree of compliance among the village girls. And, as the custom was apparently universal, there must be some trace of noble blood in all Polish veins!

On another evening we went to the Students' Theatre, founded a few years earlier by a group of university students who produced an amateur show and liked the experience so much that they decided to turn professional. The cast, a dozen strong, produced a high speed topical revue. The staging was of the simplest— the whole thing had obviously been done on a shoestring—but the personality and competence of the players were outstanding. The show was the Polish equivalent of "Beyond the Fringe", and its satire included sly digs at political ideas as well as at social customs.

By day Warsaw is busy: at the rush hours the traffic is very especially heavy. But at night the city is quiet, and the Old Town takes on a new charm. We often walked its narrow streets by moonlight. Equally fascinating were the small hours of the morning, when the earliest workers hurried to their factories. Despite its terrible sufferings, Warsaw has made one gain from the war—the Nazi destruction cleared away the slums. Perhaps the Ghetto is the most significant example of that. Its centre is now an open space, surrounded by tidy blocks of flats. Very few of these are occupied by Jews, however: there are less than 30,000 of them in the city—in which they formerly provided 30 per cent of the population of more than a million.

Many of the city's palaces have disappeared—at one time every great noble had his town house in the capital. The Nazis attempted to set the Lazienki Palace on fire, but they had to leave before they could do so. It is a charming mansion, built by King Stanislaw Augustus in a lovely park.

Wilanow Palace, just outside the city, is the finest baroque building in Poland. Here we noticed signs of intense activity: President de Gaulle was due to arrive in a few weeks' time, and was to be lodged in a wing of the palace. We inspected the apartments assigned to him. The suite was very ornate—very different from his home at Colombey-les-deux-Églises. A new bed had been bought for the occasion—black, with gold ornaments, and extra long!

The rest of the palace is a museum. We slid over its polished floors in cloth slippers, and were glad that we lived in a more humble abode.

Old Town Market Square in
Warsaw

Modern mid-town area of Warsaw

Palace of King John III Sobieski
in Wilanów near Warsaw

Wawel Cathedral in Cracow

The Germans used Wilanow as a barracks during the war, and caused widespread damage. Much of the furniture and many of the pictures were looted, but most were later recovered.

But I have not mentioned Warsaw's origin. According to legend—never to be despised in Poland, however improbable—the King of the Baltic had an under-sea palace near the mouth of the Vistula. His daughter was a mermaid. She ran away from home and journeyed far up the river. One day, near a fishing village, a prince, who had got lost while hunting, heard her singing, and then saw her in the water. She could not give him directions, but she led him to a fisherman named Wars. He and his wife Szawa gave the prince the traditional bread and salt. The mermaid then returned to the river, calling out to him: "Here you must build a city." He did so, and named it after the couple who had given him hospitality—Wars and Szawa—Warsaw.

You don't believe the story? Well, the mermaid is still the emblem of Warsaw, and represents the city on its statuary.

8

HIGH TATRAS

I

Travel in Poland can be democratic but very pleasant. When you hire a car, your driver will expect to have his meals with you. If he is intelligent, the gain is yours.

We left Warsaw with a driver and an interpreter, and journeyed to the south. After an hour or so we stopped outside a little cottage on the outskirts of a village.

"My mother lives here," the drive explained. "I'll just drop in and see her."

We all dropped in: the cottage was small, with two rooms, but proudly kept. The old lady immediately began to prepare refreshments. This is one of the difficulties of travel in Poland. Naturally you want to make contact with the people, but their hospitality is so great that you fear to over-burden their scanty purse.

There were apple trees in the garden, and we left loaded with apples. They were not really ripe, but we handed them over to the chambermaid of our next hotel: she was delighted.

The Polish countryside has a gentle peace of its own. It resembles rural France rather than England, for it has no hedgerows. It is well wooded—a quarter of the land is forested. Its little villages are as often as not built of wood—picturesque, but not always practical.

At a corner of a field you will see a little shrine, built of brick or metal, containing an image or picture of the Virgin Mary. This was built by some peasant farmer, grateful to God for a bounteous harvest. As he or his descendants pass it, they will mutter a little prayer. So will other passers-by.

The largest building in the village is the church. Its many ornaments were all presented by local men and women. The priest is more than a spiritual leader: he is consulted on many occasions when a practical decision is essential: as often as not he himself is a farmer's son, so he understands local problems.

Our first objective was Czestochowa, the Polish Lourdes, a famous place of pilgrimage. We had passed a dozen processions on the way—people making a twelve-day walk from Warsaw, carrying religious banners. Czestochowa monastery—Jasna Gora, or Mountain of Light—was of Magyar foundation, originally occupied by monks of the religious order of Paul the Hermit. In its early days it was strongly fortified, and its defences were needed.

The monastery was rich and powerful—at one time it owned one-fifteenth of all the land of Poland, the gift of wealthy men anxious for the welfare of their souls.

Its greatest treasure was a painting of the Virgin, dark with age. The wealth of the monastery attracted the attention of wandering bands of predatory knights. In 1430 it was captured and plundered. One of the Knights seized the holy picture of the "Black Virgin" and made off with it. But before he had covered half a mile a great thunderstorm burst overhead, and vivid shafts of lightning encompassed him. His intelligent horse, perceiving that a curse was on his burden, refused to move. The Knight in his fury flung the picture to the ground and slashed it with the sabre: immediately a spring began to well up from the barren earth. If you doubt this story the spring is still there as proof, and millions of pilgrims have carried away bottles of its holy water. And it is certainly true that the sacred picture still carries the marks of sword slashes.

But in 1655 the Swedes invaded and overran Poland. At Czestochowa they were halted by the monastery, defended as it was by 68 monks, 50 knights and 160 soldiers—and the "Black Virgin". The Swedes numbered 10,000.

The siege lasted a month, but it was no ordinary battle. The Swedes were not unnaturally disheartened when their cannon balls rebounded from the massive walls of the monastery, killing their own men. The climax was reached when the sacred picture projected itself on a great cloud, a colossal image of the Virgin and Child dominating the scene. The Swedes hurriedly abandoned the siege: they could fight men but not miracles. The local success at Czestochowa was decisive. Poles all over the country were imbued with a new faith and a revival of patriotic zeal. The reverse at Jasna Gora was the beginning of the Swedish retreat, the Polish people hastened its completion. A thankful people presented a superbly jewelled monstrance to the monastery, and a grateful King, restored to his throne, proclaimed the "Black Virgin" as Queen of Poland. The title is still used in official ecclesiastical documents.

It was soon claimed that the success was a miracle: it was certainly extraordinary. The credit was given not to the stout walls or the stouter hearts which had defended the monastery, but to its treasure, the Black Virgin.

According to tradition, this was painted by St. Luke. I have always understood that he was a physician rather than an artist: certainly he must have mixed his colours badly—particularly the flesh tints. Mary is as swarthy as any Indian, and the gilt embellishments around her face only heighten her colour.

We arrived on an ordinary week-day, when only a few thousand pilgrims were present. I had earlier visited Czestochowa on a Sunday, when they numbered 30,000. On a special saints' day they may exceed 100,000. But when in 1956 there came the 300th anniversary of the enthronement of the Black Virgin as Queen of Poland, then the pilgrims defied all travel difficulties as well as government displeasure as they journeyed from all corners of Poland: at the lowest estimate they exceeded a million.

I dislike the emotional atmosphere of a pilgrimage. Yet I could not deny these pilgrims' sincere devotion. It does not matter what I felt: it is their faith which matters.

The picture of the Virgin—it is painted on wood—is exhibited several times a day, and then the congregation falls on its knees. For pilgrimages, it is displayed to the crowd outside the monastery.

Is the expense and discomfort of a pilgrimage worth while? The pilgrims think so, for they always return again. "We get grace," they explained. "As soon as one pilgrimage is over, we prepare for the next. There's always someone in our village who needs divine help."

The monastery is dominated by its church, with a lofty spire, one of the highest in Poland. The interior is over-decorated baroque: the treasury of the church is rich and interesting, but the pilgrims gather in an adjoining chapel, prepared to wait for hours until the sacred picture is unveiled.

Round the monastery is the usual maze of stalls, where the

pilgrims are offered "souvenirs"—gaudy pictures, or religious trivialities. I suppose that all this is inseparable from such places, but it contrasts disconcertingly with the sincerity and devotion of the pilgrims. It always reminds me of Christ driving such people from the precincts of the Temple.

II

After Czestochowa the monotony of the Polish plain was relieved by the gentle hills of White Silesia. This was once a mining area, until richer fields were discovered nearby in the Katowice region—now appropriately called Black Silesia.

The White part of the province is pleasant, its extensive fields broken by forests: as we continued to the south, the hills grew larger—and, looking ahead, we saw mountain shapes looming through the mist. Here, indeed, was one of the spectacular corners of Poland. The road followed the course of a river between the hills: wheat and hay were growing in the fields of its valley: at its end was the mountain resort of Zakopane.

It is said that Zakopane can experience four seasons of weather in the same day. Its people are more optimistic. "It will be fine today—if it doesn't rain." But I had visited the place three times already, and each time it had rained continuously and enthusiastically. Hence my delight when I was now greeted by a warm sun.

I had known Zakopane as an overgrown village: it is now an overgrown town, of 25,000 inhabitants. Its streets are lined by an irregular maze of houses, from ancient Gooral cottages to modern shops. Even the older buildings have taken advantage of any spare yard of ground, to add an additional room or rooms. For Zakopane is a major holiday resort of Poland: with its satellite villages, it receives a million visitors a year, and thinks nothing of the arrival of 30,000 in a single day.

It lacks any special distinction in itself, but it is a grand centre, with a wide variety of mountains within easy reach: and, though it is down in a valley, the cool air of the mountains breathes invigoration to its tired guests.

Apart from its hotels and its modest boarding houses, it has a number of hostels belonging to Polish trade unions. I chanced on one used exclusively by railwaymen. It was simple, but adequate for its clientele.

"And it's cheap," said one of its guests. "Three hundred zloty for two weeks. Of course, you still need spending money for excursions—and drinks. But you can't grumble at 150 zloty a week, can you?"

"I should say not. How did you get here?"

"I applied to my trade union. In fact, I had to apply for three years before I got here. Our hostels are good, but there aren't enough of them."

"And how do you amuse yourselves?"

"We go on excursions by day, and in the evening we go out to a café for a vodka, or sit and talk."

"What about?"

"Railway timetables, mostly. You've hit on a snag there. It would be better if all trades unions combined for holiday centres, rather than each having its own hostel. We talk too much shop."

This I could well imagine. Other guests joined us, and the conversation switched to trades unions themselves.

I gather that the system is nearer to the German than to ours—the Germans have one union per industry—only seventeen altogether, as against our 390. Membership is not compulsory, but 95 per cent of all Polish workers belong to an union.

"There are so many advantages. A man pays 1 per cent of his wages to the union, and in return gets protection against dismissal—unless he has committed some crime. He gets a discount on hotel prices, and a free travel ticket every year—not just railwaymen, but all workers. The union pays a bounty to his widow if he dies, or to his wife if she has a baby. And these rest homes are good. If you can get in, you pay according to your wage. It all pays back a lot more than the 1 per cent."

But he admitted that he could afford all these privileges, and more, if he were paid a more equitable salary.

"He's right about the advantages," another man put in. "But there's one big difficulty with our unions—in effect, they represent both employers and employed. That doesn't work. It couldn't work. We are told that we can't strike, because we should be striking against ourselves. But that's absurd, isn't it? We own the railways, but we don't own them. Our union leaders are all Communists, and take their orders from the government. But you're right about the need for higher wages. What do your railwaymen get in England?"

"They aren't well paid," I admitted. I quoted such figures as I could remember. "But, of course, our cost of living is lower than yours in most respects." Again I quoted some food prices. It was obvious that my friends did not agree with my suggestion that British railwaymen were not well paid.

I must now digress to comment on the value of the zloty—after the devaluation of the £.

The Polish currency is tied to the Russian rouble, so its official rate of exchange is absurd—9·60 to the pound sterling. At current prices, a visit to a public lavatory would cost you about ten shillings.

The Poles recognize the absurdity of this, and change foreign currency for zloty at the special tourist rate of 57·90 to the pound. Even this makes shopping expensive, so Orbis—the government travel agency—issue special coupons if you change as much as 20 dollars, say £7. These coupons can be used at all Orbis hotels and many of the shops, duly indicated by a sign in the window, and give a 40 per cent advantage.

This puts the value of the zloty at 95 to the pound. But the Black Market rate is 200. Naturally, you will not indulge in illegal procedures—the penalties if you are caught are severe. But you will certainly be invited to do so.

As all prices are comparative, it does not matter which we choose. Suppose, for easy calculation, we adopt the figure of 100 zloty to the pound—i.e., value of zloty at about 2½d. Shopping at this figure is far from cheap, but as the average wage in Poland is 2,000 zloty a month, at our rate of exchange a man earns only £5 per week, as compared with £20 in Britain. We shall examine spending prices later.

Now as to the cost of tourism in Poland: as usual, it is most cheaply visited on a package tour. Booking individually, before he leaves his own country the tourist must pay for his accommodation—he can get a visa only for the number of days he pays for. The S grade, with the best hotels in Poland, costs £5 4s. 2d. a day for a nice room with private bath and all meals. First-class hotels cost £4 3s. 4d., and second-class—much simpler, but clean—£3 2s. 6d a day. There are third-class hotels—usually found in small towns—and pensions at around £2 a day, and "bungalow camps" at some resorts for as little as £1 5s. od. a day. You get what you pay for. You may also book for bed and breakfast only, or demi-pension.

When you reach Poland, the money you have paid for your vouchers is refunded in zloty at 57·90 to the pound. The all-in rate has naturally been calculated to allow for your being a hearty eater of the most expensive dishes: if you are prepared to live normally, you will have plenty of zloty left over for all your casual expenses. Poland is *not* an expensive country for the frugal traveller.

III

The High Tatra mountains are a group in the Carpathian chain, and are shared between Poland and Czechoslovakia. By tacit agreement, climbers and ramblers may cross the frontiers without formality.

The local people are the Goorals, a tough mountain tribe—tall, powerful and sun-tanned. Their costume is still to be seen in the outlying villages—occasionally in Zakopane itself: and often at weddings or other festivals. The men wear a short jacket and trousers of wool pressed into a rough felt. Underwear is not needed, but the costume is tickly and irritating, as I found to my cost when I wore it. The trousers are decorated by dark bands down the seams, and the jackets are gaily embroidered, usually in red. The effect is completed with a round billy-cock hat.

The women favour a white blouse with a flowered-coloured skirt, very full: indeed, beneath it they may wear as many as twenty petticoats. Wash day for a family must be a wholesale job.

The old houses are simple but solid: a bungalow made of logs of timber, relieved by an entrance of carved wood; sometimes the whole is colour-washed a pale blue, and the roof is thatched. The more modern buildings are larger, so as to accommodate visitors, but they are still made of wood, and are simple.

Traditionally, a cottage has two rooms, the Black and the White. The first takes its name from the stove in one corner, its smoke blackening the walls and ceiling. In another corner is a bed, assigned to the lady of the house: over it hangs a cradle, so that she can rock the baby without getting up. Around the walls runs a broad plank bench, which serves as a bed for the rest of the family. There is a table and chairs: everything is of wood, and

home-made. Religious pictures—perhaps painted on glass—
supply the decorations. It is not uncommon for young lambs or
calves to be brought up in the same room as the family.

In the hall are stored the farm implements like scythes and rakes,
and on its other side is the White Room. This is reserved for
guests: as in most mountain regions, hospitality is profound, and a
family will gladly crowd into the Black Room so as to have the
White one ready for a visitor. It has one bed in a corner, piled
high with pillows, their cases beautifully embroidered. Apart
from the bedclothes and a religious picture, everything is again
home-made.

The free use of timber is natural in a mountain-forest region.
In Zakopane there is an old timber church, but a better example
is to be found at the nearby village of Debno. This dates from the
fifteenth century, and some of its interior furnishings are older
still. It is artistically shaped, with a tower, and the inside is painted
in local motifs—seventy-seven of them in all. The paintings are
the originals, executed in home-made vegetable colours.

The church was built entirely of wood, without so much as an
iron nail. The wooden shingles protecting its exterior have been
renovated with the passing of the centuries, and modern workmen
are more hasty than those of old. Instead of using wooden pegs,
they have nailed the shingles in position. Down one side of the
church is a narrow dormitory: it has no beds, but worshippers
coming from afar can sleep the night on the floor. The church
holds about a hundred people, and is in daily use. It is wonderfully
picturesque, and I was not surprised to learn that an American
university museum had offered millions of dollars for its purchase.
Such a sum must have tempted the parishioners, but they would
not part with the church, which forms the centre of their lives.

The tradition of the timber church still prevails in the neighbourhood. At Jaczczoronowka is a modern one, built in 1901.
The Gooral lumbermen who designed and built it must have been
natural artists. And the interior decorations match their homes—
all ingeniously made of carved wood.

Many of the Goorals are part-time foresters. This is a region of
small peasant farms—there is not a huge collective for many miles.
The average holding is about 10 acres, which scarcely yields a
family living—for the soil is not rich, its crops limited to oats and
potatoes: there is however much cattle and sheep-raising.

"In the summer I take the sheep up the mountain slopes," said a Gooral. "I have eighty. I live in a wooden shack, and there is a rough barn nearby. I move the flock up the slope according to the season. Every day I milk the ewes—their milk is very good, you know. I make it into cheese—soft cheese, like this." He displayed an array of cheeses each about the size of an egg. "My wife sells them in the market. Sometimes she fries them, and sometimes she smokes them. I can tell you, smoked ewe's cheese is a real delicacy. Try it while you are here!

"While I am away for the summer, my wife looks after our farm. We have a growing family, and everybody helps. Just now they are getting in the second crop of hay. My wife comes up to me at the week-end, bringing my food for the week. She stays a few hours, or sometimes for the night. She thinks I am lonely without her. But I have my dogs."

Two large white dogs were regarding me with some suspicion. The Gooral produced a contrivance, a rough collar worked in iron, bristling with spikes. "I put one of these on when the dogs ask for them—oh, yes, they know when a wolf is about. These two, father and son, will take on any wolf. But there are few about these days. They have been frightened off—too many people about. There are a few bears in the high mountains, but they are harmless enough outside the cubbing season.

"So, one way and another, we make a living. It is not luxury, but it is a good life. And I am my own master.

"The wolf is a great nuisance to farmers, and for that reason he is being hunted to extermination: his habit of helping himself to farm stock cannot be tolerated."

He is shot on sight. Or forest rangers use a more modern device. They leave bait in the undergrowth which is laced with tranquillizers. The wolf, showing all the signs of drunkenness, recognizable without breath analysers, is then easy prey. Once I drove in a peasant cart, and a wolf staggered irregularly from side to side like any toper. My farmer companion caught and killed him: the government pays a reward for every wolf-skin brought in.

IV

The railwaymen had suggested some of the excursions which had pleased them, and we tried some of them.

The first was to the lake of Morske Oko—the Eye of the Sea. By local legend, this is connected with the sea by underground tunnels, but as the sea is three or four hundred miles away, this is unlikely, to say the least. Its older name was Fish Lake—and it teems with a small variety of trout.

The car was not allowed within a mile of the lake. We were in the Tatra National Park, where rules are stringent.

"I should think they are!" said a member of a group we had joined for the final walk. "Why, you know our anti-litter laws? Drop litter, and you are fined 50 zloty for a first offence, rapidly rising afterwards. And in the park your fine could be as much as 4,500 zloty. That's money!"

"And you mustn't pick the flowers," said another. "Not *any* of the flowers. There was one man—a Pole, I regret to say—who helped himself freely to edelweiss, and was caught."

"What was he fined?"

"He wasn't! He was sent to jail for three months. Hey, sonny!" This to a youth who was carrying a transistor radio, blaring out pop music. "I ought to warn you—those things aren't allowed in the Park."

The youth switched off the transistor abruptly. The incident was significant. We try to persuade people to behave themselves. We have Societies for Encouraging this or Preventing that. Communist leaders apparently do not believe that you can *persuade* a man to act properly: they think it necessary to *make* him. They impose punishments which really hurt, and this is much more effective than our own pious exhortations.

Later I discussed the Polish attitude to the drink-and-drive question. The police can halt a driver on the slightest suspicion. If a medical examination discloses more than a very modest percentage of alcohol in his blood stream, nasty things begin to happen to him. And if after a drink he has an accident, the results can be tough. The loss of his licence is only the beginning. Our driver liked his glass of beer—in the evening, when his driving for the day was done. For the rest of the time, he drank only soda water!

(One hint to the Polish authorities. The range of soft drinks available is very poor, and the time comes when the attractions of soda water languish. It would not be difficult to provide more palatable alternatives.)

Morske Oko is an attractive little lake, almost surrounded by high mountains—one of them, Rysy, is the highest in Poland at 8,199 feet. A dozen of its neighbours are only slightly lower. The walk round the lake takes only an hour: or you may be rowed across.

Morske Oko used to be described as wild and romantic. The words are no longer applicable, despite the majesty of its enclosing mountains. It is dominated by its visitors, who are neither wild nor romantic. In turn, they are attracted by its hostel. Such buildings in mountain districts will provide hot water free of charge, and a group of mountaineers were boiling their sausages while packing their kit.

The other excursion recommended by the railwaymen was a voyage through the gorges of the Dunajec. It begins at Czorsztyn: across the river a tall crag is crowned by a castle which used to belong to a Hungarian prince. It is now occupied by a school for architects.

You travel by a vessel called a raft—it is not really a raft at all, but consists of five dug-out canoes lashed together. Nor are these actually dug-outs; they are flat-bottomed punts about fifteen feet long and eighteen inches wide. Ten or a dozen passengers are accommodated on plank seats, and boatmen fore and aft pole the craft along—except where it is caught up in the wild rapids, which hurry it along.

On the landing stage a gypsy band plays vigorously to celebrate your departure: a hundred yards downstream another gypsy wades waist deep into the stream to play for you—and collect your gratuities. He must be a real musician. I saw him fiddling away long after our raft had passed, and before the next was in sight. There must be easier ways of earning a living.

The first two hours are unexciting. Then the gorges are at hand. The river flows in an irregular course between enormous grey rocks or mountains whose steep slopes are covered with trees to the water's edge. The voyage through the gorges covers 22 kilometres. There is one point where between the mountain called Trzy Korony (Three Crowns) and Hukowa Skala (Rock of the Thousand Noises) the course of the river is nine kilometres, whereas in a straight line the distance is only one-third of that.

The bends in the river are often completely unexpected: there are minor excitements in the rapids when your raft seems bound to hit a jagged rock protruding from the water. It never does. The voyage is exceedingly pleasant, but to sit for nearly four hours on a hard plank is not the essence of comfort.

However, it is to be shortened by half. A dam is projected above the gorges, and the journey will have to begin there. The dam will be a joint effort of Poland and Czechoslovakia, for the river is their boundary at this point.

"The boatmen work as a co-operative, I assume?" I asked.

"No."

"No? In a Communist country?"

"In a Socialist country. No, they are independent. Each boat-man gets 100 zloty for his day's work. Another 100 goes to the peasant who drives the punts back to the starting place in his cart. The rest goes to the touring agency which does the clerical work, the organization, and the publicity."

The real attraction of Zakopane lies in the many mountain walks around it. The village is of no outstanding interest: except, perhaps, for its two little markets. One is occupied by peasants, who offer ewe's milk cheese and other products. In the other, women sit knitting and selling cardigans or hats, and the menfolk display light shoes of local leather. More interesting is the second-hand market, not a bazaar, but an exchange and mart.

A woman came up to me to ask the time. Then: "Have you anything to sell?"

"What sort of thing?"

"A shirt? A pullover?"

I declined. But I saw two men bargaining fiercely, until one man exchanged an old pair of shoes for a shirt, which he immediately donned.

A final excursion by cable car to the top of the Kasprowy Wierch, which tops 6,000 feet and commands a broad view, and a brief walk carried us into Czechoslovakia. Strange, however: a quarter of the cable car passengers seemed to get no farther than the restaurant on the summit.

My last evening at Zakopane was marred by a slight argument. If a restaurant provides music, 15 per cent extra can be charged for the food. But at my hotel the music was based upon three electronic guitars, played with great heartiness.

"Couldn't you stop this noise?" I asked of the manager.

"Noise? Why, it is an entertainment activity."

"But I can't hear myself speak."

"You do not need to. You're eating your dinner."

"I'm working. Is it possible in a Communist country for a man to be stopped from working?"

"But how——"

"My friend here is a lawyer. I am asking him questions about Polish law. Such is my job. But I cannot hear his replies. And I doubt if he can hear my questions."

The manager declared that nothing could be done. An "entertainment activity" was sacrosanct. So we halted our meal halfway through, and transferred our custom to another restaurant where the predominant activity was not entertainment, but food.

Yet the electric guitars won. They twanged noisily until the early hours of the morning, and kept me awake. This is another fault of hotels in other lands than Poland. They make more money from dancing, and forget the legitimate needs of their guests.

9

ANCIENT CAPITAL

I

THE road wound northwards through the foothills of the Tatras, across the Gooral region known as Podhale. Its first town is Nowy Targ, or New Market.

In Poland, however, it is known colloquially as New York. A few generations ago this was a poverty-stricken area, and any chances of emigration to America were eagerly seized. The custom was for a family to deny itself in order to send one of its members to the U.S.A.: then, in time, he would begin to support his family.

Hence the emigrants from Podhale had families back at home, and when they became rich enough to visit their original homeland they made for Nowy Targ. This custom still prevails. Authentic stories are told of Americans arriving at Warsaw airport, and after passing through "the formalities" getting into a taxi and telling the driver: "Nowy Targ". It is a run of about two hundred miles, and even in dollars the taxi fare would be considerable.

Poland has gallantly resisted one temptation. In England the beauty of our roadside is too often spoiled by huge advertisements for this and that: in Russia such appeals are replaced by demands for harder and better work, or by quotations from Lenin. Poland has practically no wayside hoardings. But just outside Nowy Targ is a colourful poster: "Fly to U.S.A. by L.O.T. and T.W.A." This could hardly be intended for the local inhabitants.

Rain had chased us from the Tatras, and Cracow lay beneath a mantle of gloomy clouds. Yet nothing could for long dampen the attraction of this lovely city, the capital of Poland until its union with Lithuania in the sixteenth century. It escaped most of the ravages of the last war. The Russians were advancing from the east, and the Germans got ready for a bitter defence—even preparing the demolition of historic buildings. But the Russians broke through north and south, and entered Cracow, so to speak, by the undefended back door.

We at once made for the Wawel, the hill with the royal castle and cathedral. We approached by a road dominated by an equestrian statue of Kosciuszko—a copy, for needless to say the Germans melted down the original. (As a sort of retribution, the city of Dresden presented the replacement to Cracow.) A glance at an adjoining wall made me chuckle. When Cracow rejoined Poland at the end of 1918, the buildings of the Wawel badly needed repair. To raise the money, the government offered a stone in the wall bearing the name of any generous donor. The architect in charge protested—why should his beloved handiwork be defaced by such advertisement? But the money was badly needed, and rolled in. Yet the last word was with the architect. He honoured the agreement, but had the names carved in stone which would weather easily and rapidly away. The process has already begun. In another twenty or thirty years the names will have disappeared.

From the hill another and more permanent memorial to Kosciuszko can be seen—a huge mound, a couple of miles away. Hundreds of thousands of people from all parts of Poland brought baskets of earth to make this little hill. They were supported by Americans, grateful for Kosciuszko's services during the War of Independence.

Such memorials are almost peculiar to Poland. The two first began as burial barrows, with popular additions added later. They are to the memory of Krakus and Wanda. The former deserved his fame—if legend can be trusted—and he certainly gave Cracow its name. In his day the city was tormented by a fearsome dragon, demanding a virgin as its daily tribute. Many knights attempted to emulate St. George, but failed. Krakus was more cunning. He killed a sheep, and filled its carcase with sulphur. The dragon ate it, was consumed with thirst, dashed into the River Vistula close by, and drank so copiously that he burst. If you doubt the story, you will be shown the dragon's cave at the foot of the Wawel.

Another barrow was adopted as a memorial to Wanda, the daughter of Krakus. She drowned herself in the Vistula rather

St. Mary's Church in the Main
Market Square in Cracow

University celebrations in the
courtyard of the Collegium
Maius of the Jagiellonian University in Cracow

Długi Targ Street and the Town
Hall in Gdańsk

One of the new housing estates
in Gdańsk

than marry a German prince. But there used to be a modern artificial hill, to the memory of Pilsudski.

"Oh, but that one has gone," I was told.

"What? Why?"

"Well, he fought against the Soviet Union."

"It would surely be more accurate to say that the Soviet Union fought against him!"

"Anyway, it's gone."

Extremist political parties have a habit of destroying memorials to people who do not agree with their "ideology", but an artificial hill is not so easily disposed of as a statue. And the Pilsudski memorial was still there. Only its name has disappeared, and not even the Communists have dared to turn it into a memorial to Karl Marx! They hope that the memory of Pilsudski will die with the older generation. Then, maybe, they will pass off the huge mound as an old colliery tip.

II

The royal castle was rebuilt by Italian architects early in the sixteenth century. Its courtyard is beautiful, surrounded by graceful colonnades: and the interior is indeed that of a palace— large, lofty rooms, with carved surrounds to doors of lovely timber: each room has a great stove, enclosed within a pattern of decorated tiles.

The feature of the palace is its collection of huge Flemish tapestries. Many of them have biblical themes—the story of Noah and his ark was a special favourite. There is some grand old furniture, and the floors of marble or walnut are very fine. At one time they were even finer, for they were inlaid with mother of pearl. But successive military occupations inevitably involved serious damage: soldiers are seldom careful with other people's property. The Chamber of Deputies was used as a German army cinema during the last war.

Franck was the Nazi Gauleiter, and his main interest was not so much maintenance as loot. Some of the Wawel treasures were hurriedly rushed to Canada for safety when war threatened: others were eventually traced to various places in Germany, and have been recovered.

The Chamber is colloquially known as the Hall of the Heads.

8

The fine ceiling is divided into compartments, and in each there used to be a carved head. There are now only thirty: the rest have disappeared: the blame rests not with the Nazis but with earlier vandals.

One of the heads is that of a garrulous woman, a bandage tied firmly about her mouth—so realistically that surely the sculptor was working from a familiar model! Another is alleged to have intervened when the king gave an unfair judgment. "King, judge justly!" it enjoined: and the monarch was so startled that he amended his decision.

The Armoury is outstanding, with one sword of especial interest—it was that used during the coronations of the Polish kings. It was looted during the partitions of Poland, and after a long stay in Germany it found its way to an auction room in London. This was after the last war, when a number of Poles had settled in Britain. They co-operated to buy the sword, and restored it to its rightful home—the Wawel in Cracow.

It is not possible for large groups of visitors to be taken through some of the rooms, but if you travel in twos and threes it is easy to get permission to visit them. On the top floor is a marvellous collection of Turkish and Persian tents captured by John Sobieski after his great victory at Vienna. Some are enormous marquees, the Turkish ones decorated in red motifs, the Persian in blue. They are of course set up properly, and are unique.

Adjoining the palace is the cathedral: here kings were crowned and buried. Some of their tombs are magnificent. I took my wife, Helen, first to a crucifix, the Cross and the figure of Christ carved in black ebony. Here Jadwiga prayed when she was told that she was to marry the pagan Duke of Lithuania; and, according to legend, Jesus spoke to her, asking her to make the sacrifice whereby Lithuania would accept Christianity. More authentic is the story of Jadwiga's stairs. The poor girl shuddered at the thought of marriage to an ill-featured pagan: she had a Christian lover, and sought to flee with him. But on the narrow stairs a monk met her, and pleaded that she should consider the progress of her faith rather than of her own happiness.

She died young, but had established a dynasty. Her statue on her tomb reveals her as very beautiful.

Certainly she was and is loved by the Poles. Her father was a Hungarian who became king of Poland; and during the Hungarian revolt of 1956 the tomb of Jadwiga was loaded with flowers, each spray bearing a message of sympathy.

Between the Wawel and the city centre is a maze of the narrow streets of old Cracow, some lined with palaces of nobles or rich merchants. Often you will find a narrow passage: it will lead to a courtyard with old houses and shops of great interest.

A number of buildings form the famous university, second only in Central Europe to Prague for age. One of its students was Nicolas Copernicus, who was born at Torun, and as a scientist was far ahead of his age.

The Germans claim Copernicus as one of their own great men, and the inscription on his statue in Warsaw was changed more than once as the city changed hands during the Second World War. But the Polish claim is stronger. And would a German desire to study at a Polish university?

Less authentic is a connection with Dr. Faustus, whose alleged hand-print is shown on the door of the university museum: he really belongs to Germany. Or Pan Twardowski, a Polish magician whose stories were based on the alleged exploits of a Cracow student.

Like Faust, he sold his soul to the devil, who promised to make him the greatest magician on earth. In return, Mr. Twardowski would be safe unless he met the devil in Rome, when he must surrender his soul.

The devil fulfilled his part of the bargain. Among the magic he provided was a giant cockerel, on whose back Twardowski would fly—after Daedalus and Icarus he must have been the first aviator in history!

At one time Twardowski was lost in a great forest. He stumbled on through the darkness, and at last he was delighted to chance across an inn. But as he prepared for bed, the devil appeared.

Now Twardowski had naturally been very careful to avoid Rome in his travels. But to his horror he found that the name of the lonely inn was Rome!

The devil took him, and flew high into the air. Twardowski, very frightened, began to pray: or, by some versions of the story, the sound of a monastery bell was heard. It was now the devil's turn to be scared—and in his alarm he dropped his prey.

Twardowski was free, but in mid-air—and so far from the attraction of the earth that he fell upon the moon! And, if you wish for proof of the story, can you not see Twardowski, the Man in the Moon?

And you meet him frequently in Cracow—in the souvenir shops, where he is offered in effigy or picture, flying on his cockerel or sitting on the horn of the moon!

III

The centre of Cracow is its great market square, spread around the Sukiennice, or Cloth Hall. This is an interesting building, and an excellent example of the "Polish attic". The architects were Italians, who despised the steep roofs so essential in a land where there are heavy snowfalls in winter. So they hid the steep sloping roof by an ornamental wall following the line of its eaves.

In one corner of the square is St. Mary's Church, whence the *heynal* is sounded hourly, and which is the home of the famous triptych of Wit Stwosz. This is indeed a remarkable piece of work. The church itself is somewhat sombre, but the gilt of the triptych, dominates the gloom. The many figures, in their flowing robes, are beautifully sculpted. The carvings represent scenes in the life of Jesus Christ and the Virgin Mary. Maybe the huge object is rather too colourful. In Germany you will find the sculptor's masterpieces in plain wood—in some ways more pleasing. But this is not to denigrate the wonder of Cracow.

It was hidden when war threatened, found, looted and damaged by the Germans, but restored when peace came. The restoration work occupied skilled craftsmen for 64,000 hours, and cost 17 million zloty. Earlier I had met one of the men who helped with its repair.

"It was a labour of love, to work on such a masterpiece," he said. "Did you know that it consists of 300 pieces of sculpture, ingeniously fitted together? And, when Wit Stwosz constructed it, he selected lime trees 500 years old. That was 500 years ago—so the triptych is actually a thousand years old."

It has one failing. Naturally, it stands behind the altar: there, it distracts attention from its background—a series of magnificent fourteenth-century stained glass windows.

The church at a Saturday evening service was crowded: on the Sunday it was packed. The sermon was slightly disturbing to a few members of the congregation. A new school year would soon begin, and the priest was primarily addressing parents. In our time the Church was hard pressed by its enemies, he said. Parents must insist on such rights as they had for religious education of their children. The publication of religious books and journals was declining—the excuse was shortage of paper. There was plenty of paper for political manifestoes, but little for religion. He criticized an article in a leading magazine, whose author declared that the sex instinct was purely individual. But this was not so—it was a matter of concern to society and the Church, of social and religious behaviour. He switched to the danger of indifference to the problems of youth, and concluded with a dissertation on the subject of harmony. But there was little trace of this in his words: he was emphatically a member of the Church militant. He was at least right in one of his statements—that the Church is strongest when it is oppressed.

"He was right," said my companion. "Today we talk about 'before Gomulka' and 'after Gomulka'. In the earlier period the Church was so wickedly persecuted that it received the sympathy of many who were not by any means fervent Catholics. Gomulka has eased a few of its heaviest burdens, and since then the influence of the Church has diminished somewhat—especially among young people."

The Communist intention is to rid Poland of religion—if it can. Perhaps its most cunning plan would be for Gomulka and his friends to become Church members! Then the religious hierarchy would have nobody against whom they could issue a call to battle.

I have mentioned only a few of the attractions of Cracow, which cannot be exhausted in a casual visit. Helen and I walked for hours, by day and by night, about the little streets which converge on the Market Place. Almost by accident we found ourselves in the ancient Ghetto. Jews came to Cracow by invitation in the Middle Ages, and played a considerable part in the development of the city's commerce. When the war began in 1939, there were 60,000 of them in the city. Today the number is 2,000.

Doubtless there are others who evaded Hitler's madness, possibly by escaping to Palestine, yet the bulk of the Jewish population formed the earliest victims of Oswiecym. The Ghetto has now lost its name as well as its earlier inhabitants, but there is still an atmosphere of sadness about its narrow alleys. I pictured them as I had seen them before the war, peopled by men in long black coats and round velour hats, and boys wearing ceremonial curls beside their cheeks. Their synagogue on a Saturday morning was crowded: the women were herded upstairs in a gallery. The men were below, swathed in striped prayer shawls, their bodies swaying in a fervour of religious ecstasy. Did Rembrandt find his models in Cracow?

Festivals in Cracow have a long history. Every spring the Rector of the University hands over his authority to the students for just one day—on which the students also enjoy the freedom of the city. There are processions and dancing—and no work.

"Cracow Days" are another annual occasion in June. The atmosphere is that of carnival. There are bands, giant masks, and historic figures—including, naturally, Krakus and the dragon. Nor are the invading Tatars omitted, but now they have become comic characters. The *Laikonik*, the Tatar horseman, with his skirted horse and an outsized moustache, is the villain of the parade, and is heartily booed and hissed. But children like him: they eat his effigy in sugar or gingerbread.

A gentler celebration is seen just before Christmas. Different organizations, especially those of builders, compete in constructing Szopkas, or cribs—some of which are so ornate that they resemble cathedrals. Christmas rivals Easter as a Christian festival in Catholic Poland.

IV

I met some local Polish authors at dinner at the ancient Wierzynak restaurant. As far back as 1364 it served the famous "Feast of Kings". Cyprus was threatened by the Turks, and the German Emperor, the kings of Poland, Hungary and Poland, the Duke of Austria, and many other princes met in Cracow to decide on their action—if any. They were given a Lucullan meal, followed by expensive presents. These latter are now dispensed with, but the food is still good.

We called in at the Michailik, for many generations the favourite haunt of literary men and artists—who, if impecunious, used to pay for meals by drawing or painting cartoons or sketches on the walls. But I was disappointed when I revisited the Hawelka.

It had one story which was no legend. In the days of the

Partitions an Austrian officer had his dinner there every night, sitting at the same place by a fixed table or counter. The food was so nourishing that he began to get fat. The Polish proprietor realized the growing difficulties of his client, and had a rounded segment of wood sawn out of the table to accommodate the officer's tummy. This space had to be enlarged every year or two.

Then the owner died. In his will, he directed that the officer should dine free every evening at the Hawelka for the rest of his life. And so he did, the segment of the circle in front of him ever enlarging.

The restaurant is now state property and has been "popularized". Its young energetic manager had never heard of its story: and quite plainly was more interested in chromium fittings than in tables shaped to fit corpulent clients. And I am quite sure that he will never will free meals to *his* regular guests. On my next visit I shall doubtless find a juke-box installed. Times and manners do change.

But not always. We went down the famous salt mine of Wieliczka, which has been in use since the eleventh century, and as of old the galleries are flooded, the salt dissolves, the water is pumped up to the surface, the salt evaporated and refined.

Visitors descend by hundreds of steps—but there is a lift to bring them up later. A miner conducts a small party along about three kilometres of the tunnels—in the mine these total more than 300 kilometres, or nearly 200 miles! If this were all, it would be monotonous, but over the centuries the miners have carved out novelties in the rock-salt, which is easy to work. There are great halls, and several churches. The walls of the huge chapel of St. Kinga are decorated with a quite remarkable statuary. One miner, Wyrobak, demonstrated such talent that one of the directors of the company sent him to an art school. On his return he sculpted a great panorama of the Last Supper. Its craftsmanship is noteworthy. From a distance its depth is normal, but close examination shows that it amounts to no more than 17 centimetres.

The next hall contains a tennis court and a basket-ball enclosure. Another is used for an annual party for the miners and their families. The Germans adapted the mines as underground munition factories during the war—but nine soldiers fell into one of its lakes and were drowned.

The mine has 1,300 employees, of whom 400 work under-ground. 200,000 tons of salt are produced every year.

"No, we are not well paid," said a miner, emphatically. "We are not included in the mining industry, but in the chemical industry. True, chemists can do a lot of things with our salt—but so they do with coal. But we are paid 2,100 zloty a month, and a coal miner gets 3,600. It's all wrong."

Maybe the gap is too wide. But a coal mine has its special dangers: the salt mine little more than the casual risks of a factory.

On our return journey to Cracow we passed a fine, large and modern hospital, with a thousand beds, for children. And it had been built by the subscriptions of American Poles. Their organiza-tions have also financed the building of schools all over the country. Americans for two or three generations, they still retain a great affection for their ancestral home.

V

A village adjoining Cracow has become a large town. Nowa Huta is built around a vast metallurgical plant. It was constructed in 1949, and already has 120,000 inhabitants, thirty-one schools, two cinemas, a theatre, a hospital, many libraries and "palaces of culture", parks, sports fields—but no church.

The lack of this has aroused endless argument. When the town was first projected the Church authorities were granted a suitable site. Ironically, it was in Marx Street! But the council refused to issue a building permit. Nowa Huta was modern, it was claimed—it did not need a church. But the people made it quite clear that it did!

True, on the southern edge of the town there was a monastery, with an old wooden church beside it. But Nowa Huta is a Communist (the word used in Poland is Socialist) production from start to finish, and its bosses could not bear to see their project spoiled by a church.

Now they claim that the site on Marx Street is required for a school. However, under the pressure of public opinion they have allocated another site for a church "if it is still wanted". It is: the people have made this quite clear.

Nowa Huta consists largely of huge blocks of flats. Most are monotonously ugly, but some are gay and colourful. Extensions to the original plan have incorporated neighbouring villages.

"We drew 7 per cent of our workers from other plants," said a foreman. "We recruited the rest in the villages."

"But they were not engineers?"

"Oh, no. But we taught them. Some of them *are* engineers, now. We had a lot of trouble at first. The wages here are more than a villager ever thought of, and we had much drunkenness and absenteeism."

"What are the wages?"

"A skilled worker gets around 2,300 zloty a month. A technician will get at least 3,000. Unskilled workers as low as 1,200."

"You have a Works' Council?"

"Oh, yes. I am on it."

"It is elected?"

"Of course. Secret ballot—no official list. The Council includes twenty-six technicians, sixteen economists, and lawyers and office staff—which is large."

"And workers?"

"They make up the rest."

"They are only a minority?"

"Yes."

"Why?"

"Well, it is a free vote. And workers don't necessarily vote for workers. A *free* vote, I said. Less than 20 per cent are Party members."

"Your functions are advisory?"

"Yes. We are allocated a production quota—for the plant. We don't have individual norms, setting man against man. A worker gets a basic wage per hour, plus a bonus for achieving the quota, shared according to the work of his section. Collective norms, you might say. We are a new plant, and are doing well."

I suppose that a man who makes enough money is oblivious of his surroundings. Nowa Huta is entirely functional, but I prefer ancient Cracow to this newfangled human rabbit warren.

10

BLACK COUNTRY

I

THE road to the west from Cracow passes through a region of green hills decked with woods and spinneys. Approaching Ojcow we drove along a narrow valley flanked with great rocks, which in turn are pierced by numbers of caves exciting to explore. The picturesque valley ends at Pieskowa Skala, commanded by a castle of the Radziwill family.

Here the character of the villages changes. The houses are still constructed of timber, but many of them are colour-washed in a delicate shade of eggshell blue. No other tint is used. "Who first chose this colour, and why?" I asked. No one could say.

"It started with our grandfathers' grandfathers, or much earlier," an old man guessed tentatively. "I think they were trying to reflect the sky."

Our next halt was a place of horror: Oswiecym, or Auschwitz. The death camp has now been converted into a Museum of Martyrology, and is visited by large crowds, including children. True, you need imagination to picture the gruesome horror of the scene, and the children do not understand death, so they are not afraid.

Above the iron entrance gate is an ironic motto, *Arbeit macht frei*: literally, work makes (or gives) freedom. But this promise was fulfilled to very few of the five million people gathered from every region of Europe to satisfy Hitler's megalomania: not all of them were Jews. Oswiecym consisted of three camps. That of Bizezinka (or Birkenau) has been retained as a gruesome museum.

A string of cattle trucks would arrive from some distant corner of Europe. A German doctor would sort out the arrivals. Little children—they were useless—they ate but did not work.

Old people and weak women also. The stronger men would be marched off to an adjoining camp. They would be worked, hard, on meagre rations—the Nazis calculated that a strong man could last for four months under such conditions. The moment he weakened was almost his last.

The "useless" prisoners were herded in wooden huts. Oswiecym had been a Polish barracks, and now 1,200 people were packed into a hut designed for a couple of platoons. There was a triple row of bunks not three feet high, in which the victims were herded like rabbits.

Some did not have to endure this misery. They would be marched straight from the station to the camp, and ordered to strip for a bath—often they undressed in the open. Then they would be packed into the "bath". But instead of water, gas poured in, and within twenty minutes all were dead.

The dirty work of the camp was done by other able-bodied prisoners. I met one such man when I visited the camp soon after the end of the war in 1945. (Then the place was far more horrible than it is today, for trenches of dead were left open so that relatives might attempt to identify them.)

"At first I was afraid that I would weaken and die," the man said. "I was always sick. Think of it. A gang of us would be sent to clear one of the gas chambers. In it would be the bodies of hundreds of women, indescribably distorted. Some, when the gas came, had tried to scratch their way out with their fingernails. Others had a look of surprise, when they realized that the expected bath water was a lethal gas.

"We had to carry the bodies out. First we cut off the women's hair—the Germans made cloth out of it. Then some of us, armed with carpenter's pincers, pulled out any teeth with gold fillings. We could almost identify Jewesses by their teeth. Their men looked upon gold teeth as an emergency reserve, and often we found gold covers on perfectly healthy teeth. Then we carried the bodies to one of the crematoria, which could deal with 2,000 a day. Our final task was to clear the crematorium of the dust to which our fellow human beings had returned.

"My worst days came when I was allocated to the children. Can you imagine what it feels like to lead little children deliberately to their death. And I have a family of my own! Chubby little boys and girls used to take my hand as I led them into the gas chambers. I learned to cry and sob quietly. Had the Nazi guards seen me, it would have been interpreted as a fatal weakness.

"The only children who escaped were twins. The Nazis wanted to use these for medical experiments—they were trying to discover how their own women could breed little Nazis two at a time."

I could feel for such unfortunate men as we walked round the Museum. Here was a great heap of women's hair, and among it the neat plaits of little girls.

Some of the rooms in the brick blocks were reserved for "criminals"—men who had tried to escape (about two thousand succeeded in doing so) or who had insulted the Führer. Sometimes they could not even lie down, but had to stand packed in their cells for days on end while awaiting death. They were given no food, and there are records of horrible reversions to cannibalism.[1]

These atrocities are illustrated in the Museum by photographs, enlarged from snaps taken by the German soldiers to send home to their own people. Their letters show that they were told that all their victims were Jews, and that they were playing a valuable part in Hitler's "Final Solution".

How could men believe in such a manner, even under orders? How could intelligent men participate in such horrors and not go insane? I think I was most affected when I attended a war crimes' trial in Austria. Here a dozen members of a local Home Guard unit were proved to have deliberately and brutally murdered hundreds of Jews in a convoy they were guarding. Yet the accused men were typical of the benign-faced Austrians you would meet on a mountain path, who would greet you with a cheery Grüss Gott, and go right out of their way to aid you. That such men could descend so low was almost incredible—and inexplicable.

Everyone should see Oswiecym, or one of its fellows. The visit will hurt, but will never be forgotten. Many years ago I advocated that when statesmen were discussing policies which might lead to war, they should do so not in a comfortable palace, but in an open marquee in the midst of a war cemetery. For this, I would now substitute a death camp like Oswiecym, with the plaits of murdered children decorating the walls.

[1] Similarly among Russian prisoners of war, systematically starved by the Nazis—see The Devil on my Shoulder, by Hans Becker (Jarrolds, 1955).

I got into conversation with a man who was obviously affected by the atmosphere of the death camp.

"My sister died here," he said. "She lived at Torun, and in the district was a prisoner-of-war camp. One day two English officers escaped, and she sheltered them. The Germans found this out, and sent her here. You know what affected me most?"

"The pile of human hair?"

"No. My sister was a very precise woman—a Victorian, I think would be your term. She would not fear death; in war-time it was always near. But what appalled me was that picture of a group of naked women walking to their 'bath', as they were told. My sister was much too intelligent to believe that. She would have walked calmly to her execution, but to walk naked, with those smirking Nazi soldiers looking on! That would have hurt harder than the thought of death. These poor people were not even allowed to die in decency."

Almost every Pole can tell such a story of his relatives. One-fifth of the nation perished, generally by murder. Assuredly nobody can understand the Poles and the "Polish madness" unless he has seen Oswiecym, so as to realize their incredible sufferings.

II

Our next halt was Katowice, the capital of Upper Silesia: its German name was Kattowitz. The plebiscite following the First World War, with its indecisive results, led to the adoption of a fantastic frontier. A farm would be in one country and its barns in the other, or the boundary might actually pass through a house. So if its owner lit his pipe in the kitchen and smoked it in the living-room, he was smuggling!

The confused frontier was used by Hitler—not merely for propaganda, but to start off the war.

Gliwice (then Gleiwitz) was just inside Germany, and was an example of such anomalies. It had a radio station, used to beam propaganda into Poland. This was the objective of a fake raid just before the war began.

Polish prisoners were gathered from German concentration camps. They were dressed in Polish uniforms and put under a German leader—who has now told the full story. The Polish "partisans" attacked the radio station at Gliwice, but were all shot dead—no wounded. Excited broadcasts described the Polish "aggression". Even in Nazi Germany few people believed the story, however: similar ruses had been tried previously, and subsequently revealed.

"Even apart from that, the war began here," said a Katowice man. "Hitler had decided to start fighting on 26th August. Then he postponed the date until 1st September. He was depending on German residents in Poland for aid—to make diversions and arouse alarms. Not all of these people were warned of the change of date, and shooting began and some of these were killed on 26th August."

We found that Katowice was preparing to commemorate an earlier war. In 1919, 1920, and 1921 there were local insurrections or fights with German armed guerrillas protesting against the plebiscite. Now a monument had been erected, and awaited its formal inauguration. It was as queer as the *avant-garde* sculptors could produce. Entitled "The Wings of Hope", it consisted of three mounds of irregular sculpture. To me it was meaningless: nor could I find anyone who could explain it. The best comment came from a local councillor.

"None of us could understand it, so we thought it must be good," he said.

In the countryside we had seen occasional memorials in honour of Polish guerrillas killed fighting against the Germans— in the small Communist organization, not the Polish Home Army, who were often ignored by the régime. Most of these monuments were fantasies. One reminded me of a guillotine!

Katowice is the centre of the richest corner of Poland, the mining and industrial region. It is the country's smallest province, with only 3 per cent of the land area—but 11 per cent of the total population.

We called on the Vice-Chairman of the Provincial Council.

"Yes," he said. "As soon as you are out of one town you're in another."

I assured him that we had regions like that in England, too!

"There are thirteen towns in the group around Katowice," he went on, "and they have a total population of 3½ million. We are considering their reorganization into four cities.

"This is an intensely industrial region—there are eight coal mines within the boundaries of Katowice alone. We have the Ministry of Mines here, you know. The Minister has a small office in Warsaw, to keep in touch with the Seym, but his staff is here.

"Our production has doubled since the war. Unfortunately, the world price of coal is low, but we export a good deal—even as far as Japan. Our steel commands better prices. Our coal mines are very far from nearing exhaustion, and our seams are thicker than yours in England. Not all of them, of course, but seams two and a half metres thick are quite common.

"Our air is admittedly dirty." We began to talk of smokeless zones, not yet essayed in Poland. "But our accident record in the mines is good.

"The average earnings of all workers is 3,000 zloty per month. The skilled men working at the coal face can earn much more, of course. They are allocated a norm—you understand the term?"

"Oh, yes. In England we call it a stint. It is an old practice." He seemed to be surprised. Maybe he thought that the Communists had invented the norm.

"A man who produces more than the norm makes very good money, of course," he went on.

"But if he fails to produce the norm?"

"Then, naturally, he gets less. But most do well. Their savings are the highest in Poland. They usually have TV and a refrigerator."

"And a car?"

"Not yet. Some could afford one, but there is a shortage of cars. Some miners earn as much as 6,000 zloty a month. We provide houses at low rents—around 300 zloty a month. And there is a financial scheme whereby we make it easy for a man to buy his own house."

"And the salary of the manager?"

"It is good. 6,000 or 7,000 zloty—more if his pit beats the allotted norm. And there are certain perquisites attached to the job. Quite apart from skill, you have to pay for responsibility."

"Yes. But the Russians would not agree with you."

"Then we do not agree with them. Responsibility, like success, deserves reward."

"There seem to be signs that the use of coal is going out of date."

"Yes, that could be true. But you can make so many things from coal. We work very closely with our chemical industry."

"You have no difficulty in recruiting labour?"

"No. Not at the wages we can offer."

He recommended us to visit the local Palace of Youth. The Poles are not as well placed in this respect as the Russians, who were able to seize real palaces for their young people. The premises at Katowice were not ornate—the building had once been used as a store for pit-props. However, its equipment was adequate, and its space was far greater than would be available for a youth club in England. There were facilities for most hobbies and for training for trades. The age limits were ten to eighteen.

"It is very active in the evenings. The boys and girls come here after school."

"All of them?"

"Oh, no. We could not hold anything like all of them. Our members are selected on the basis of their school record. It is a great incentive to good work, the fact that it can mean membership of the Youth Palace, which is very popular."

Katowice was interesting, but an industrial mining town is scarcely beautiful. And we were quite glad to get into the air of the green countryside.

III

We moved into the Piast country, that of the family which provided the first dynasty of Polish kings. It began at Opole.

This was an ancient settlement long before its dukes attained national importance as relatives of the king: or even before they became dukes at all. The tombs of three of their number lie in the Franciscan church of Opole. They were known by the name of Bolko, which was later transformed into Boleslas. They were the chiefs of a Slav tribe, originating from both Polish and Czech sources. The long period of German rule, however, affected the local architecture. It is, indeed, important to realize that most of the towns of the region were built in the days of German supremacy, and those which were spared war damage are not very different from other towns in the adjoining German provinces.

The River Oder runs through the town in several channels.

Outdoor fashion parade at Zakopane

Youth parade in Gdansk

Castle of the Teutonic Knights at Malbork

The main course is a large stream, carrying a lively traffic of barges. The market place was also lively. September 1st was near— the beginning of a new school year, and parents were busy buying new outfits and books for their children.

We were now well into the New Territories, or Oder-Neisse provinces, taken from Germany after the war and allocated to Poland by Stalin in recompense for the eastern part of Poland which he had seized for Russia. There was then a strong rumour, probably of Nazi origin, that the Poles would be unable to settle the provinces. I had denied that in 1945, when I saw the Germans expelled and the Poles moving in. Today the question does not arise. The provinces *are* settled, and are doing well.

Stalin's argument was simple. He wanted half of Poland—Russia had an ethnic claim to part of the eastern territory. And he pro- posed to compensate Poland with land taken from the Reich. The Germans had started the war—his own pact with Hitler was con- veniently forgotten—and had vilely attacked the sacred Soviet Union. For this they must be punished, and the loss of territory was part of their punishment.

The Polish outlook was different. The lands up to the Oder *had* been Polish centuries ago: the Poles were merely re-occupying their ancestral home. There are limits to the historic argument, however. Mussolini claimed to restore the Roman Empire, but we did not propose to hand over to him England south of Hadrian's Wall.

However, the historic claim was well founded. The Piasts pro- vided the first dynasty of Polish kings, and this was their country. After the reminders we had seen in Opole, there were more in Brzeg, an ancient Silesian settlement populated by a Slav tribe. It is beautifully situated on the Oder, in a lovely countryside.

The Brzeg-Lignica line of Piast princes made Brzeg their capi- tal. Their castle, or palace, was in process of restoration from the depredations of war and time. Its chapel is a Piast mausoleum.

The princes were in close contact with their cousins, the Polish kings, at Cracow. It was Prince Ludwik I who initiated the "Chronicle of Polish Princes", the local Debrett of its time, and a great source of information on Polish history.

"More than that," said a local schoolmaster. "It was at Brzeg that the Polish Hymn Book was first published. That was in 1673. It was a masterpiece of the old Polish prints.

9

"The Germans complain that we recovered these regions by force. But they were seized by force by the Prussians. If their argument is sound, so is ours."

The little town is recovering from the devastation of the last war. It has one interest other than historic. Near Brzeg the Eastern or Klodzko Neisse joins the Oder.

From now onwards almost every village was connected with the Piasts. Olawa has a Piast castle—which remained in the hands of the Polish royal family until Silesia was seized by the Prussians in 1741. And Wroclaw—known in its German days as Breslau—was also a Piast city. The last of the princely line was Henry VI. On his death, without a direct heir, his province was inherited by the King of Bohemia, and thereafter shared the fate of that country.

"It was a Polish-Czech city when the Prussians took it in 1741," said a priest. "Seven hundred years earlier the Poles had defeated the Germans at the battle of Psie Pole, just outside our city. Then, in 1241, came the Mongol invasion of the Tatars. They were halted at Lignica, eighty kilometres to the *west* of here. In the battle, the Polish king, Henry the Pious, was killed, but his army had resisted the invaders so valiantly that the exhausted Tatars were glad to withdraw from Silesia.

"The Prussians began to Germanize the province. Frederick the Great turned Wroclaw University into a barracks for his soldiers. Bismarck was worse—but even he could not remove all Polish influences. True, as the city grew and its industries flourished, the overwhelming majority of the population was German, but its greater part was not local, but had been drawn from other parts of Germany."

Obviously I had to pursue the argument further. First I must see how Wroclaw had recovered from the tremendous battering it received during the war: and how the Poles were settling down in the ancient city.

11

WEST OF THE ODER

I

IN 1945 the defeated German armies were reeling before the advancing Russian hosts—which included a strong Polish force. At times the retreat became a rout—the Russians captured one German camp, near Katowice, in which a meal had been prepared in the officers' mess and the soup was still warm on the tables.

But Breslau was strongly garrisoned, and its strategic position demanded resistance. Yet the Russians, aiming for Berlin, would not be halted: a force was detailed to besiege Breslau, while the main armies pressed on.

Conditions in the besieged city were appalling. The garrison resisted fiercely, and the Russians could only advance in the suburbs by flattening a path with their powerful artillery fire. And the Germans deliberately destroyed great areas of the city to improve their field of fire.

When in East Berlin I heard one story of the siege of Breslau. I had witnessed one of the frequent parades—armed services, factory fighting units, and youth organizations armed with carbines. As these youths and girls marched by, an old lady whispered to me: "Only the colour of the shirts is changed."

"She was right," a German acquaintance said, later in the day. "I was in Breslau during the siege, which lasted for three months. Conditions became intolerable. One evening a large group of elderly people demonstrated in front of the office of the Nazi *gauleiter*.

" 'Surrender the city!' they cried. 'The war is lost—the Russians are in Berlin! So why should we suffer and die when all is over? And we are hungry.'

"The *gauleiter* ordered the police to disperse the crowd. They failed. He ordered them to shoot, and they refused—maybe their own parents were among the demonstrators. He called out a company of German infantry, and ordered them to fire. They would not. So he brought along a Nazi youth unit, armed with carbines, and ordered *them* to fire. And they did."

Nearly 70 per cent of Wroclaw was totally destroyed. As usual the Poles decided to restore the historic buildings in their original form, and in this they have been successful. The ornate Gothic town hall has arisen from its ruins, and was crowded with people queueing for licences for this or that. Its principal façade is gaily decorated with varied statuary. Among the decorations, need I add, is the Piast coat of arms.

In the Town Square are some fine old houses, of wealthy burghers, now restored to their former grandeur. Among them is one where the Polish kings used to stay when visiting Wroclaw. Most of the old churches have been restored. The red brick cathedral, dating from the twelfth century, was seriously damaged in 1945: the Nazis used it as an ammunition store, and an explosion wrecked it. It has an altar-piece reminiscent of that at Cracow, and perhaps sculpted by pupils of Wit Stowsz. The stained glass windows are certainly Polish. The Holy Cross church is unusual, in that it is built in two storeys.

One of the quarters of the town had a curious history. The Nazis, using forced labour, tore down the houses and a monastery, and made the open ground into an airstrip. This was to be available for the evacuation of Nazi dignitaries when the position became critical. The *gauleiter* did in fact make his escape at the last moment, but most of his staff fell into Russian hands.

The River Oder breaks up into several channels through the city, and islands are thus formed. This may have been the reason for the earliest settlements, as the islands were defensible. The first known people in the district were a Slezanic tribe of Slav origin—probably the ancestors of the Poles. They took their name from a river bearing the Polish name of Sleza. From this was derived the provincial title, Silesia.

In the tenth century, Wroclaw was included in that part of Poland ruled by the Piasts, and later the growing city was the seat of a Piast dukedom. It was at that time one of the most important cities in Poland, and capital of the province of Silesia. The Piast dynasty of dukes at Wroclaw lasted for three hundred years

longer than the Piast royal dynasty at Cracow. By that time it was
a rich city—its trade extended as far as England and Scotland.
Then it shared the fate of its province, and passed under Czech
and then Prussian rule. The process of Germanization was intense,
and by 1939 the Poles in Breslau were numbered only in hundreds.

II

At Lubiaz is a famous old monastery. I was advised to apply for
admission to the Slaski or Silesian Museum in Wroclaw. There I
was told that it was impossible to see it, as the whole place was in
the confusion of reconstruction. "War damage, you know."

But I knew that the damage was not due to the shells or bombs.
The Russians had occupied it, and their soldiers—like those of all
other nations—were not careful of other people's property. When
they left, the monastery was in a sad state, its ancient decorations
ruined.

However, another monastery was available, if I needed one. So
we journeyed to Trzebnica. Here was an early Slav settlement,
brought to fame by Henry the Bearded, of the Piast dynasty, the
ruler of Silesia. He had an unusual reason for wanting to endow
a shrine, for his wife was a saint! Other men have claimed this
distinction for their wives, but Hedvig, or Jadwiga, was actually
canonized. She was famous as a founder of churches.

Henry built a basilica, with a convent of Cistercian nuns
attached. Its abbesses were for many centuries members of the
extensive Piast family, and ranked as duchesses. St. Hedvig was
buried in the church, which became a famous place of pilgrimage.

The basilica is overwhelmed by Baroque decorations. As
gentler relief, a dozen pictures illustrating the life of the saint are
hung about it. The church is a good example of the old Polish
architectural custom of using brick for building and stone for
decoration.

One doorway, however, has a peculiar lintel. A monk (the
convent is now a monastery) described the carved figures as
Samson and Delilah, but corrected his identification to David
playing the harp to Bathsheba. But his instrument is not a harp,
or even a lyre, but a rather fat-bellied guitar. Nor does Bathsheba
seem to be at all pleased with the performance.

On our return to Wroclaw we passed by the scene of the battle known as Psie Pole, or Hound's Field, where in 1109 King Boleslas the Wry-mouth defeated the German army of the Emperor Henry V, who was attempting to seize Silesia. The battlefield was strewn with corpses, and according to tradition, starved dogs devoured the bodies: hence 'Hound's Field'.

The other famous battlefield, near Lignica, was off our itinerary. It was the capital of a Piast dukedom, and still has ruins of a Piast castle. In fact, the whole district is rich in historical reminders that in older days it was part of Poland.

III

I called on Professor Jwaszkiewicz, the mayor, to gather modern information about Wroclaw. He gave a knowledgeable lecture.

"When the war ended, there were only about 6,000 Germans left in Wroclaw. The siege had involved many casualties, and before it began thousands of people had taken refuge in the countryside. They began to make their way back, but most of their homes had gone, and perhaps they were not sorry to be directed westwards.

"Of the Poles who then moved in, 18 per cent in the town and 42 per cent in the rural region were from the provinces around Lwow or Vilno. The rest were from central Poland.

"You must remember that very many thousands of Poles had been taken to Germany for forced labour. As the war ended, they began to make their own way homewards. And Wroclaw was the first big town they came to. Despite the damage, since the Germans had evacuated the city there were homes for all. Incidentally, 40 per cent of Wroclaw's initial population came from villages.

"And most of our settlers were young. In 1950 over 32 per cent were between seventeen and twenty-seven years of age. You can imagine what this implied—a high birth-rate. It rose to the very high figure of 30 per thousand. This could not last indefinitely, but our birth-rate is still far above the Polish average. Fifty-two per cent of our people have been born here—since the war. Only 6 per cent of our people are over sixty. You must have noticed the comparative youth of our population."

I had already done so. It was remarkable.

"At first some of our settlers were apprehensive—because of the confusion among the victorious Allies about our frontiers. Some of the immigrants left. But gradually ideas stabilized, and it became apparent that Wroclaw had returned to Poland for good. Since 1958 all apprehension has vanished. The city is building more houses—and many people are building their own.

"We were a very mixed lot to begin with. Our people came from every corner of Poland, spoke different dialects, and often had peculiarities arising from a local way of life. Soon this changed. If a young man sees an attractive girl, it does not matter if he comes from Cracow while she is from Vilno. And the schools were wonderful mixers, of course. Today we are a Polish entity, with a strong local patriotism."

I asked if any Germans had stayed behind.

"We have only about a hundred Germans in the city. A few are old people who could not pull up their roots. Others did specialist jobs which they did not wish to leave, and we were happy to take advantage of their skills.

"The industry of the city is expanding at the rate of 10 per cent per annum. Maybe this is too rapid. There are some people who believe that more of our effort should be devoted to housing. But as one industry ceases to expand, another begins. In the region we have sunk new copper mines. And natural gas has been discovered. So it is difficult to see how our industrial expansion can be halted.

"Perhaps because Wroclaw is a youthful city, it is a happy one.

"The countryside? That, too, prospers. But doubtless you would prefer to see for yourself. Call in and see me on your way back."

IV

I adopted the professor's advice. During the following days we called at every type of farm. Seventy-four per cent of the farms of Lower Silesia are privately owned—small peasant farms, in fact: only 0·8 per cent are co-operatives (or collectives), and 24·9 per cent are State farms.

Our first calls were at peasant farms, selected at random. We would see a man working in the fields, or his wife busy about the

farmyard, and would stop and talk. There was never any difficulty here. They were quite willing to talk, and frankly. At least,
there *was* one difficulty—how to escape after our conversation
without allowing the wife to provide refreshments.

The first farms we visited were much of a pattern. The usual
peasant farm averages ten hectares: twenty-five acres and a cow,
so to speak. The main crops are wheat and roots, with fodder.

The farm houses are of brick—a contrast to the timber
cottages which most of the families had left.

"Yes, indeed, this is much nicer than my old house near
Lwow," said one farmer's wife. "There we only had two rooms—
here we have five. It's true that at first I wasn't happy here. This
was not my home—it was another woman's, and I longed to go
back to my own. But not now. I have had two babies here, and
that makes all the difference, as your wife will agree. Now it's our
home."

I asked her husband a few financial questions.

"Yes, we make a living," he agreed. "Of course, we are not too
far from the town, so my wife drives the cart into market one
day a week with a load of cabbages. And the children collect
mushrooms. That means that I don't have to take another job, as
some men do. I like farming."

I mentioned the Polish average income.

"Oh, I don't make as much as that in cash," he said. "But you
would have to add the value of our produce which goes into the
kitchen. There's our cow, for example. She doesn't cost us
anything. She grazes off the wayside grass—there's plenty of it.
One of the children takes her to a different spot every day, stakes
her there—a light chain fixed to her horns, and pegged to the
ground—and collects her in the evening. And we grow enough
fodder to keep her and the horse in the barn for the hard months
of the winter. And we have forty hens. So there's plenty of milk
and eggs—you can get a lot of meals out of them. Cabbages—
they are one of our standard crops: and we grow enough
potatoes for ourselves.

"So we live. The children go to school—we have a new one in
the village now."

"Were you ever in a collective?"

"Oh, yes. Soon after I came here. I was forced into it. Resisters
were arrested and imprisoned in those days. But I didn't like it—

I had always been an independent farmer. I did not like working for a wage. Nor did many of our friends. And it was monotonous —too much time doing the same thing. With your own farm you do a dozen different jobs every day. So as soon as Gomulka said that we might dissolve the co-operatives, we did.

"Now the government takes a proportion of our crops, but pays a fair price for it. The rest we can sell ourselves, at any price we can get. Oh, yes, there is a risk, but that's farming. Ah, here is my wife with some refreshments!"

Life on a small farm is not easy. We called on one peasant who worked a 5 hectare (12½ acres) small-holding.

His wife was the business director of the concern. She told us that in a very good year they might make as much as 30,000 zloty, including the value of the produce they consumed—practically all of it, in fact. Three thousand went in taxes, and a small proportion (not more than 10 per cent) went in compulsory deliveries to the State. For this, however, reasonable prices were paid.

"It is when the weather is bad that we face disaster," the farmer's wife said. "Rains or frosts can be ruinous. But thank goodness that we are healthy. We do not come under the National Health Service. A doctor's visit costs 25 zloty, and a hospital charges 55 zloty a day. That is a lot of money to us."

Most of the large farms in the region, it will be seen from the quoted statistics, are State farms rather than collectives. This is not at all incomprehensible, for the collective system was very unfair. I work on a collective which has good soil and communications. You work on one fifty miles away, where the soil is thin and the nearest railway some distance off. You work as hard as I do, but get little more than half my remuneration. Men sitting in offices and splitting up the land into farms forget that soil and climatic conditions vary very considerably. It is impossible to draft out a plan whereby all farms are equal.

So the collective is abandoned and converted into a State farm, with the workers paid a regular wage. You gain, but I lose. It is not surprising that the State farm is gaining—though it has little to do with Communism. A man ploughing for the State is no better off than if he ploughed for a private employer.

We called at a State farm at Lagiewniki, and spoke first to its manager and his technical adviser. Both were practical farmers—

the days when a man got a job as farm manager because he was a good Communist are over.

The farm was a large one—4,500 hectares, or 11,250 acres. It had 480 employees, including 24 clerks—bureaucracy is the bane of the Communist world. Sixty-five per cent of the workers were women.

"Naturally we do not give them the heaviest jobs," the manager explained. "Our principal crops are sugar beet and wheat—we raise 420 quintals per hectare of beet, 31 quintals of wheat. We also grow some flax, and rape—for making oil.

"We raise a lot of cattle—we send 20 per cent of our beef to you in England. At any given moment we have about a thousand bullocks, 240 breeding cows, and 3,500 calves—we buy these off independent peasants as well as rearing our own, and fatten them up. We have 800 pigs—we kill them for bacon and ham when they reach a weight of from 96 to 103 kilos. England and Germany are good customers.

"We have ample machinery, including tractors and combines. We take our beet to a sugar factory a few miles away."

"And your workers?"

"Each man gets a house free, but pays for his own electricity. He is allowed a quarter of a hectare of land for a garden—more if his family is large. He gets 35 chickens a year, as well as free milk, and can keep two pigs. So he is not badly off. And, of course, his wife works as well."

Certainly we encountered few grumbles as we wandered around. The workers were organized in teams, each under a foreman. Norms, or standard days' work, are fixed, and there is overtime at the busy seasons of the year. The farm was well managed. I showed its statistics to an English farmer on my return.

"My biggest criticism would be the use of twenty-four clerks," he said. "Do they count the grains of wheat individually?"

But the bureaucracy has nothing to do with farming: it pertains to the political system.

V

Our next halt was at the little town of Nysa—the Polish form of Neisse—on the eastern river of that name.

Here I had had an unusual experience in 1945. Only a few of the historic buildings of the old town had survived the war. The rest of Nysa was a maze of ruins—it had changed hands two or three times in the bitter fighting, and hundreds of burned-out tanks littered the surrounding countryside.

I borrowed a bicycle from a Russian soldier—who had looted it from a deserted house—and rode to the south, as far as the Czech frontier. The journey was not easy: all the bridges had been destroyed, but the rivers were neither wide nor deep, and I waded across.

The green hills were very pleasant as I rode back towards Nysa in the evening glow. Suddenly a man appeared from the bordering trees. He wore a tattered German uniform—a fairly common sight: evidently a demobilized soldier. Yet he did not speak German. He might be Czech, I thought—there are many Czech families on the wrong side of the frontier. He held up his hands at our lingual helplessness, accepted a cigarette, and at least understood that I was English. His language was certainly Slav.

I got back to my billet. A Polish official had called on my host.

"I've got the toughest job in Nyasa," he said. "I'm responsible for law and order. Imagine it: the town destroyed, no lights, no roads, no anything. No police—a few men who call themselves militia, but who are the biggest thieves in the town. Fortunately I can call on a few troops. My biggest difficulty is with our Russian allies.

"Their discipline has cracked. Or they don't realize that they are in Poland now, not Germany. There are shots and hold-ups every night. Keep indoors!

"And there are the mines. Our troops have already removed thousands, but there are plenty left. Don't go down the lane at the back of this house, by the way—it hasn't been cleared yet.

"There are German deserters too—a nuisance. But at least I can deal with them—I can't with the Russians."

This reminded me of my encounter with the man in the tattered German uniform—by this time I had decided that his language was Russian.

"Oh, hell!" said the Pole, wearily. "More trouble! I'd better go and warn everybody."

He explained his anxiety. The Germans had captured a total of more than a million Russian prisoners. I have mentioned a general named Vlassov, who was urged by the Nazis to form the "Free Russia" movement, and recruited a large army from among the prisoners-of-war. His principal supporters were Ukrainian Nationalists.

When the Germans collapsed, one of Vlassov's divisions was on the Czech frontier, among the mountains south of Nysa. It dissolved, and its members lived by raiding and looting. They were desperate men—they knew that they could expect no mercy from their own people.

My Polish acquaintance expected trouble, and he was right. In the middle of the night I was awakened by a fusillade. I got out of bed, and sheltered against a wall.

When it was light I went out, and marched to the sound of the guns. Russian soldiers were blazing away into a desolation of weeds. There were raiders hidden there, an officer explained. His unit was keeping them occupied while another company worked round to the rear.

Two light tanks appeared, and the battle was soon over. Three prisoners were brought in—Russians in German uniforms. I did not envy them. Vlassov was captured later, and hanged from a meat hook.

And in my excitement I walked back to my billet along the lane which had not yet been cleared of mines!

Today the restoration of Nysa is almost complete. The town was once the capital of a principality ruled by the bishops of Wroclaw, and acquired so many churches that it was known as the "Silesian Rome".

The burghers' houses surrounding the market place had been restored as of old; so have most of the historic churches. The region about is rural, but a few small factories have been erected in the town.

We had left the plain behind, and were in a land of gentle green ridges, well forested, and with the promise of higher hills to come.

VI

Nysa's neighbour, Paczkow, has been described as the "Polish Carcassone". The title is somewhat grandiloquent, for Paczkow is no more than a large village. It has retained its ancient walls, however, though they are so crude that they have not needed a Viollet-le-Duc to restore them. They and the whole place are dominated by an enormous church: it was once included in the local defensive scheme. It has buttressed walls and an interior wall! Like Nysa, Paczkow belonged to the bishops of Wroclaw. It may not be a rival to Carcassone, but it is a very pleasant little place.

We followed the river to Klodzko, the town from which it takes its name—although it rises many miles to the south, near the Czechoslovak frontier. It was ruled for centuries by Polish princes, until it was taken over by the kings of Bohemia. Frederick II of Prussia took it and fortified it so strongly that Napoleon failed to capture the place. Its old quarters are akin to those of Nysa, save that the war damage was not nearly as serious.

Now when in 1945 the Germans were expelled from the Polish New Territories, one exception was made. Walbrzych (German, Waldenburg) was the centre of the Lower Silesian coalfield. Skilled workers were needed, so some Germans were allowed to stay on. But in 1957 there was inaugurated the "uniting families" policy. Many a German was working in a Polish mine while his wife and family had fled to Germany. They were now allowed to leave Poland, if they wished: or his wife and family might join him in Walbrzych. But one condition was attached to this concession: he must become a Polish citizen. Hence an emphatic "None!" was given to my question: "How many Germans are now left in the coalfield?"

The German armies surrendered it without a fight in 1945, so the mines were captured almost undamaged. The district had long had Polish connections, through the Piast family. And now it is second only to the Katowice region as the most important coalfield in Poland. The town of Walbrzych itself is unusual—it really consists of a dozen villages, joined together. And around are pleasant green hills, a foretaste of what lay ahead.

The region between the two Neisse rivers was of some economic importance. The Walbrzych coalfield provided hard coal, excellent for coking, and thus important for the manufacture of steel. The rest of the Silesian coal—though easy to mine—was suitable only for domestic and industrial fuel. The iron ore of Silesia had already been exhausted, and today most of the ore for the plant at Nowa Huta has to be transported from Russia—to which country Silesian coal is exported. Polish economists believe that the long hauls could be avoided if Sweden replaced Russia, and waterways were used instead of the more expensive railways. This, they believe, would be the "natural pattern" of trade.

12

ODER-NEISSE PROVINCES

I

WE picture the Sudeten mountains as in Czechoslovakia, but their northern slopes are in Lower Silesia—and now in Poland.

We made our headquarters at Jelenia Gora (German, Krumm-hübel), an old town enclosed by a ring of green mountains. In 1004 the Polish King Boleslas the Brave ordered one of his knights, Jelnek, to build a castle here, as a defence against the Czechs of Bohemia. The settlement around the castle was known as Jelnek's Mountain—Jelenia Gora.

It flourished as a weaving centre, but the plague in the seventeenth century ruined the town—by 1640 no more than eight families remained. But it recovered, and under the Germans developed as a tourist centre. This distinction it has retained.

We wandered along the valley to Karpacz. On a nearby mountain are the ruins of a castle which long appeared in Polish folk-lore.

In the Middle Ages the castle of Chajnik belonged to a beautiful duchess of the Piast family named Kunegunda. Many knights were attracted by her beauty—and her wealth—and in the fashion of the day she set them a task to prove their love: each aspiring suitor had to ride his horse along the battlements. The cynical Kunegunda watched as one after the other they fell into the valley below. The supply of aspirants ceased.

But then a knight arrived from distant parts, and demanded to be put to the test. Kunegunda demurred, for she had been greatly attracted by the man—and the supply of eligible knights had been gravely reduced.

The newcomer rode his horse along the battlements, and Kunegunda was delighted. But the knight did not ask for her hand: he rode off, never to return: Kunegunda, utterly humiliated, flung herself to death in the abyss below. Old-time minstrels drew a good many morals from this legend.

From Karpacz we took a chair lift to Mala Kopa. Its route lay along a wide swathe cut in the forest of mountain conifers, and we travelled over a carpet of ferns, shrubs and deep blue gentians. The summit commanded a wonderful view, including the highest mountain in the Polish sudetens, Sniezka, 5,343 feet.

The Germans used to call these mountains Riesengebirge: now, in Polish, they are the Karkonosze, both names meaning the Mountains of the Giants. Some are regarded as extinct volcanoes, and obviously there were once glaciers here. Some of their beds have now become little lakes, bordered by rocks of fantastic shapes. The region has abundant rainfall, and is the birthplace of any number of streams, some of which are very picturesque. There are plenty of deer and wild boar—so we were assured by the locals, for we ourselves saw nothing larger than a black squirrel. Mountain sheep imported from Corsica have also settled down quite happily.

The valley leads on to the little village of Bierutowice, named after the Polish president installed by the Russians in 1945. It has one unusual curiosity.

Frederick William IV of Prussia, travelling in southern Norway, came to Wang, on the lake of that name. Here was a fine old wooden twelfth-century church, doomed to destruction as no longer large enough for the population. The traveller bought it, and re-erected it in the village then called Brückenberg.

The *Stave-kirke* is an amazing example of ancient Scandinavian architecture. The portals are elaborately carved, some of the motifs being derived from Viking culture. The church has double walls, and we could walk round the building between them.

Small black squirrels climbed the adjacent trees, but I was more interested in the caretaker. He was a Pole who had reached England after his country's defeat, and had fought in North Africa and France. I do not know if the district houses an unusual proportion of these men, but I encountered six of them in the same day.

In an adjacent valley is a picturesque waterfall, its approach lined with huge boulders. Here a photographer offered his services: he would take your photograph alongside a well-trained St. Bernard dog which would pose at the word of com-

Bison in the Bialowieza Forest

Concrete slabs marking the siding—the Railway of Death—at Treblinka extermination camp along which thousands of Polish Jews travelled to the gas chambers

Bernard Newman in search of his characters (Chapter 16): (*above*) at the rocket-launching site near Blizna-Pustkow; and (*below*) by the River Bug at Sarnaki where the rocket fell in the reeds

mand: or you might hire the dog for your own pictures. In the next village another photographer had copied the idea, and had added a stuffed bear as a model!

Alpine climbers would despise the five thousand feet of the Sudetens. But the mountains are very pleasant, clothed in every shade of green. And while they offer no rock-climbing perils to mountaineers, they provide wonderful country for hikers, ramblers, or even ordinary walkers. Small wonder that Czechs, Germans and Poles in turn have made this pleasant region a holiday resort.

II

At Szklarskiej-Poreba is a glass factory, an unusual one—cut glass: it has a branch a few miles away at Pieckowice. This is modern, but the other uses the methods of well over a century ago. So far as I could see, the products were identical—the modern methods simply apply more efficient ways of feeding molten glass into the same moulds, or blowing it into the same shapes.

The most interesting process follows. The glass is "cut", or ground, into its patterns. It has been moulded into thick shapes, but the rest of the processes are by hand. The patterns are conventional: they have not changed for a long time, and do not need to change. It is easy for a man to make a mistake, but every article is scrupulously examined, and on the slightest fault being detected the piece is smashed and melted down again.

There was an amazing range of patterns. A man might spend months on decorating a delicate vase of one particular shape and then turn to a massive bowl. This was real craftsmanship.

"Our workers begin to train while they are still at school, you might say," the manager explained. "Then they serve a long apprenticeship; in a sense, they are training for ten years. In that time they may still produce as many imperfect as perfect goods. It is all a matter of delicate touch, skill, and intense concentration.

"We employ 1,100 workers, of whom 30 per cent are women. The average wage is 2,350 zloty per month. This includes the unskilled labourers, who get about 1,400 zloty, and the craftsmen, who can earn as much as 4,000. They work to a norm, and are paid according to their production.

"We export 70 per cent of our products. Twenty per cent go

to England. The English are keen buyers, and know good glass when they see it. They prefer the traditional patterns and designs. They appreciate, too, that good lighting is essential to bring out the beauty in cut glass—the many facets reflect the light in all directions."

Jelenia Gora does not pretend to night clubs, nor did we want them. Instead, we walked round to another kind of club, which had served us well in other places as a home of interesting conversation.

Each large factory has its own social club. But workers can get tired of continuous contact with fellow workers, or their factory may be at a distance from their home. The Society of Peasants and Workers is not primarily political, but cultural. Its town-club serves the employees of such plants as do not have one of their own, or people who are tired of the company of their colleagues. A trifling annual subscription is charged: the remainder of the finance is provided by local factories.

In the district of Jelenia Gora, I learned, were 16,000 workers, of whom 4,800 were members of the central club. Its activities include dances, films, books, newspapers, lectures, discussions, and poetry readings—the last always a popular cultural feature in Poland. There are dramatic, film and musical societies, intellectual games such as chess: and handicrafts.

I recognized one man in the club—I had seen him during the morning at the glass works.

"I like this place better than our own club," he said. "I get tired of talking shop. I see enough of glass by day without talking about it all night."

"Your work is very demanding."

"Oh, yes. But I like it. There is something satisfying in the creation of beauty. But when it comes to discussions, our local Communists take the floor, and keep it.

"I'm not a politician, but a craftsman. Before the war I worked for a boss, and he paid me. Now I work for another boss, the State, and it pays me. What's the difference?"

"Some people would say the difference lay in the extras provided—medical service, holidays, and so on."

"Yes, we get them, true. But I have always had medical service and holidays. It seems that the Communists don't trust people. They organize everything for everybody. But if they would pay a wage which would enable a man to pay a doctor when he needs one, or pay for his own holiday—well, what's the difference?"

He began to talk about a lecture given at the club the previous week—on Viet-nam. Now in any country will be found two opinions on American policy in that country, but my glass-worker friend—a very intelligent man—had heard only one. Naturally, it was the one followed and promulgated by the government.

"Hell, what you say makes it all seem so different!" he exclaimed. "I've often wondered how the Americans managed to get into such a mess. But that's our trouble. We have discussions—but how can you discuss a problem when you only know one side of it? Tell me your last bit again."

"I only suggested that at your next discussion of the Viet-nam war you should raise two points. First, who started it? Second, have the Communists the right to impose a government by force?"

"That last one will startle them!" he chuckled. "Why, that's what happened in Poland! I can see some fun when I raise that point."

"Don't get yourself into trouble."

"Oh, there's no danger of that—now. Anyway, I shall talk about Viet-nam, not Poland. Our people are very good at reading between the lines."

I was sad to meet a man who wanted to acquire knowledge but was unable to do so. But I was encouraged to find that free speech was returning to Poland.

III

One day I shall return to the Polish Sudetens. High on the hills are chalets which act as pensions. I shall settle down in one of the quietest of them, and write a book. In between the chapters I shall walk in the forests: and all the time I shall breathe the invigorating mountain air.

We left Jelenia Gora in the early morning. For many miles the road wound its way through the green hills: often it is bordered by forests, occasionally broken by villages which have not yet lost their German character. Their inhabitants are Poles, but the houses are German, and might have been transferred across the

Oder from neighbouring Saxony. Many are painted and half-timbered, very picturesque. Most are substantial. I could picture the wonder of the Poles who had been transferred from the wooden cottages near Lwow.

Even more substantial are the old castles dotted about Lower Silesia. Many are now in ruins; some have been converted into museums. One, Grodno, bears the proud title of Museum of Old Polish Knighthood.

Most of the castles were founded or acquired by members of the ubiquitous Piast family. They were built as defensive posts, but later some were transformed into residential mansions. One was occupied until the beginning of the last war: military pillage left it the familiar wreck.

Jelenia Gora marked the end of our stay in southern Poland. It is a lively little town, as befitting a wine centre: it is situated in a valley almost surrounded by vine-clad hills. Its prosperity was formerly based on cloth, when Flemish weavers settled here in the thirteenth century, and it still has its factories. But its heyday is its wine festival every autumn.

We were making for Szczecin, but could not resist a side excursion to Poznan, which I had visited many times previously. The little towns and villages are neat and tidy, and nearly every one has some point of interest. Sulechow, for example, for long was the home of a Polish Calvinist community, and one of its first ministers was a Scotsman, Andrew Malcolm—who used to preach eloquently in Polish. And at Wolstyn Dr. Robert Koch discovered the bacillus of tuberculosis in 1876.

We were now on the right bank of the Oder, and had returned to the Polish plain. We crossed the border of 1919-45, to see the distant towers of Poznan.

It was the first capital of Poland, and prior to that was the seat of the first Polish bishopric. Its cathedral holds the sarcophagi of the first rulers of Poland—Miezko I and Boleslas the Brave. The building suffered grievously during the last war, because of the Nazi habit of using churches as ammunition stores.

Poznan began as a fortified village on an island in the midst of marshes: this was in the ninth century. It expanded rapidly in commerce and political and religious importance. After the Partitions, it was known as Posen, and the process of Germanization was intense. The Kaiser Wilhelm II built a castle here—it is now used for local government offices. Then in 1939 it was seized by the Nazi invaders, and incorporated into the Reich, and its Polish population massacred or expelled. In January, 1945, the city was surrounded by the Soviet army, but 20,000 well-armed Germans fought on for another two months. In that time the central section of the city—the historic Poznan—was completely destroyed.

It has now been restored, and the city is itself again, with a lively economic and cultural life. The reconstruction of the decorated Renaissance Town Hall has been most delicately accomplished: it has as neighbours colourful houses, also brilliantly restored.

To the Poles, Poznan is of an importance which is likely to become traditional: it was at the Bazaar Hotel in December 1918 that Paderewski proclaimed the new Polish Republic. And it was here in 1956 that the strike of the Poznan workers led directly to the overthrow of the Stalinist government of Poland and its replacement by the more modern rule of Gomulka.

Not far from Poznan is Gniezno, associated by legend with the early days of the Polish race. And close to this old town is an older one: Biskupin, where archaeologists have unearthed a large fortified Slav settlement of 2,500 years ago.

13

POLISH BALTIC

I

SZCZECIN and the surrounding region of Pomerania were captured by the early kinds of Poland. It had begun as a Slav fishing village, and developed into a port during the tenth and eleventh centuries. But not until 1121 was Christianity introduced —by a Polish king. The town had to withstand invasion from Danish as well as local invaders: it suffered no serious danger until the thirteenth century. Then Poland was weakened by internal dissensions, and Szczecin (the German Stettin) became a free city. It was a member of the Hanseatic League, and prospered greatly as one of the important ports of the Baltic. English, German, Swedish, Norwegian and Spanish ships docked here.

Then a stream of German settlers infiltrated into the town. During the Thirty Years War it fell to Sweden, which ruled it for a hundred years—and then sold it to Prussia for two million thalers. Thereafter its progress was rapid: it became the principal port serving Berlin. Its quays extended towards the mouth of the Oder—Szczecin is thirty miles from the sea, but its subsidiary Swinoujscie can accommodate very large ships.

It lost a small part of its hinterland after the First World War, and suffered badly in the Second. It was a favourite target for R.A.F. and American raids, and its capture by the Russians in 1945 entailed further destruction. When I visited the port ten years ago, the old city in its centre was still a mass of ruins. Since then, however, much restoration has been accomplished.

The general plan was to build first factories, then communications, and then homes, in that order. (De Gaulle, who is *not* a Communist, adopted the same priorities in France.) Now the centre of Szczecin is lively again, despite occasional gaps in among the buildings.

The historic buildings in the city centre have been restored much as they were. Modern buildings have also been added, and Szczecin has almost reached its pre-war population. The old lay-out has been followed. In 1875 the Germans had rebuilt the town on plans prepared by Baron Haussman, the creator of modern Paris.

Today Szczecin is the largest port on the Baltic, handling goods of 11 million tons. It also has busy shipyards, turning out many 15,000-ton ships.

"But soon we shall be able to build ships of 24,000 tons," said Professor Janowski, the town planner. "Our progress is real. Our population today is 345,000. By 1980 it will be 500,000. We are a young people. One-third of our number are under sixteen.

"At the end of the war Szczecin was almost deserted—only 6,000 Germans were left. The rest had fled as the line of battle advanced. We drew our new settlers from Central Poland and Vilno, but now we have our own population—40 per cent of our people were born here. This makes for a strong civic spirit.

"The restoration of the old city has not been easy, for most of the documents and plans had been destroyed. We adopted the idea that the old quarters should be restored as far as possible, and on the same general plan. In the suburbs we could modernize.

"We have the port, shipyards, and factories for steel, iron, clothing, chemicals, and paper. Fertilizers will soon be added to our list. Wages—good, for we have a large percentage of skilled men. Say, an average of 2,300 zloty a month. The manager of the shipyards, about 12,000, according to the production. Yes, like his men, he works to a norm, and his salary goes up if the plant exceeds it.

"Our prosperity can be gauged by the number of private houses being built. Normally a married couple with children are allocated eleven square metres per person. Allowing for kitchen and corridors, this means about seven square metres of living space. It is hoped shortly to raise this figure to nine. Our rents are low—five zloty per square metre in a modern flat with central heating: 3·8 zloty otherwise.

"We have been experimenting in prefabrication. Not by the Russian method, but by pre-casting large slabs of concrete for walls and floors."

"You build with them like a child's house of cards?"

"You might say so. But we build. We need seven new schools a year."

"At least you are more favourably placed than Los Angeles. There the annual figure is twenty-six."

"You would doubtless like to see some of our buildings?"

Naturally, we did. The blocks of flats are utilitarian, but the private dwellings are interesting. The maximum floor space is 110 square metres for a small family, rising as it increases. A professional man or a craftsman earning good money may in some circumstances build up to 150 square metres.

As space is restricted, architects are ingenious in inventing devices to give the maximum living space within the standard 110 square metres. But to us, despite economies on corridors, the rooms would be small. A modest garden is attached to the house, often used for the growing of flowers.

The price of the standard house is 180,000 zloty: a larger building may run to 250,000 zloty. A rich man, by installing labour-saving and other gadgets, may add considerably more to the price of the house.

If you build or buy a house, it is yours. You may leave it to your son, or sell it—but not at a profit. You may let a room or rooms at a fixed proportion of the house's value: that, at least, is the theory, but it often seems to be ignored.

The Poles have introduced one interesting variant to the world of property—part-purchase. Instead of buying your house or flat outright—a small flat costs around 40,000 zloty—you make a semi-purchase at about half price. You live in your house or flat, but you may not sell it. When you die, you may leave it to your wife or children, but if you have neither the ownership reverts to the State. In effect, you have paid the rent of the house for years ahead in a single process.

(Incidentally, until 1961 Poles did not have to pay rent. Then Gomulka explained that money was needed to pay for new accommodation: either a rent must be paid or taxes increased. The rental system was adopted as being the fairer.)

II

Across a channel of the Oder from Swinoujscie (German Swinemunde) is Wolin Island.

This is delightful. The greater part of the island is covered with forests—often primeval, the trees growing as they were planted by Nature. The roads seemed to be miles of green tunnels as branches from either side met in the middle.

The central part of the island is a National Park. Its centuries-old trees are interspersed with a wide variety of wild flowers—the flora of forest, marsh, hill and sand dune are represented. Deer and boar inhabit the forest, whose tall trees are frequented by sea eagles and cormorants. The infrequent villages are quite charming. Some have pretensions as holiday resorts.

The little town of Wolin itself is modest enough today, but played an important part in local history. Centuries ago it was the leading port of the tribe called the Wolmiania. It is mentioned in ancient German, Scandinavian and Arabian chronicles. It lost its character as a trading centre when a sand bar began to form across the river mouth.

Wolin and its environs were annexed to Poland in the tenth century, but were ruled by Prussia after a century under the Swedes.

Our road east ran parallel to the sea. It had rained, and I have never seen so many frogs jumping across the wet road. They must have had some set and group purpose, for they all moved in the same direction.

In a moist evening we arrived at Kolobrzeg, another ancient town—it was the site of the first bishopric established by the Poles, by Boleslas the Brave, in 1000. There was no difficulty about accommodation—the town is now a resort as well as a minor port, and hotels are plentiful.

Its recent history was stormy. In March, 1945, the Russians were engaged with a strong German rearguard in East Prussia. Hitler had ordered that Kolobrzeg should be held to the last man—it was an important supply point for the Nazi forces farther east.

The First Polish Army, with an attached Russian division, broke through the "Pomeranian Wall" of German defences, and reached the sea to the west of Kolobrzeg. After a bitter struggle lasting ten days, the town was captured. The Polish army took a solemn oath on the beach that the port which had once been Polish was now once more Polish: and so it should remain. There followed a ceremony later described as Poland's "Marriage with the Sea". A woman officer flung her wedding ring far into the sea as a symbol of the ceremony.

Recently a monument has been erected on the scene: the intentions of the sculptor are so modern that the ordinary man would find them obscure.

Outside the town is a military cemetery—the Polish losses were heavy. Russian graves are marked by a star, Polish by a cross. Polish soldiers are named individually. A Russian stone will bear the inscription, "Here lie 47 Russian soldiers".

There is one individual grave—that of the Polish woman officer who flung her wedding ring into the sea. She was killed a week later.

Koszalin, our next halt, is an undistinguished town: so are those which followed, but the countryside between them is green and well-wooded, and little lakes appear among the hills. Here is Kartusy, in the midst of the Kashubian Lakeland—or, as it has been more extravagantly called, the Kashubian Switzerland—and in the heart of what used to be called the "Polish Corridor".

The name Kartusy is obviously derived from the Carthusian monks who long ago built a monastery here. In their day the rural element of the population still retained some pagan traditions, and a hill outside the town is indicated as the site of the witches' sabbath.

The statesmen at Versailles were puzzled. Obviously the revived Poland must have an access to the sea, and President Wilson's Fourteen Points had promised that the country should contain all regions with an indisputable Polish population. This included the Kashubians, who were a Polish tribe: hence the "Corridor".

But the life-line of Poland was the Vistula, which enters the Baltic at Danzig—and this, whatever it had been centuries ago, was now a German city. In those days peace-makers tried to please everybody, including defeated enemies. So Danzig was declared to be a Free Port, with local government under the League of Nations, and with its port available for use by Poland.

The scheme was complicated, but could have worked. However, the Germans of Danzig did not intend it to work. The local dockers demanded that they, not the Poles, should decide which cargoes should be loaded or unloaded at their quays.

Such a situation was intolerable. Further, Polish trade was

developing so rapidly that soon Danzig would not be able to handle it all. The Poles decided to build a port of their own.

Their choice was limited. The northern boundary of the "Corridor" was a short stretch of sandy, Baltic coastline. It contained one small fishing village, Gdynia, with about a thousand inhabitants.

Work began on the construction of the port. In 1923 a merchant ship docked at a small landing stage. The growth of Gdynia then became remarkable. By 1939 the population was 130,000 and the port had eight miles of quays—and its traffic far exceeded that of Danzig. Shipping lines plied thence to all parts of the world.

Danzig was always jealous of the newcomer, and was dear to Hitler. During the war the port of Gdynia was completely destroyed, and finally the *Gneisenau* was sunk across the harbour entrance. She was removed by the Poles, and the warship tied up at a quay, and now a museum, is the Polish ship *Bursa*, with a fine war reputation.

The bay which includes Gdynia and Danzig is protected by a sand bar from 300 yards to three miles in width. It terminates at Hel. If you wish to go to Hel, it is best to go by boat. By road, around the bay, the journey is nearly 100 kilometres; by sea it is eight.

These sand barriers have one peculiarity, the "Wandering Dunes". (Maybe the best are to be seen at Leba, a few miles to the west. Near here a complete village was once engulfed by the sand.) The sand is exceptionally fine and light. Strong winds blow the grains at the surface up the slope of a dune and over its crest: in windy weather the whole summit of a dune may move several feet in a day. Hence the "wandering". Such dunes could have been dangerous to coastal villages, but experiments with afforestation have kept potential offenders in hand.

Gdynia is now itself again, and is busier than ever. So, in a different way, is Sopot, Poland's largest seaside resort. It has a good beach, a pier, a race-course, and a remarkable theatre, the "Forest Opera". This is described as open-air, but actually it has a nylon roof to protect an audience against rain: but the natural background of the stage is a delight, a mountain-side covered with fir trees.

The Communist countries have commercialized folk-lore in a different fashion from the West. We have "pop" singers who specialize in what they claim is folk music, but which actually is indistinguishable from modern "beat" themes. In East Europe the genuine folk-lore music and dances have been retained, but are now seldom encountered at village festivals. Instead, professional song and dance companies are formed, and the performances they stage are expensively produced—and sometimes are very attractive. Some, indeed, have appeared in many foreign countries.

One of these is Slask—the word meant Silesia—which we saw at the Forest Theatre at Sopot. It was gorgeously staged, with all the beauty of the old Polish costumes—now, alas, seldom seen except in museums. The music had been adapted from folk airs of Silesia and Cracow, and was lively and pleasing. A company of about a hundred, with its own choir and orchestra, danced with energy and delicacy. It was, indeed, a performance to remember. I did not wonder that Slask was chosen to entertain de Gaulle during his visit.

Gdynia–Sopot–Gdansk are often called the "Tri-City"; indeed, they are closely associated. After the Second World War there was no argument about Free City status for Danzig: its people had had their chance, and had fumbled it. Now the city has reverted to its ancient Polish name of Gdansk, and is incorporated in Poland.

III

Gdansk began as a Slav settlement. By 997 it had acquired a name, Gyddanyzc. A Papal Bull later described the place as Kdanzc, a castle in Pomerania belonging to a Polish bishop. Later it passed under the rule of the Polish kings. Its situation was important—at the mouth of the River Vistula, whose basin was the main artery of Poland.

Then came the Teutonic Knights. When they had exterminated the rural pagan Bo-Russians in the name of their faith, they turned their attentions to the Poles, who had long been Christians. In one savage massacre in Danzig 10,000 people were slain. Any who escaped were expelled, and the city was re-peopled with German settlers. But the eventual defeat of the Teutonic Knights reunited Danzig to Poland, and so it remained until the Partitions. A process of Germanization was then resumed, so that Danzig became thoroughly German—and, after the rise of Hitler, thoroughly

Nazi. Danzig had a prosperous future ahead as a Free City, carrying all Poland's foreign trade. Her people chose otherwise. They
supported Hitler enthusiastically in his demand for the liquidation
of their Free City status, and their incorporation within Germany.
At last they had their way, at the cost of a bloody war which left
the city a complete ruin.

In 1945 Danzig once more became Gdansk—a shattered city,
it is true, its population fled, and its port devastated. The Poles
began a long-term policy of reconstruction along the now familiar
lines—restoring the old city to its former glories, while the
suburbs were made completely modern. I had seen the old city in
its ruins, and now examined its reconstruction—beautifully done,
with historic buildings and burghers' houses as they were before
the war—but needing the passage of fifty years to give them the
patina of age.

Dluga Street was the very centre of old Danzig, and so it is in
new Gdansk. Tall, shapely houses flank the street, most of them
delicately colour-washed.

There is an ancient gateway at each end of the street, and in the
centre of this is the old town hall, with a commanding spire. Not
far away is St. Mary's church, a vast pile which can hold 25,000
people. Outside, its red brick is gloomy, but the interior is
bright enough—it has lost its stained glass windows, and the
sun's light streams through.

The cathedral for the region is, however, at Oliwa, a suburb of
Gdansk. It is an undistinguished building, but has a remarkable
organ. Its church was originally a monastic chapel, sacked twice
by the pagan Bo-Russians and three times by the Christian
Teutonic Knights. Since then it has become over-ornamented.
The organ shares this decoration, but has a compensatory interest.
It has a remarkable mechanism, contrived by a monk. Angels
hold trumpets, which they raise to their lips and blow at appropriate places in the music: others ring bells, the sun and the stars
move in their orbits, and the 6,000 pipes combine to produce an
impressive sound.

There are short organ recitals during the day, and just in front
of us was a party from a Polish Communist organization. They
ostentatiously brushed aside the priest who came round with the
collection plate—except for one man, who boldly stood up in his
pew and insisted that his coin should be passed along.

I met one member of the party as we went out, and commented on the incident.

"Oh, I'm not going to support these reactionary blackfrocks," he said. "I didn't want to come here, but the committee which organized our holiday trip said we ought to go because it was cultural. I couldn't argue with that. We believe in culture, you know. I don't see anything in it myself, but it's the party line, and so of course I go along. But I've had enough."

That evening I chanced to meet the same man as I emerged from the Forest Theatre at Sopot. He was enthusiastic about the Slask performance.

"Now, *there's* culture for you. Lively music, a riot of colour in the costumes, and the dancing—did you see how the girls made their underskirts twirl around? Yes, the party line is right. Culture is the thing for the people!"

Gdansk was preparing for the visit of President de Gaulle. As a practising Catholic, he naturally wished to hear Mass during his week's stay. The Polish government did not want this to happen in Warsaw—it might arouse too much enthusiasm. So it arranged that on the Sunday he should be at Gdansk. There he could hear his Mass. Not in the huge St. Mary's church, where again a congregation of 25,000 might be disconcerting to an atheist government, but in the modest cathedral at Oliwa, where the congregation could be kept to manageable proportions.

IV

One of the terms of the First World War led directly to the opening of the second.

The Vistula enters the sea by several channels at Danzig. One of them flanks a narrow peninsula, the Westerplatte. Here the Poles were allowed to have a military depot, guarded by eighty soldiers.

In the last days of August, 1939, it was obvious that something was afoot. Danzig teemed with German "tourists"—all of whom were strong, healthy young men with a trick of slipping into marching steps as they did their sight-seeing. The Poles surreptitiously increased their garrison to 182.

The situation should have been eased by the arrival of the battleship *Schleswig-Holstein* on a courtesy visit: she moored in the river. Local residents were invited on board for parties. They did not know, but might have guessed, that below-decks were crowded more German soldiers.

At 5.30 a.m. on 1st September shells from the German war-ships—there were others off-shore—began to pour into the Polish depot. The men rushed to their duty posts: the main attack began later in the morning. The Germans seemed amazed to encounter resistance—apparently they thought that the Poles would be frightened into surrender.

Here the Nazis had made a big mistake. The little garrison held out against 4,000 Germans for seven days. (Astonishingly, the Poles lost only 15 dead: the German losses were 400.)

A council of officers considered the situation, which was of course hopeless from the beginning. Should they continue to hold out? The Westerplatte had become an inspiration to the Polish people, their army rapidly crumbling before the Nazi onslaught. Or was it fair to ask their men to risk their lives any longer? By the seventh day it was obvious that Poland was beaten, and the heroic but unhappy commander of the Westerplatte walked with a white flag towards the German lines.

Recently a monument was unveiled near the tip of the Wester-platte—to the Polish soldiers killed during the war. Around are trees and red roses: and a giant banner in red, "Never again war!"

"We mean that," said a man who kept a kiosk near the entrance to the Westerplatte—a sergeant during its epic defence.

"What happened to your comrades?"

"Ah, you might ask! At first they were treated properly, but then the Nazi rot set in. Some were murdered, some died of starvation. Very few of us survived."

That evening we went to see a new film, *Westerplatte*, admirably timed, and produced almost as a documentary. Its saddest moment, naturally, was when the commander led his battered men to their surrender.

There were other epics in the seizure of Danzig. One of the earliest Nazi attacks was on the Post Office. It had no garrison, of course, but some of its Polish staff were reservists, and decided to fight. They could do little more than to endure the German attack, for they had very few weapons, but they withstood heavy fire for a whole day.

Poland had many anniversaries to commemorate during the

first week of September. It was fitting that the defence of the Post Office was one of them. A "demonstration" had been organized. Communist "demonstrations" are usually political, but this was a genuine memorial—with political overtones.

We chanced upon some hundreds of Scouts and Guides preparing to march—they have replaced the Soviet-type Pioneer organizations. They were headed by a rather decrepit band, its instruments so battered that I wondered how they could play in tune. But the veterans rallied nobly, and marched off the youth of Gdansk.

Every band in the city was on duty, and processions streamed from every direction bringing the members of the innumerable Communist organizations. Banners were carried. "We want peace!" demanded the Scouts and Guides, which was reasonable. "We do not agree with American imperialism in Vietnam," proclaimed adult groups. Others deplored American bombing in Vietnam. Doubtless the demonstrations would persuade the Americans to withdraw from Vietnam post-haste.

Great wreaths lay outside the door of the Post Office, with a guard of honour of two soldiers, two Scouts and two postmen. A contingent of the army and navy arrived briskly with their own band; they were armed with modern sub-machine guns, and marched well—but their drill in a limited space was confused.

Then the city council came out of the Post Office on to a platform. Its President made a lengthy speech to the large crowd—far too long, it appeared, for the many juveniles present, who talked among themselves, or began to play games where space permitted. The President said the proper things about the postmen and the Nazis—whom he equated with West Germany, not East: apparently no one in East Germany was ever a Nazi, or, if he had been, had now been converted to the Communist cause. A few side comments on American imperialism, suitable music from the military band, and the demonstration was over.

"Do your people really think that this kind of thing actually does anything?" I asked a group of teachers.

"To the Americans, no. To our own people, yes."

Manor in Żelazowa Wola —
place of Frederic Chopin's birth

Rural landscape in central
Poland

A scene of the Masurian Lake District

Beach on the Baltic in Sopot

Winter view from the Kasprowy
Wierch in the Tatra Mountains

14

"LAND OF A THOUSAND LAKES"

I

THE Poles call Masuria the Land of a Thousand Lakes. This is an understatement. The region has more than *two* thousand lakes.

Our first halt was at Malbork—the Germans used to call it Marienburg. Here the Teutonic Knights built the great castle which was then their headquarters, the home of their Grand Master. In its day, the castle was very powerful—one of the strongest in all Europe—and could stand a long siege.

When the Poles defeated the Knights, Malbork and its region passed into their hands—until the days of the Partitions. Then the Prussians showed scant respect for the work of their ancestors. The castle was converted first into a barracks and then into warehouses—only the palace of the Grand Master was spared. But German scholars protested against this desecration, and the process was halted. The Second World War, however, inflicted grievous scars on the noble pile.

Most of the repairs are now complete, and the most interesting parts of the castle can be visited. It is bounded by the River Nojat —an arm of the Vistula—whose waters used to fill the moat.

The High Castle was a strange combination of stronghold and monastery. The Teutonic Knights were originally monks, though in their later history they were joined by knights and men-at-arms from other parts of Europe—all seeking adventure or loot, or both. The Middle Castle was added later, to house the Grand Master, who moved from Vienna in 1347. He must have lived like a king: nor were his attendant monks badly housed.

There are refectories and barrack rooms, beautifully vaulted. The Grand Master's apartments were indeed sumptuous.

Students of military architecture would delight in Malbork. It had its own wells, storehouses, workshops, flour mills, and even its own foundry. The only war casualty not yet restored is the church, which received a direct hit from an Allied bomb. But the whole pile, in red brick, is massive and monumental, forming a remarkable relic of a stormy past.

The Teutonic Knights dominated our day, for we moved on to Grünwald, a green field of bitter memory to those war-lords.

It was in 1409 that the Knights began to raid the Polish border provinces. At that time Poland was united with Lithuania, which ruled a great swathe of Eastern Europe, extending into the Ukraine. So the army of King Jagiello consisted of Poles, Lithuanians, and Ukrainians—including even a detachment of Tatars.

Jagiello was tempted to attack, but refrained. Then the heavy cavalry of the knights charged his Lithuanian and Tatar right wing, and drove it back in confusion. But the Poles held their ground, and the Lithuanians recovered. The army of the Knights was split in two, each section surrounded, and the slaughter was fantastic.

This was the end of the power of the Teutonic Knights. Within a few years the Order had been secularized—and its Grand Master had sworn allegiance to the Polish king!

The Poles have only recently erected a memorial to the great victory of Grünwald. At the crest of some rising ground, in the centre of the battlefield, is a stone monument, dominated by three rough and stern faces. By its side is a group of tall steel pylons, each crowned by a banner. And nearby the plan of battle has been set out in stone, while in a room below it visitors can see an excerpt from the Aleksander Ford film about the Teutonic Knights.

Hundreds of years later another battle was fought almost on the same site. In August, 1914, East Prussia was invaded by the Russian "steam-roller"—actually two armies. Rennenkampf attacked from the east, Samsonov from the south. At first all went well.

But the German commander was a man with ideas. Hoffmann planned the battle long before Hindenburg and Ludendorff arrived on the scene. The two Russian generals were notoriously on bad terms—years earlier, Hoffmann had seen them boxing each other's ears on Mukden station. One would not hurry to the aid of the other, he realized.

So a German cavalry screen held Rennenkampf while the main

force marched to meet Samsonov. The German victory was complete—and they could now turn to repel Rennenkampf. Hoffmann noticed that he was near to Grünwald—or Tannenberg, as the Germans knew it. So the first victory in the east was called the Battle of Tannenberg.

The victory was decisive. The Russians lost 90,000 prisoners and tens of thousands of dead—Samsonov's army was annihilated. When he realized the extent of the débâcle he walked into the neighbouring forest. A single revolver shot was heard. His body was never found. The wolves of the forest had merry feasts in the autumn of 1914.

Hindenburg's personal part in the battle was meagre, but he was the Commander-in-Chief. And he was born at Olsztynek, only a few miles away. It was natural for the Germans, even in the moment of final defeat, to erect a memorial on the site of one of their great victories—eight massive towers, joined by arcades, filled with mementoes of the battle and memorials to the regiments involved. When I passed this way in 1914, Hindenburg was dead, and his body was temporarily buried in the Tannenberg memorial.

Later it was transferred to the Rhineland. And the memorial is no more. The Russians destroyed it. They did not like monuments to Russian defeats, even if the Russian armies were those of the Czar. This made me wonder what would happen to the new Russian monuments scattered all over Central Europe. At the moment the host countries are friendly, but no one can foresee the situation in fifty years' time. What will happen to the memorials when the Russians retire to their own country—if they ever do?

II

I have often regretted that we have no national folk-museum in England: there is a small one in Wales. Pride of them all is Sweden's Skansen. Here old houses doomed to destruction have been preserved and rebuilt, and some are still inhabited by people wearing local peasant costumes. We enthuse about our beautiful thatched cottages, but one day we shall realize that we have none left: they will all have become victims of road-widening schemes. We have left it late, but there is still time to rescue memorials of our national and provincial heritage, and to present a picture of bygone England.

The Poles have begun their own Skansen at Olsztynek. It will expand, for a considerable area has been allocated outside the little town. There have been transferred buildings from all parts of Masuria: there is a lovely old wooden church, with a separate belfry: a windmill: a manor house; and many picturesque cottages illustrating rural life long ago.

On to Olsztyn (in German, Allenstein), the capital of Masuria, completely surrounded by hills, lakes and forests. It was the seat of a Polish bishopric; here one of the thirteenth-century bishops built a castle, and its defence was entrusted to a canon of the chapter. The most famous of these canons was Nicolaus Copernicus, who defended the castle stoutly against the Teutonic Knights.

Today the castle is a museum. Its exhibits include handicrafts of the Bo-Russians, the tribe annihilated by the Knights. There is a statue to Copernicus, who was in effect governor of the castle for four years. His rooms are shown to the public.

Olsztyn is a pleasant little town, and we decided to use it as a headquarters for our stay in Masuria—it is an excellent centre for such a purpose.

Lidzbark Warminski was close at hand. Its magnificent castle—built, needless to say, by the Teutonic Knights—has been described as the best preserved example of medieval architecture in Poland. It is square, with a tower at each corner. In its centre is an arcaded square reminiscent of, but older than, that of the Wawel at Cracow.

The Hohenzollerns meant to demolish the castle and its contents, so as to obliterate all evidence of Polish culture. The Polish bishops protested strongly—and the local people refused to take any part in the demolition. Thus this idea was abandoned, but the rich furnishings of the castle were removed to Germany.

The second part of Lidzbark's name reminded me that we were in Warmia. The history of this province differed from that of other regions of Pomerania. The Prussian bishops were Protestants, but the bishopric of Warmia remained Catholic and as such was closely associated with Poland. The residence of the bishops—who were for long also the rulers of Warmia—was at Lidzbark of Warmia. The bishops were remarkable men—most of them were scholars and scientists.

We drove eastwards through charming undulating country, much of it forested, and dotted with innumerable lakes, large and small. Ketrzyn—once known as Rastenberg—promised interest of another kind. Some miles outside the little town is a great forest: our driver led us along a narrow forest ride.

"Goering's bunker," he announced, as we halted before a huge mass of concrete, one end of it shattered.

We were on the site of the Wolfschanzer, Hitler's Wolf's Lair, from which he directed the war against Russia. It covered a considerable extent of the forest—eight square kilometres in all: every senior member of the Nazi hierarchy had his own bunker. Each was protected by a great concrete mass, fifteen to twenty feet high. Iron steps led up the vertical sides, so that anti-aircraft gunners could scramble to their defences.

There was only one entrance to each bunker—well guarded, of course—and the whole building was surrounded by minefields and electrified fences. Below were eight floors of offices.

A few hundred yards away was the main group of head-quarters bunkers. That of Hitler resembled that of Goering, and was the key to a vast underground city. This was so well guarded that no intruder could penetrate its defences. And the forest was not apparently enough to guarantee its secrecy from the air. From tree to tree hung a vast network of camouflage—wire net-ting to which fragments of green material were fastened. The camp had its own railway—also camouflaged.

As a drastic precaution, in Hitler's bunker was a plunger which would blow up the whole headquarters complex. Naturally, nobody expected it to be used. But the Russian advance in 1945 forced Hitler to flee. When all the staff had gone, an officer pressed home the plunger. There was a series of fantastic ex-plosions. Walls and ceilings of concrete six feet thick were hurled dozens or hundreds of yards. Trees were shattered: the brick houses of the guards disintegrated. Everything above the ground was devastated or destroyed—except the bunkers: or, at least, much of their concrete protection. These sustained cracks, but no more: they were strong enough to resist any explosives.

The minefields have been cleared, but the eight storeys of rooms have not yet been opened up. Their entrances are hope-lessly shattered by the explosions. It can reasonably be assumed, moreover, that the place was liberally strewn with booby traps.

This underground city was constructed by prisoners-of-war. Every three months or so the whole gang of workers was massacred—they knew too much. The only ones to survive were a few Poles who were employed above ground. But some of the German guards have been traced, and their information helps to form a general picture of the Wolf's Lair.

I stood beside the enormous blockhouse guarding Hitler's own bunker, and pondered over the drama of 20th July, 1944.

There had always been anti-Hitler elements in Germany. Most were of the class he despised—the aristocrats. These included senior army officers, who realized that Hitler's megalomania would lead to disaster for Germany.

Only as a last resort can assassination be justified. But Hitler's death—and that alone—could put an end to the slaughter of the war he had produced. That the assassination was to be carried out by army officers did not affect the issue. In the pre-Nazi Prussian code of military law there was a clause which said that orders of criminal intent were not to be obeyed. It was only in Hitler's day that the "blind obedience" idea was introduced in the German army. This was invalid from any ethical point of view—obeying orders cannot be admitted as an excuse for committing, or even condoning, a crime. The conspirators felt that in planning the death of Hitler they were animated by an ethical sense of duty and patriotism.

One of the leaders of the conspiracy was General Henning von Tresckow. Although he disliked the task of an assassin—everything in his family tradition and upbringing was against this—he determined to do the "dirty job" himself.

The first difficulty was the choice of explosive. The fuses used by the German army made a slight hissing which might have been noticed. However, the British had dropped supplies of explosives for their saboteur-agents, and some had been captured—and their fuses were silent. A bomb was prepared: it looked like two square bottles of Cointreau brandy.

When Hitler was to fly to his headquarters, the bomb was placed in his aircraft. The conspirators prepared to take over Berlin and assume power—but nothing happened. The bomb was later recovered, and the detonator proved to have a tiny fault. Had some inspector in a British factory not been negligent, Hitler would have died in March, 1943. The conspirators would then have made peace, and the world would have been spared untold misery over the next two years.

The "generals"—though they were not all of that rank—prepared to strike again, and to take over immediate power as soon as Hitler was dead. More British explosives were collected, and hidden in the forest near the Wolf's Lair. For some unexplained reason, they suddenly blew up!

Another scheme was that an officer who was prepared to sacrifice his own life should hide a bomb under a new uniform he was "demonstrating" to Hitler. Then, at the right moment, he would throw his arms around Hitler and both men would be blown to pieces. But, almost as if he had some premonition, Hitler kept postponing the demonstration.

General Tresckow was willing to make another attempt, but the task was at last handed over to Count Claus Schenk von Stauffenberg, a colonel on the General Staff—he had lost an eye, his right arm and two fingers of his left hand with the Afrika Corps in Libya. He had long been the leader of the conspirators. He was a sincere Christian, and to him Hitler was "evil incarnate".

He was summoned to a conference at the Wolf's Lair. When he arrived, he found to his surprise that the meeting was not being held in Hitler's concrete bunker, as was usual. It was a warm July day, and the conference had been transferred to the Tea House—a wooden structure in the forest. Stauffenberg was not an expert on explosives: otherwise he might have held his hand.

He carried the explosives in a briefcase. This, after pressing the switch which lighted the fuse, he placed against the leg of a table near Hitler. Then he was called to the telephone, and went out.

Minutes later he heard the explosion. Had the bomb exploded in a concrete building, its results would have been fantastic. But the wooden walls collapsed under the air pressure.

However, four people were killed, and others gravely injured. Stauffenberg took a quick glance at the holocaust. Its victims lay about in pools of blood. Hitler had been hurled out of doors by the force of the explosion: his clothes were torn to pieces, his body covered with blood, and he was lying where he fell, apparently lifeless. Surely nobody in the room could be alive.

Stauffenberg managed to get out and hurried by air to Berlin, where he announced Hitler's death. The agreed procedure for taking over power was set in motion.

But Major Remer, commander of the Guard battalion in

Berlin, was persuaded to telephone to Goebbels before he obeyed the generals' orders. Then he learned that Hitler was still alive!

Remer led his men *against* the conspirators. He was promptly promoted for his services, and later became one of the leaders of the revived National Socialist Party in Germany. But Stauffenberg and his friends were shot—on the same day as should have seen their triumph. As he was about to die, Stauffenberg cried: "Long live our sacred Germany".

Hitler's revenge was swift and terrible. The conspiracy was completely broken. So was "our sacred Germany".

The first attempt on Hitler's life was made in Warsaw in 1939. The Nazi leader entered the Polish capital to celebrate his triumph. A group of Polish conspirators had placed a bomb in a lavatory under a street along which Hitler would pass.

An officer in a nearby house prepared to set off the bomb. But to his horror he found that ten or twelve people were standing on the selected spot—and Hitler was approaching. He hesitated: could he deliberately kill his own people? The critical seconds passed, and Hitler was beyond danger.

It is easy to criticize in retrospect. He did not know it, of course, but at the cost of a dozen Polish lives, the officer could have saved millions. But what would you have done, at the time?

III

On to Gizycko, between two lakes connected by a channel. The town has the inevitable castle of the Teutonic Knights, not so fine as the rest, and is now a holiday centre.

We took a speedboat and swept across Lake Mamry to the island of cormorants. Alas, our organization must have been bad: we circled the island twice, but saw not a single cormorant. Disappointed, we turned round, but as we passed another island we saw a whole flock or covey of cormorants—which promptly dived at the sight of us. I presume that they must have come up again some time and somewhere, but their underwater swimming defeated us. So we gave up, and passed through the connecting channel to Lake Neogocin. Both these lakes are large—over a hundred square kilometres each.

Many of the Masurian lakes are used for passenger traffic—a

voyage of several hours is commonplace. Here and there the boats are pulled overland from lake to lake.

The banks of the lakes are usually forest-clad and slope gently. This is a land of villages, some of them very picturesque. One is of outstanding interest—Wojnovo.

In 1830 there was religious trouble in Russia, when the hierarchy began to make alterations in the Orthodox creed. Some people objected: in fact, some of the Old Believers were so upset that they decided to leave Russia. The Prussian king offered them hospitality, and allocated five villages to them. Wojnovo was one of these: the other four are not far away.

The village seemed quite ordinary—one long street, lined with cottages. In the centre is an Orthodox church, and we tried to find its priest. We failed: his was only a part-time appointment, and he was a farmer as well: now he was at work in his fields—nobody knew exactly where.

We were advised to consult the monastery, near the shores of the lake. This was a Roman Catholic establishment, but nearby was an Orthodox convent for aged women. One of these greeted us at the door—in Russian.

"Oh, yes, we all speak Russian. Our grandparents brought their speech with them as well as their faith, and we have abandoned neither. The village? Ah, it is very mixed these days—about half and half, Russian and Polish—with some people who do not know what they are—usually the product of mixed marriages. But even the Russians in Wojnovo speak Polish—I suppose it is useful to anyone who is out in the world.

"Here we are retired. There used to be twenty-four of us, but now there are only eight. I fear that we are a dying community. The Poles have been very good to us. We have a small pension, and some fields and cows. We manage. Those of us who are able work in our fields. But we are very old. I am one of the youngest, and I am over eighty. Come and see our chapel."

It is small, but ablaze with gilt, in the Russian style. Dozens of holy icons cover the walls: many of them had been brought by the original Old Believers from Russia. The chapel is lighted by an extravagant candelabra, a strange contrast to the evidence of poverty about it.

"It was given to us by a merchant in memory of his dead wife. It is wonderful, is it not?

"We have prayers night and morning. We use the old Russian tongue and liturgy—not the modern version.

"Our great festival is Easter. Then Russians from miles around rally to us. People call us Phillipians, you know—it was the name of our sect. I think it was because of certain verses from the Epistle, but I am not quite sure.

"Our symbol is the Cross." She pointed to the gilt cross which dominated the chapel. "It is a symbol that Jesus came from heaven to make our souls free. And the slanting bar indicates that our souls go direct from church to Paradise."

Other members of the little community entered. And as we prepared to depart we saw one of the sisters driving home four cows: once they were in the barn, she began to milk them.

This strange little community has withdrawn from our world and has created a world of its own. It is poor, but far from unhappy. There can be contentment in poverty, and certainly there is happiness in faith.

15

FORESTS

I

WE had visited a number of farms in the New Territories. Some were small, though at ten hectares the average is above the national figure. At anything less than this, the peasant needs either very fertile soil or an additional job.

But one man was doing exceptionally well. The maximum for a private farm is supposed to be 40 hectares, but by a series of legacies he had acquired 54 hectares, and had been allowed to keep them. His economic standards were well above the average. He had a house and adequate barns: two horses, 21 cattle and a tractor: geese, ducks and hens. He cultivated wheat, oats, barley and fodder.

"I don't make a fortune, in spite of the size of my farm," he said. "My trouble is the quality of the soil. My land is graded in one of the lower of the six classifications of quality.

"But I raise 30 quintals of wheat per hectare. The government takes 10 per cent in tax, and I sell the rest where I like. The government pays 100 zloty a quintal for its purchases—I can usually make more in the market.

"Most of my neighbours in the village here have about 15 hectares. They can live on that. A man with such a farm usually has two horses, one cow and no tractor. He has to work hard, but he can make a living—he does not need to take another job. There is a good deal of co-operation—peasants help each other at busy seasons.

"Of course, I have to work very hard, with such a large farm. My wife helps me, and it will be easier as the children grow up. I have to hire a little extra help for sowing and harvest.

"No, I don't have a car. I would like to have one, but I want to start the children off well first. Education is more valuable than a car."

171

He was a happy man, with a happy family. The smaller farmer, on the other hand, lives in an atmosphere of strain. He *can* make a living, true, but a casual accident like the failure of the rains can bring him too close to serious difficulty.

There are very few co-operative farms. They comprise only 0·8 per cent of all Polish farms, and we had a great difficulty in finding one. Most of the large farms are State owned, of the type already described.

The 1,800 co-operative farms are of three different types.

1. The peasant surrenders the whole or part of his land to the co-operatives. He is paid what is in effect rent for the land he surrenders, and he is also paid for all the work he puts in. He keeps his own livestock.

2. He surrenders all his land except a private plot of up to one hectare, and all his farm buildings. The State will grant credits to this type of farm, for purchasing equipment or building barns. The peasant is paid rent for whatever he puts into the co-operative.

3. A modification of the foregoing. The peasant surrenders his land (less a garden plot), buildings, cows and horses. He is paid rent for them—or the co-operative may buy his cows and horses outright.

The co-operating peasants are paid according to their work. A farm committee decides on standard "norms"—which are *not* imposed by the government. Each piece of work is given a valuation. Eighty per cent of all co-operatives come into the last two categories.

The system is not perfect, and can never be so. The tractor-driver may complete his work in five hours, and then carry on and work another norm. But the norm of the shepherd, whose work is much less intensive, will take twelve hours, so it can scarcely be duplicated. So the tractor-driver earns twice the shepherd's pay.

The co-operatives pay less tax than the private farmers. The government takes from 6 per cent to 8 per cent of the crops, according to the quality of the soil.

After Gomulka's famous speech in 1956, in which he said that inefficient co-operatives might disband, so many did so that only 1,300 remained. This figure has gradually mounted to 1,800—and not because of government pressure: the movement has been

voluntary. The new co-operatives have almost invariably been
formed by peasants farming less than 5 hectares, which do not
yield a living.

The co-operative peasant's income depends upon his work, the
soil, the type of cultivation and machinery. On an average he
receives around 1,800 zloty a month, but he also receives fodder
for his cow and food for his pigs, and some chickens. (If he has
no cow, he can buy milk from the co-operatives at a reduced
price.)

The millionaires among the farmers are the horticulturists.
Working on a good farm near a large town, a hard worker can
earn from 3,000 to 4,000 zloty a month.

Another call was at an Agricultural Centre, which is in effect
another form of co-operative. It has only 150 hectares of land, but
has large workshops.

It serves six villages. Farmers—mostly private—pay a subscription of 50 zloty per hectare per year, and for that they can have
tractors and other farm machinery at 20 per cent less than the
standard price. It has a staff of mechanics to keep the machines in
repair. As can be imagined, it is a boon to peasants who cannot
afford to buy a tractor of their own.

These "Agricultural Circles" are traditional in Poland, and
their activities cover more than three-quarters of the villages.
They are very useful in the provision of machinery, seeds,
fertilizers and advice to their members. Some Communists regard
them as a stepping-stone to collectivization, but their effect on the
peasant is the opposite—because of their aid, he is able to farm his
smallholding more efficiently and profitably.

"Our young people don't find farming attractive," wrote a
Warsaw journal. "Today, a young man wants to make a lot of
money and to have his two to four weeks holiday."

Poland is not the only country with the problem of the attraction of the bright lights of the towns. Contrary to the position in
most Communist countries, the private farmers are doing well—
their incomes are estimated as averaging 40 per cent above the
national standard. But in the last fifteen years the farm population
has fallen from 47 to 38 per cent of the national total. The
proportion of old men and of women has increased.

The Communists believe that they can check the flight from
the land. In some countries they simply make it illegal. The Poles

would never suffer this. Their leaders suggest capitalist inducements like incentive bonuses and provision of larger farms. I wish
them well. In grave emergency a man can live without a television
set, but he must eat.

II

Until quite late in the war it appeared that the whole of East
Prussia would be allocated to Poland: the Russians had suggested
this. Eventually Stalin could not resist grasping a little more
territory: he took the northern section of the province, with the
important port of Königsberg—now Kaliningrad. The German
population has been completely expelled.

Near the little town of Mikolajki we plunged into the heart of a
great forest. There we found an establishment of the Polish
Academy of Science, at Popielno.

The Deputy Director took us round. His work was with
animals—horses, beaver, cows, and deer.

The horses are unusual. They are Lipyans, once common in
Eastern Poland, probably originating from a cross between the
local horses and wild ponies. They themselves are technically
ponies, a couple of inches below fourteen hands.

They are beautiful creatures, with a mousey-brown and smooth
coat. They move with dignified ease, and are very friendly. We
found twenty in the home paddock, and they crowded to the
fence beside us.

"The Germans seized most of our stock during the war," our
host explained. "But we are now breeding again. Apart from these
in the paddock, we have fifty living wild in the forest.

"We are domesticating the horses in the paddock—see, there is
one drawing a cart. We sometimes sell one to a peasant—or even
to a circus.

"Would you like to see some of the Lipyans running wild in the
forest? We shall have to go on foot."

We set off at once. Though fifty horses were at large in a
forest exceeding six square miles, it was a delightful ramble. The
forest was virtually primeval, and quite beautiful. But we
encountered no Lipyans.

Or any deer—until the Deputy Director led the way to a series
of large paddocks, each inhabited by Masurian deer of a different

species—red, fallow or white. These lovely creatures were shy, but our host revealed himself as a remarkable imitator of animal sounds. His attempt at the cry of the red deer brought an instantaneous response from a large stag. And a wild boar outside the paddock joined in the duet with his high-pitched grunt—and must have been astonished when he got a reply in kind.

The habits of the deer are being closely studied, under natural conditions, by the scientific staff. In other pens Guernsey cows are bred, and these also are the subject of research. And in darkened enclosures are beavers, sleeping in their beaveries by day, and coming out by night—with trunks of trees available for their amusement.

III

Our last forest was the grandest of them all—probably the finest as well as the largest in the whole of Europe.

Bialowieza is indeed primeval. Its trees were planted not by man but by Nature, in an irregular complexity over the centuries. They are packed so closely that the forest is quite dark: and in any square yard to which rain and sun could penetrate, a dense undergrowth flourishes.

I had first visited Bialowieza in 1934, but now found great changes. The tiny hamlet is now developing into a holiday resort. In 1934 the whole of the forest was in Poland; now the Russian frontier runs through it. Then a visit was an adventure: now it can be included in a package holiday.

Indeed, Bialowieza had then given me a real adventure. It is the last home of the European bison, which roamed wild in the forest, and a Ranger had taken me into the forest in search of his charges. At last we had stumbled on the king of the herd, an enormous creature a good ton in weight. He, too, was startled, and angry: he charged—and we ran.

We took different paths—and the bison followed me! It was gaining on me. An isolated tree in a small clearing offered an escape, and I swung myself on to its lowest branch. The bison paced around the tree, breathing furiously, waiting for me to come down. I did not intend to come down!

I was rescued by the Ranger. I heard his shouts of "Bove! Bove!" I laughed aloud. "Bove" is an affectionate diminutive, as one calls a cat "Pussy". The idea of calling Pussy to this angry giant was really comic.

But the Ranger had also brought food, and enticed the bison away. On the walls of my study hangs a photograph; it shows a very angry bison stamping around a tree: I took the photograph myself—from up the tree.

In older days the forest of Bialowieza was the personal property of the Czar of Russia: only he and his guests might shoot the bison. They must have been very poor shots, for the number of bison remained consistent at between five and six hundred. Then came the First World War, and the Germans occupied the forest: their soldiers were often hungry, and a bison represented at least half a ton of meat. By the end of the war the bison had been almost exterminated.

The Poles, now owners of the forest, decided to preserve the breed. They obtained three specimens from zoos and private collections, and encouraged them to breed. Gradually the herd was built up—in 1934 it was forty strong. The process was repeated during the Second World War. A dozen bison then survived: they were carefully preserved. In the Polish section of the forest there are now 157: in the Russian section, 82.

Some dozens of bison have now been transferred to other forests in Poland, and some have been sold to zoos in different parts of the world—including London. But they all came from Bialowieza.

Other inhabitants of the forest include elk, deer, boar, wolf and lynx. There are more than two hundred species of birds—and a thousand of butterflies.

A Ranger conducted us over the museum which has been erected in Bialowieza, with specimens of flora and fauna from the forest.

"Would you remember the Ranger who was in charge here in 1934?" I asked.

"Yes. Wagner."

"That was the man. What has become of him?"

"He went out to South Africa—he died there, about two years ago."

"Did he ever tell you how he took an Englishman into the forest to find a bison: they found one—and had to run for it?"

The Ranger laughed aloud. "Indeed he did! It was his favourite yarn, and grew with every telling."

Panorama of the centre of Wro-
cław

Industrial landscape in the Tu-
roszów region, Lower Silesia

The folk dance ensemble from
the Łowicz region

Mountaineer folk band from the
Silesian Beskid

"I am that Englishman!" I announced.

"What? Well——" He turned to one of the stuffed specimens close beside us, and patted it affectionately. "Then here is your bison!"

It seemed to be even bigger than my photograph suggests! The beast had died in 1936, I learned.

Today you may explore Bialowieza in comparative comfort. You hire a local cart, with a guide. First you are driven to the paddocks, about five kilometres away. Then you explore the forest, looking for bison in the wild: the trip takes about four hours. Or, of course, you can walk. There are faint paths, but they are way-marked, and you ought not to get lost more than once every half-hour. Your greatest danger does not come from bison, but from the possibility of wandering over the Russian frontier.

The Polish section of Bialowieza covers 58,000 hectares, the Russian 72,000. A forest with a total extent of 500 square miles is indeed large. From its dense mass spring spruce trees 150 feet high, and 700-year-old oak trees with girths of twenty feet. Other indigenous trees are pine, ash, oak, birch, maple, elm and poplar. And in the dense undergrowth is found the *zubrowka*. The bison love this herb, but it is also used in the preparation of the famous "Bison" vodka. (*Zubry* is the Polish word for bison.)

We made first for the stockades, a few miles along the Hajnowka road. Here indeed was a surprise—the large enclosures are now overlooked from a grandstand! You are not permitted to get closer to the six-foot stockade, over which an angry bison can jump. A year or two ago a Ranger entered the enclosure, startled and frightened a bison, and was badly mauled.

One large stockade contained some youngsters, but in another was the present king of the herd, with his wife. He refused to take any notice of us, or to pose for a photograph. I remembered Ranger Wagner. "Bove! Bove!" I shouted, and the bison got up and posed almost professionally. Then he treated himself to a sand-bath.

Not far away was yet another enclosure with more of the Lipyan horses. In winter they lose their brown hue and turn white—except for a dark band on the backs of their necks.

IV

The journey back to Warsaw was across the Polish plain—a green land of peasant farms, with villages of timber cottages. We travelled on a Sunday, and the churches had large congregations. Outside were parked dozens of peasant carts, each of which had brought six or eight people to worship. Some had combined business with religious duty, and after the service the scene was one of a Bazaar, Exchange and Mart. Some families bartered plums or tomatoes for potatoes or apples. Or, if no such bargains were available, they sold their produce. Then they sat back for a chat—this was the social occasion of the week.

In no country are there so many memorials as in Poland, as no country has suffered so much. Many of them are very *avant-garde*, and I did not pretend to understand them. But in the midst of a little forest was one which affected me strongly. It marked the site of a horror camp. All the world knows about Oswiecym (Auschwitz), but there were twenty-seven others, many of them on Polish soil.

Some years before the war started, a gravel pit began operations near the village of Treblinka, north-east of Warsaw. A special railway siding was built to serve it. The Nazis took it over, and used it for the supply of materials for military constructions in preparation for their attack on Russia. Thereafter it was used for general purposes.

It was at first staffed by "stubborn elements" among the Poles—farmers who refused to deliver their produce, or men who avoided obligatory work. The guards were S.S. men, assisted by Ukrainian mercenaries.

The forced labour camp expanded. The prisoners were shockingly treated, and half-starved. The Nazis chose only strong, healthy men, and calculated that they could get from two to six months' labour before their victims dropped.

This was bad enough: but in 1942 a second camp was added to Treblinka—an extermination camp. This was meant to play a big part in Hitler's "final solution".

The subterfuges adopted by the Nazis were fantastic, probably designed to entice their victims to go quietly to their fate. It was explained to the Polish Jews—and to Jews in many other European countries—that they were to be settled in Eastern

Europe, and would first be assembled at a labour camp. They were given railway tickets to a place named as Treblinka.

There a Potemkin railway station was built. It had the usual notices—booking office, waiting-room, refreshment buffet, cloakroom, and the like. But none of these things existed! They were merely to inspire confidence, to allay suspicion.

The strong young men were marched off to the labour camp: their death was postponed for a few months. The others made the short walk to the "factory of death". The German executioners called it *Himmelfahrt Strasse*—"the road to heaven".

Just across the way was a wooden building with the Red Cross flag above it. The old and crippled people stumbled across to this—and at once received a bullet in the back of the head.

Some of the evidence given by the few survivors taxes belief, but is only too true. Consider the evidence given at the Nuremberg trials by a Jew who was rescued from death by a friend working in the camp, and then owed his life to the Germans' need for an interpreter.

"They brought an aged woman with her daughter to this [the Red Cross] building. The latter was in the last stages of pregnancy. She was laid on a grass plot, and several Germans gathered to watch the delivery. This spectacle lasted two hours. When the child was born, Menz (the executioner) asked the grandmother—that is, the mother of this woman—which of them she preferred to see killed first. The grandmother begged to be killed. But of course they did the opposite: the newborn baby was killed first, then the child's mother, and finally the grandmother."

The able-bodied people marched about a hundred yards: they believed the resettlement ruse until the very last moment. West-European Jews, warned of the Nazi genocide policy, would not believe such a fantastic idea.

Men and women were separated, and ordered to undress—ostensibly for a bath. The men undressed in the yard, the women in a barrack room. They moved on to bathrooms—very hygienic, lined with white tiles. Above were contrivances which looked like showers. Still no suspicion—except that an inordinate number of people were crammed into each room—an uncomfortable bath. Then the showers began to discharge—gas.

It was carbon monoxide, exhaust gas from motors: the room quickly filled. The scene can be imagined—the terrified people—

including many children—screaming in their agony, fighting in a hopeless attempt to escape. They must have suffered appalling pain before they collapsed in heaps. The Nazis held that their system was very efficient—from the arrival of a train to the removal of the corpses occupied only two hours.

A thousand prisoners did all the dirty work—stripping the victims who had been shot, cutting off women's hair, extracting gold-filled teeth, collecting jewellery, watches and money—though the guards took their pick of this before handing it over—burning the bodies and burying the ashes. From time to time these workers were changed: one set would be placed among the victims and a staff "recruited" from newcomers. The officials were S.S. officers, while the ubiquitous Ukrainians formed the guard.

Attempts at escape were infrequent, and the escapees were usually shot. But in August, 1943, the guards had to face an armed mutiny among the working prisoners. These, of course, knew what their fate was to be, after escorting so many thousands to their last "bath". They, who had nothing to lose, attacked guards and seized their weapons. Many were shot, but three hundred escaped. It was these who provided much of the information about the extermination camp.

In all, three-quarters of a million people died here. Most, but not all, were Jews, drawn from Poland, Czechoslovakia, Austria, Belgium, France, Greece, Yugoslavia, Bulgaria, Germany and Russia. Sigmund Freud's sister was among the victims. The money collected suggested that there were some British and Americans among the victims, but these have not been identified. Escaped prisoners have declared, however, that they saw British prisoners killed.

As the Russian armies advanced from the east, the Nazis got frightened. The remaining prisoners were killed or evacuated, and the guards were ordered to destroy the camp and leave no trace of it. This they failed to do.

Oswiecym (Auschwitz) was the largest of the extermination camps, but Treblinka came next—it could dispose of 25,000 people a day. Majdanek's daily limit was 20,000, while Belsen could only deal with 15,000 bodies.

All over Poland I had heard arguments about Treblinka. A man believed to be the war-time commandant had been captured in

Brazil. This man was Franz Stangl, who had charge of the camp for its final year, and had previously been chief of the similar camp at Sobibor. He was an Austrian, and had long been on the "wanted" list of Poland, Austria and West Germany.

After the war he had been arrested by the Austrians, but escaped—helped by an underground S.S. organization—which, the Poles believe, still exists. Via Italy and Syria he made his way to Brazil, and in 1967 was arrested at São Paulo.

But Poland had no extradition treaty with Brazil, and Stangl was handed over to West Germany. The Poles had supplied evidence and sent witnesses to Bonn, but they had little confidence in German justice. Recently a man accused of atrocities after the Warsaw rising had been acquitted by West German judges on the grounds of insufficient evidence. The Poles had suffered too much to be able to understand what they regarded as legal quibbles.

Every man, obviously, must have a fair trial. But the Poles do not pretend to like the German adoption of a time limit for the trial of offences. If a man has committed a dastardly crime, they say, he should be punished—however long afterwards he may be arrested.

The trial of Stangl should have taken place before this book appears. The evidence—and defence—should be interesting. Our newspapers get excited about a murder, especially if a woman is involved. But here is a man who is alleged to have been responsible for the murder of 700,000 men, women *and children*. If the charge is true, imagination boggles at the punishment his own soul must have already have inflicted upon him—or the years of terror lest he should be found out.

One can well understand the lingering anger of the Poles. But not all those responsible are to be found in West Germany or Brazil. Some of the S.S. men of Treblinka are at large in East Germany, and some of the guards in the Ukraine—both countries to which Poland is allied. And the Nazis were not the only exponents of mass murder. If they *had* liquidated the Polish officers at Katyn, they would have done it much more efficiently!

The memorial at Treblinka is an unusual but not an incomprehensible fantasy.

On the site of the fake railway station is a line, hundreds of yards long, of concrete sleepers. It leads to the main memorial, which is surrounded by a thousand irregular standing stones: the taller ones represent the adults, the small ones the children—names will be carved on them when the list is complete. And the road between the station and the camp has been laid out in huge boulders, to mark the path of death. The muted singing of birds in the forest served only to emphasize the atmosphere of tragedy.

"The birds didn't sing at all when I was here," said a man wandering about in the midst of the standing stones.

"When was that?"

"1942."

16

AN AUTHOR IN SEARCH OF HIS
CHARACTERS

I

POLISH television invited me to join in an interesting experiment.
In 1952 I published a book, *They Saved London*, concerning the
Nazi flying bombs and rockets. Poles played a great part in the
Intelligence work which revealed these weapons to us before
they went into service, and Winston Churchill paid a grateful
tribute to our Polish friends.

My book—which was later filmed—was written in documentary form, for it was comprised of items of information culled
from hundreds of sources. Not all of these were accurate—
sometimes one contradicted another: my informants especially
tended to get confused between the V.1 and the V.2.

Now I was invited to visit the scenes of the actions I had described. What was more, I might meet some of the men who had
played an active part. Pirandello wrote a famous play, *Six
characters in search of an author*. My assignment worked the other
way round—an author in search of his characters.

We drove south to Tarnow, which was to be our headquarters
for a few days. A television van, loaded with equipment, accompanied us. We passed through Sandomierz, often described as one
of the oldest and most interesting towns in Poland. It is situated
on a high ridge flanking the valley of the Vistula, and its larger
buildings emerge from little woods on the steep slopes. The
Baroque cathedral has some Oriental and Byzantine touches, for
Sandomierz used to be a famous centre on the East–West trade
route. Here the caravans divided, to follow the Vistula either to
Cracow or to Danzig.

I found St. James's Church more interesting. It was a Domini-
can foundation, and the source of widespread tradition. The monastery was raided by the Tatars, and only one of the brothers

escaped—the other forty-nine were slashed to death by the raiders.

The story, with ancillary details, was regarded as a legend for seven hundred years. Then it was found to be true! The bodies of the forty-nine martyrs were discovered, and the skulls of most of them had been slashed by swords. What is more, the man who escaped had compiled a list of his fallen brothers, and inscribed it in stone. The tradition is now revealed as fact.

"An island of history" is another of the names given to Sandomierz. The town has many ancient buildings, but nearby is a modern industrial region—including a sulphur "mine" where the sulphur is excavated open-cast fashion by a huge grab.

The German threat in the 1930s drew attention to one obvious weakness. Poland was self-supporting to a remarkable extent. If she could maintain her frontiers she could fight a war, but her drawback lay in the fact that her native supplies of metals and coal were largely drawn from Upper Silesia, adjacent to the German frontier.

The problem was tackled with foresight and energy. The French loan of 25 million pounds in 1937 was applied very largely to its solution. It was significant to note that while Russia and Germany were talking of Five Year Plans, the Polish Press and Polish conversation re-echoed with the continual mention of C.O.P. The initials stood for Centralny Okreg Przemyslowy, or the Central Industrial Area. In a triangle within the confluence of the rivers Vistula and San, about the town of Sandomierz, was developed a new industrial district. Existing towns and villages increased their population by thousands per cent: one new town of thirty thousand inhabitants sprang up within a year. A rural countryside found itself an industrial district. By 1939 dozens of factories were in production, and I noted that considerable reserve stocks of essential commodities had been accumulated. The mountain streams of the Carpathians had been tapped to yield the precious power, and there was even a direct supply of earth gas from the Polish oilfields.

The C.O.P. was well planned and magnificently developed. It was an achievement of which any nation might be proud. But the weakness of long-term calculations lies in the lack of secrecy—and it is possible for a potential enemy to make long-term counter-plans. So long as there was an independent Czechoslovakia, then the C.O.P. area was capable of defence. The events of March, 1939, altered the situation in the course of forty-eight hours. The German seizure of Bohemia and Moravia meant added anxieties to the Polish defence. But the occupation of Slovakia meant that the entire strategical idea was shattered. A mere glance at the map is sufficient to show how the extension of the front to the south meant that the C.O.P. was outflanked from the very moment of the war.

The foundation of the new industrial area could not of course be kept secret, and the Nazis adopted a plan of campaign which led to its capture by overwhelming armoured forces. Now it has been rebuilt and considerably extended.

II

Tarnow, despite its long history, is an undistinguished town. I was interested in the mausoleum of General Josef Bem, a native who achieved the distinction of becoming a national hero of both Poland and Hungary. This is in a park: but the cathedral contains magnificent tombs of the Tarnowski family, who restored the town after its destruction by fire in the fifteenth century.

The search for my characters began at two neighbouring villages, Blizna and Pustkow, near Mielec. Here was another vast forest. In 1940 the Nazis adopted it as a weapon trial centre: its barracks housed the famous "Battery 444", which specialized in this work. All the adjoining villages were destroyed, and new roads and railways were built. The whole area was strongly fenced and guarded by special companies of the S.S., who had their own depot here.

Most of the work was done by prisoners of war, mostly Polish. A monument records that 15,000 men perished in the camp: the usual Nazi policy prevailed—the men were worked until they could work no more, and then they were herded into gas chambers. One of these has survived: it is half underground, and had two holes in the top—one was for the admission of the poison gas, the other served as a window, so that the jailers could see that all their victims were dead before the doors were opened.

Four thousand Russians died shockingly—literally starved to death. They tried to subsist on grass and roots, but only eleven survived.

Defensive precautions were so elaborate that the camp soon

invited the attention of the Intelligence Branch of the Polish Home Army. Local men were encouraged to seek employment in the camp, but the Germans chose only those of low intelligence, unlikely to be interested in what they saw. But one of these men was not as simple as he looked. He was the first of my characters.

"I was engaged on building work," he explained. "One day I was repairing a window, and I noticed that a German officer left a large document on his table. So I looked at it—it was a complete plan of the camp. So I just stole it, and gave it to my Intelligence Officer."

"And I sent it to Warsaw, whence it was passed on to London," said the latter. "We had already ascertained that the Germans were testing new weapons—tanks, guns and even gas.

"We knew about the rockets before the first one was fired. We identified the place where the weapons were assembled—a large concrete building. I will show it to you—or what is left of it.

"Close by, on the top of a ridge, were concrete launching pads. They were defended by pill-boxes all round them. But, though we could not get near the launching pads, we could spy on them through the glasses from a nearby wood. One of us would climb a tree.

"A rocket was fuelled and fired from an upright position on the pad. Then it took off—under its own power—leaving a white trail behind it. The rise was very slow at first, but gained in speed.

"It was obvious that not all the technical difficulties had been overcome—about half the rockets failed to rise.

"We noted carefully the exact times of those that did leave. Our headquarters in Warsaw soon found that they were aimed at Sarnaki, over two hundred miles away. Their arrival was timed, of course, so it was possible to calculate their speed.

"The rocket was about 14 metres long, and was gyroscopically-stabilized, with fins and vanes. From our observations, our experts (the Home Army had set up a special Commission of Research Workers, professors, and scientists, to examine all the evidence received) calculated that the rocket was pre-set on its calculated course by turning the vanes—we saw this done. Later the missile was made to ride a radio-beam.

"In the meantime, we had received some very interesting news from Warsaw."

One day in 1943 there was a serious motor accident on the

roundabout known as the Washington Rondo, in the Praga suburb of Warsaw. One military car was completely wrecked, and three German officers were killed.

Next day a German N.C.O. visited a Polish undertaker, and ordered three coffins.

"They must be good ones. They are for three senior officers, clever scientists, who were killed yesterday."

"Would those be the officers killed on the Rondo?"

"Yes. A pity. We needed them!"

The undertaker duly reported to Intelligence, which always welcomed any scraps of information. The number of the wrecked car had been noted, and inquiry more fitted to police work than military Intelligence revealed that it had been seen at Sarnaki, on the River Bug, and Blizna, much further south.

This linked up with other items of news. There was a German soldier, registered as an Austrian because his mother was of that nationality, and he had lived with her. But his father was Polish.

We often hear of "security checks", which are often in fact applied with severity, but most of which are quite useless. We can take a lesson from this incident. The Austrian was a radio operator, and he had been drafted to a camp near the German Pomeranian village of Peenemünde. And, despite his life in Austria and his natural love for his mother, his sympathies were Polish!

He reported unusual activities in this camp. The news was duly passed on to London, where astute men asked for a strict watch. This revealed that Peenemünde was an experimental centre for flying bombs and rockets. On 18th August, 1943, the camp was raided by the R.A.F. on a tremendously heavy scale, and great damage was done. It was an easy guess that the Germans would remove their experimental centre beyond the reach of the R.A.F., and soon it was confirmed that the rocket experiments had been transferred to Blizna-Pustkow, and that the reception area for the trial shots was the region of Sarnaki on the River Bug.

Now the widespread Home Army Intelligence service swung into action. Then came one of those strokes of luck on which police work and espionage so often depend. Sometimes the enemy makes a mistake: sometimes sheer chance plays against him. The rockets were enormous, 14 metres long: spies in the camp had actually seen them. The assembly shed and firing pads had been identified—from a distance, for they were rigorously guarded. In the experimental stage the rockets carried no explosive warhead.

Several of the rockets had fallen in and around the village of Sarnaki. But many disintegrated in flight. Of the fifty-seven attempted launchings from January to March, 1944, only twenty-six were successful—and of these only four actually reached their target.

We duly recorded a conversation beside the launching pads near Blizna-Pustkow, and then headed north for Sarnaki.

Here, one morning in 1944, a Polish angler was wandering along the banks of the Bug when he came to a stretch where the river bank was clustered with reeds. Then he saw something unusual protruding from the marshy reeds. He quickly covered it with branches and leaves.

A Home Army officer—a local doctor—was soon on the scene, and rapidly identified the object. A rocket had fallen into the reeds. Ten metres were immersed, the remaining four protruding. So far as he could see, the rocket was not seriously damaged.

"I knew how badly full details of the rocket were needed," said Dr. Norwid-Niepokoj, as we surveyed the scene. "I borrowed two pairs of powerful horses, and the rocket was pulled clear and hidden in that forest over there. Engineer Kocjan arrived from Warsaw with a team of mechanics. Feeling their way, they took the rocket to pieces, and soon a lengthy technical description was on its way to England."

There it was received with jubilation. "But if only I could see the real thing!" said the British scientist. But he little thought that his wish would be fulfilled! It was, however, as a result of one of the most audacious operations of the war.

Not far from Tarnow is the village of Zabawa, to which I made my way in the last stage of my investigations. My companion was a potato exporter who during the war had been second-in-command of the local branch of the Home Army. Like all his companions, he adopted a pseudonym. The Germans got to know this very well, but never identified "The Pirate" with the reserved man whose sole interest seemed to be potatoes.

"It's a pity," he said. "The colonel won't come."

"What do you mean?"

"The colonel—my commander. He lives in Silesia—in the New Territories. Maybe he is nervous of revealing himself, or he may not have been well lately. But to come all this way from Silesia, and then not to appear—that is absurd."

"Where is he?"

"In the house we stopped at, in the last village."

"Turn the car round!" Words are my trade, and I was confident that I could talk the colonel over.

I began to speak as soon as I met him, and was prepared to go on until he yielded from sheer weariness. But it was not left to me. My wife Helen took him by the arm and smiled at him, and he agreed to come with us.

Not far from the forest was a stretch of open ground—it had recently been cleared of wheat. Here twenty or thirty partisans of the Home Army had gathered—the men who had participated in the dramatic episode.

The open stretch of ground was used by the Germans as a reserve airstrip for their fighter planes. The Poles called it Motyl—butterfly. Already a British aircraft had landed there, but since then the local German forces had been increased by units retiring before the Russian advance. There were 4,000 Germans within a mile of Motyl: one of their posts was within four hundred yards of the field.

The conspirators very soon got a shock. The Germans had not used the airstrip for some weeks, but now two fighters landed! However, they took off before dark.

Four hundred men of the Home Army were on guard—in the forest as well as the open country. Every German post was covered—if its occupants moved, battle would be joined. But it would be best if the enemy could be contained—quietly.

It was an eerie scene, as the men crouched in the darkness. Others, in the forest and village, prepared torches and stable lamps to act as a flare path.

Soon after midnight the waiting men heard the sound of an aircraft above. An R.A.F. Dakota had made a remarkable flight over enemy-occupied territory from Italy. Signals were exchanged, and the plane prepared to land. Its headlamps switched on, it swooped down. The pilot saw that there was not enough room to land, so he flew on.

"I was frantic," said the colonel. "For the moment he forgot to switch off his lights, and they were blazing as he flew over a German post. But they did nothing."

The Dakota circled, and then landed safely. It unloaded some passengers and half a ton of precious supplies: then the partisans began to load the essential parts of the captured rocket—in an amazing assortment of parcels, suit-cases and crates. Within five minutes of its arrival, the aircraft was loaded. A Polish technician was to accompany the spoil, and with him two leading Polish politicians, urgently wanted in London. The engines of the aircraft were boosted and the pilot applied his controls. But the aircraft refused to move!

There had been prolonged rain, and the ground was soft— the wheels of the aircraft had sunk in. The heavy packages were hastily unloaded, and the pilot tried again: useless. Home Army men produced spades, and began to dig. Twigs were laid in the muddy depressions. Still the aircraft refused to move.

The pilot reluctantly prepared to abandon his machine. Petrol was thrown over it.

"One more try!"

As the spade men dug, others pushed at the wings and fuselage of the Dakota. And it moved!

Reloaded, it took off, bringing to Italy, and thence to London, the secrets of one of Hitler's Revenge weapons.

I heard the stories of the partisans. Some had had experiences far more exciting than any James Bond thriller.

All my characters were of course amateurs: none had previously faced a TV camera. Some were bold, many nervous, and some shy. There were no scripts, and every item was impromptu. Except one.

In the evening, at The Pirate's home in Tarnow we shot some interior scenes. One elderly man, I found, had come prepared.

"I believe that you organized the transport of the rocket to the airfield?" I asked. This interview was to establish one connecting point in the story, and was scheduled for fifty seconds. But the ex-Home Army officer had other ideas.

"I was born in 1892," he began, and gave a long account of his life. He spoke for nearly an hour: then the camera crew reported that they had run out of film.

On the airfield someone was chosen to tell the story, while the others listened. Few of the partisans had met since the episode, and some did not even know one another!

Finally I answered their questions. The last was simple: "Was the work we did of importance?"

Was it of importance? The word was far too small. My reply was well received. It is not often that a principal actor gets a hearty round of applause from the "extras" of his picture, but such was my experience on this airstrip which had been the scene of an episode.

III

We were to leave Warsaw for home very early on a Tuesday morning. I completed my assignment with Polish TV at lunch on the Monday. They paid me—quite a substantial sum—in zloty. As it is forbidden to take Polish currency out of the country, Helen found herself confronted with a woman's dream—a pocket full of money which *must* be spent in an afternoon.

We made a good start. We had been very impressed at the quality of the cut glass we had seen at the Julia factory in the Sudetens. A shop in the old market place offered a good selection, and half our money disappeared in one transaction. I began to think out an explanation to give to the Customs Officer at London Airport.

A week earlier we had visited the Warsaw fashion centre—a state affair, but run by experts who had full authority. As the girls paraded before us, the lady manager explained that in the past most of their designs had been drawn from Paris, but now Polish artists were creating their own, and they hoped one day to enter the uneasy market of world fashion.

There was scarcely time for Helen to order a new frock, but we had been impressed by the quality of Polish silk and the beauty of its designs. It was expensive, and a dress length made a further inroad into our fortune.

In the Cepelia shops there was a wide selection of folk-art—carved wooden boxes to hold cigarettes or cards; hand-made lace and beautiful embroidery; dolls in authentic Polish costumes; pictures of Polish dancers in costume made out of coloured straw; even Pan Twardowski flying through the air on his cockerel: and necklaces and brooches of amber. Before leaving home we had warned our family that for once presents might not be forthcoming; we had spent some time in Turkey[1] earlier in the

[1] See *Turkey and the Turks*. Herbert Jenkins, 1968.

summer, and this journey had used up most of our travel allowance. But now we could be quite generous.

I kept back enough for our evening meal: then a friend called at our hotel and carted us off for dinner. So the last of my zlotys were spent at the airport shop the following morning.

Helen thought that the Monday afternoon had provided an admirable climax to a very pleasant journey!

17

POLISH MISCELLANY

I

THERE used to be more than three million Jews in Poland—most of them were descendants of those sent "beyond the Pale" by the czars of Russia. Some were rich: others were not. This distinction did not have any effect on the Nazi executioners who sought to implement Hitler's "final solution".

Today the Jewish population of Poland is about 50,000. Not all were massacred during the war, but Poland had such unhappy memories that many of the survivors preferred to emigrate to Israel.

Before the war there was a strong anti-Semitic prejudice throughout Poland. The millions of Russian Jews had not been absorbed into the national life—and many of them seemed to prefer to live apart. The sharing of common sufferings tended to bring Poles and Jews closer together.

Then, after the war, the old feelings revived. The unpopular Stalinist government, a Russian puppet, contained a high proportion of Jews: so did its secret police. With the end of that rule, anti-Semitism subsided.

It was again revived, not among the ordinary people, but in government circles. It arose as a result of the Israel victory over the Arabs of 1967. Gomulka dismissed three generals and dozens of officers for the crime of pro-Israel sentiments.

When the Middle Eastern war began, Gomulka took the sensible view that Poland was not concerned. But then Russia strongly supported the Arab cause. Gomulka delayed his own declaration for forty-eight hours.

Previously the Communist countries had met in conference at Karlovy Vary. The West Germans had made a friendly approach to the solution of outstanding problems. The Russians were disposed to accept it, but the Poles were suspicious, and were not yet ready to forgive and forget. Gomulka argued strongly, and brought the Russians around to his viewpoint. Hence, when the Soviet leaders took a strong line on Israel, Gomulka felt called on to support them.

So he took a firm line with officials who did not agree with them. Many of them were of part-Jewish origin: but there could be no dual loyalties, Gomulka declared. Men not loyal to Poland had better go to Israel.

But the people of Poland expressed their own opinions very frankly: nor did they always follow the government line. The Poles appreciate military virtues, and the defeat of sixty million Arabs by three million Israelis was so remarkable as to encourage the view that it was really due to British and American aid. The Jews owed their victory, I claimed, to (a) better organization, (b) higher military qualities, (c) far better leadership, and (d) the fact that the Arabs were fighting for prestige and revenge, but the Jews were fighting for their very lives.

The Poles agreed with my third point, and in fact they drew a little reflected glory from the Israeli victory. For General Dayan, the organizer of the victory, came of a Polish-Jewish family and was trained at the Polish Military Academy at Lwow!

Gomulka is not fundamentally anti-Semitic. His wife is Jewish: so are some of his ministers.

Senior officials in several of the ministries were victims of his purge. It was announced that these men "had not returned from holidays". Minor offenders were punished by the withdrawal of their party cards, but all this was done without fuss or publicity. The government merely announced a scheme "to appraise the ideological and moral level of party members". This would "purge the party ranks of people who are passive".

Local party meetings loyally passed the conventional resolutions, condemning Israel's "policy of conquest", "contacts with Nazis" and "terrorism in Arab territories".

The Jews in Poland were naturally jubilant at the Israeli victory. I heard reports of drinking parties to celebrate it. But one Pole had an original outlook. "The Jews won because they struck before the Arabs were ready. Illegal? Maybe. But look at its result. Why didn't we do this to Hitler in 1938, or earlier?"

There is a Jewish theatre in Warsaw. It is often attended by Poles, attracted by the quality of the acting. The seats are fitted with automatic translating sets, so that the Hebrew can be followed.

Israel has honoured many Polish citizens who, at the risk of their lives, helped the Jewish population during the Nazi terror. These included a number of Poles who took part in the Ghetto rising.

The Jewish hold on Polish commerce has almost completely disappeared, save for some of the small shops. Jews are still well represented in the Polish professions, however.

II

There is plenty of political wit in Poland. Some of it is borrowed: stories about the humourless East German Ulbricht have been remodelled to fit Gomulka. Today stories about China are also very popular.

"How lucky we Poles are to have a buffer state like Soviet Russia between us and China!"

A Soviet plane comes in to land at Peking Airport. The stewardess announced: "We are landing in China. Please tighten your seat-belts."

A young Chinese responds angrily: "Please, no politics!"

"In Russia all the cats have been killed because the Soviet government could not bear to listen to 'mao, mao, mao' all night long."

China conquers the world. Two Russians are standing in the winter snow, clad in thin traditional blue Chinese overalls.

"Come to think of it," says one, "things weren't too bad under Stalin."

About 1975. Johnson and Kosygin are sitting in a Chinese prison. Johnson says: "I told you it was a mistake to concentrate on the German problem."

Polish humour reflects the uneasy feeling that the future may belong to China. Definition of an optimist: "A man who is learning to eat caviar with chopsticks."

War breaks out between Russia and China. In the first week, the Russians capture a million Chinese; in the second, five million; in the third, ten million.

In the fourth week Kosygin gets a telegram from Mao: "Had enough? Capitulate?"

In an effort to reach the moon, Chinese stood on each other's shoulders. But when the top man was a mile from the moon, the pyramid collapsed.

The cause of the failure was announced in Peking: the six men who formed the base of the pyramid had not read "The sayings of Mao" carefully enough.

A Polish baker was summoned for hygienic negligence—a dead fly had been found in a bread roll.

"That isn't a fly—it's a sultana!" he declared in court. He seized the roll, and ate the "sultana"—thus destroying the evidence against him.

Poland, like most of the other Communist countries, faces a serious problem of alcoholism. It was frequently explained to me that the well paid workers get drunk because they can do little else with their money. The government has initiated a campaign against drunkenness—and logically enough, makes the vodka pay for it: one zloty out of the price of each bottle goes to the campaign.

One man charged with being drunk and disorderly complained to the magistrate: "But in one day I contributed ten zloty to the fight against alcoholism!"

Gomulka spoke severely on the rise in consumption of vodka. "Can any conscientious, patriotic peasant acquiesce in such a state of affairs? And what can we say of local or national councils which build profitable drinking dens instead of homes for the people?"

But the government has a monopoly of the manufacture and sale of vodka, and makes a large profit out of both.

The Polish consumption of spirits is double ours, but that of beer is much less. In the rural regions illicit stills are by no means unknown.

After the German attack on Russia, General Sikorski arranged with Stalin the formation of an army drawn from Polish prisoners-of-war. This army was transferred to the West, where it rendered yeoman service.

But in 1943, when the Katyn disaster was followed by the establishment of a Communist government, a new Polish army was formed in Russia. This Kosciuszko Division was placed under the command of General Berling, and eventually became the First Army: a Second Army followed. By the end of the war some 400,000 Poles were under arms, and 150,000 had been in action.

After victory, some Poles returned from the West, but received scurvy treatment. Half of the officers in the Polish army were Russians! The first post-war action was a joint effort. Anti-Communist or Nationalist factions in the Ukraine—and Ukrainians in south-eastern Poland—formed the Ukrainian Insurgent Army (U.P.A.—Ukrayinska Povstanka Armeya), and waged guerrilla warfare for some years. By 1948 the combined efforts of Soviet and Polish divisions had quelled the revolt.

Thereafter the Polish forces grew in strength, but were Russian-controlled—even wearing Russian uniforms. Hundreds of Polish officers were "purged", but the situation changed after Gomulka achieved power. Now the Polish army was Polish. The Chief of Staff was General Spychalski, who had previously been one of the officers "purged" by the previous Stalinist government.

Today the Polish armed forces are the largest and best-trained and equipped of all the satellite states. The army numbers over 200,000 men, including several armoured divisions: the air force has nearly a thousand aircraft: the navy is small—a few destroyers and submarines.

By treaty, the Russians were entitled to keep forces on Polish soil to protect their lines of communication to East Germany. In 1956, by agreement, the strength of these forces was reduced from three divisions to two. Perhaps the Russian confidence was influenced by the revelation that 70 per cent of the army officers were party members.

Mr. Gomulka once visited a kindergarten. The headmistress wanted a number of expensive improvements, but Gomulka pleaded the poverty of the State.

He went on to a prison. The governor demanded a cinema for the convicts, and Gomulka agreed.

"But you turned down the request from the kindergarten!" his secretary protested.

"Yes," Gomulka smiled. "But I'm not likely to spend my old age in a kindergarten!"

(The same story is told about many other leaders in the Communist countries.)

At a party meeting a man was asked his opinion of a disputed point.

"Well, Marx said——"

"No. We want your own opinion," the chairman interrupted.

"Well, Lenin said——"

"Your own opinion!"

"Well, before I give my own opinion let me make it quite clear that I do not agree with it."

III

The *Morning Star* (late, the *Daily Worker*) is usually on sale in the big towns. *The Times* and *Telegraph* may also be offered. Most large hotels have a club room, where the leading newspapers of many countries are available.

More interesting is the International Press and Book Club. Anyone can enter this—there is no subscription. There are classes in English, French, German, Russian and Swedish, and the principal newspapers of these countries and of U.S.A. are on the stands—usually about a week late—either for sale or to be read on the spot.

So it is quite impossible for the government to confine world news to its own journals. Such an attempt would in any event be countered by the very large number of Poles who listen to foreign broadcasts.

I found that the premises of the International Press and Book Club in different towns were admirable places for conversation. They are usually frequented by the more intelligent members of the population.

"Letters to the Editor" have become a feature of "Socialist Democracy".

"It is no use anybody complaining to officials," said a woman doctor. "But publicity yields practical results.

"Most papers, and the radio, employ special staffs to reply to letters. Not all can be printed or broadcast, of course, but the staff gives practical advice to the writers. Many are personal complaints—the treatment of children at school or of patients in hospital. Very few people know their own rights, and a complaint to an authority is answered on a printed form, or a copy of rules. Even fewer people understand these—maybe not even the people who send them.

"The newspapers are doing a real job. Some of the nationals get over 100,000 letters a year—Polish radio and TV even more."

Opinion polls are not unknown in the Communist countries. In 1963 samples of Polish opinions on the Sino-Soviet conflict were collected. Which country was right? As might be expected, Russia led easily, with 40 per cent of the votes: a year later, however, this had decreased to 24 per cent, while the Chinese support had increased from 7 to 9 per cent. There were many odd answers—for example, 10 per cent declared "Neither". But in 1964 no less than 51 per cent returned the answer "Don't know".

Polish newspapers are at least not afraid to publish figures which contradict the glowing terms of official pronouncements. One Warsaw journal revealed that in durable consumer goods Poland was much behind Czechoslovakia, and still much more behind West Germany. It quoted figures—per thousand inhabitants:

	Poland	West Germany
Refrigerators	26	185
TV sets	54	122
Radio sets	185	322
Cars	0·6	119

A Warsaw weekly commented on the results of a survey or poll: "The dreams of the Polish citizen are rather modest." The survey showed that half of those questioned had an income no higher than 800 zloty a month, and only a little over 10 per cent received 1,500 zloty or more. Almost a third had a one-room residence. Only 59·8 per cent had running water. "The main dream is a more comfortable apartment and a higher income."

The Poles have been so indoctrinated in the natural need for foreign exchange in "hard" currency that the average man is almost a human computer in working out its value. One result of the official propaganda is that the Poles tend to despise their own currency and to follow the "cult of the dollar".

It is quite illegal, but if you stopped almost any Pole in the street and offered him dollars, pounds, escudos, marks, or francs he would promptly buy them—at the correct black market rate.

A Polish magazine published a cry from the heart. "We are living in a strange country—a funless country." It went on to list the distractions available—if you had money. "Man hungers for luxury. . . . He needs a choice, a range of possibilities, not an identical existence. . . . Why are we second-class citizens? . . . Why is there such a yawning chasm between the everyday greyness and the out-of-the-ordinary occasions?"

The magazine did not attempt to answer its own queries. But without doubt there *is* a hunger for luxury in Poland. It has been stimulated by foreign visitors—officially welcomed because they bring with them invaluable "hard" currency.

IV

Humour is a very useful safety valve. I do not know if Gomulka has deliberately permitted the political joke—it might be so, for he is very different from the humourless Ulbricht. He himself appears in very few of the apochryphal stories—his Puritan character and his personality scarcely encourage fun at his expense.

Cyrankiewicz, the Prime Minister, is different. He is reputed to be the only Pole who is not afraid to go to Moscow. He declares that the Russians would never harm a hair on his head. He is completely bald.

The butt of many jokes is Stalin's "present" to Warsaw, the Palace of Science and Culture—"the nightmare of a drunken confectioner", a Polish poet described it.

The happiest man in Warsaw is alleged to be the caretaker. He lives on the 30th floor, and is the only man in Warsaw who cannot see the Palace.

But a wittier comment described the building as "God's punishment for blowing up the Orthodox Cathedral"—a reference to the Russian church in what is now called Victory Square, demolished by the Poles soon after the First World War.

Polish humorous magazines are banned in Russia. It is claimed that Czechs learn Polish in order to read them. Even in Stalinist days humour was not repressed. One cabaret had resident censors. They sat through a series of jokes about one of Napoleon's generals—a most unlikely subject for humour. But the audience knew that the biting satire referred to the hated Marshal Rokossowski.

The mythical Radio Erivan is alleged to provide Marxist comments on events.

"Can a child be produced by the intercourse of two men?" "No, but experiments continue."

"Will there be another war?" "No, but the struggle for peace will leave no stone standing."

Feliks Dzierzynski, the Pole who became the head of the Russian secret police, features in many of the stories.

"Daddy, was Dzierzynski really fond of children?"

"Yes. But he hated parents."

A Communist lecturer announced that the Russians would soon go to the moon.

"What—all of them?" someone asked, hopefully.

There is a touch of modern "sick humour" in some wisecracks.

"What is Russia?" "The poor man's America."

"What is a hundred metres long and lives on cabbages?" "A Polish meat queue."

"Can one build Socialism in our country?" "Yes, but one should live in another."

V

Some general comments by a well-informed Pole.

The Catholics in the Seym are not formal representatives of the Church—indeed, they do not always agree with the Cardinal. Other countries have Catholic political parties, but not Poland. The Church does not want political representation.

The Independents do not form a real opposition. They may have their own opinions on certain points, but in the main they support the government. Otherwise their names would not be on the voting list!

In theory it would be possible for the Independents to gain a parliamentary majority. But in practice it is impossible, as the government makes out the lists of candidates.

But Poland *does* have a political life. There are all kinds of different trends of opinion within the party, and sometimes this leads to lively debate. There is quite a vivid political life inside the party—and, since the Stalinists, even a certain element of democracy.

So if a man doesn't like the system, and wants to play politics— he has to join the party. It includes plenty of groups—he ought to find one to suit him. Today there is no definite party line.

Poland is the most liberal of all the Communist countries: Hungary next. There are some members of the Seym who definitely try to represent the people. And the party likes it that way—when possible.

You know the most Soviet country in the world? Britain. You have in practice what Russia has in theory—government by Soviets, that is, councils. Russia, France and Germany are ruled by Civil Servants. France can have frequent changes of government. It makes little difference. The bureaucrats are always there.

We have our share of bureaucracy—I don't deny that. But if there is such a thing as National Communists, you will find them in Poland. There are lots of technocrats in parliament, and they are getting more and more powerful.

The ordinary people don't babble about freedom these days. What they want is efficiency. Freedom is scarcely a topic, but efficiency is. Hence the power of the technocrats. It is the same in all or most other countries. You have been ruled by capitalists, like Henry Ford. Today you are ruled—or soon will be ruled— not by the capitalists, but by the general managers of the big concerns.

No matter what our political ideas, we have to keep close to Russia. Germany is still there, and does not impel trust.

In twenty years' time? No one can tell. It is certain that Russia will not be the same then, so it is probable that Poland will be different, too. A liberal socialism here, I should guess.

You know the Polish nightmare? That Russia and Germany should join hands again. That is *not* impossible, any more than it was in 1939. If opposites like Hitler and Stalin (or *were* they opposites?) could make a deal, any of the present type of leaders could do it. And you have often pointed out in your books that when Germany and Russia are friends, there is trouble ahead for Poland.

And some notes by one of the directors of planning.

Our gross national product has been rising at the rate of 6 per cent a year. The population rises at more than 1 per cent. The net gain in real incomes is around 3 per cent.

Our principal exports are agricultural products. But we may have to limit these, in view of the increase of home demand. We expect very soon to become a full member of G.A.T.T.

There is no actual unemployment—in some towns there is indeed a shortage of labour. But in others there is hidden unemployment in the form of over-staffing.

Two thousand zloty a month is the average wage: 900 will shortly be the minimum. It is not enough—unless the man's wife also has a highly skilled job. You can observe the feminization of Poland. Because of our shocking war losses, women form 52 per cent of our population—a million more than men. They are very much to the fore in such professions as medicine, law and teaching.

In our economy the principal factors are—apart from agriculture—sulphur, copper, shipbuilding, fertilizers.

Some of these, like shipbuilding, are quite new to Poland.

And from a senior member of the war-time Home Army.

General Bor had to fight (at Warsaw). Stalin planned to take over Poland—not merely to impose a Communist government. He lowered his sights when he saw the potential opposition.

If Bor had not fought, he would have played right into the hands of the Nazis. Do you know that in Warsaw the Gestapo had a special section with but one objective—to capture Bor. There were car loads of them on a twenty-four-hour alert, awaiting a telephone call. They offered huge rewards, but no Pole was ready to play the Judas.

The French restored their own morale by the part they played in the capture of Paris. We hoped to do the same at Warsaw.

Stalin was pleased when the Warsaw rising failed—he had refused to co-operate. He hoped that the Nazi terror would be blamed on the Polish leaders.

No man fought more bravely against the Nazis than did Bor. But your government never gave him a decoration—nor was it represented at his funeral. Our own government did nothing at all. The ex-soldiers of Warsaw subscribed to send a huge wreath to England. It was held up by the Polish Customs for twenty-four hours—but then allowed to go through.

Here in Warsaw there was a Requiem Mass in Holy Cross Church. There was no announcement—such was not allowed. But the grape-vine was active. Long before the service the church was packed, and a great crowd swarmed across the road outside, holding up the traffic. The service was most moving, and men and women alike were in tears. The theme was: "I have fought a good fight, I have finished my course, I have kept the faith."

I wish I could describe the Warsaw rising to you. The front was everywhere. Old men and women dug up pavements to make barricades. Women acted as messengers, and many of them took part in the fighting. So did boys.

I had some of the Communist's People's Army in my section. Not many—there weren't many of them, anyway. They fought well—and I only wish Stalin could have heard what they said when he let us down! The fact was, of course, that Stalin didn't want the Poles to win. Not only the battle—the war. A broken Poland would have been easy meat for him.

I was lucky. The Nazis didn't catch me in Warsaw. So I got out—through the sewers—and carried on the fight farther south.

Just look through these papers. They give you an idea of the Polish Home Army from the *German* point of view:

"The Home Army was active even during the first winter of the War. At that time its chief activity was sabotage—especially of Russian supplies pouring into Germany, which were a great help to our war-time activity. The Poles attacked the trains with home-made bombs.

"In March, 1940, the Gestapo and the Soviet Secret Police held a conference—on how to fight the Polish Underground. The importance of the subject can be gauged by the fact that the conference lasted for several weeks.

"In the early spring of 1941 the Home Army Intelligence officers noticed huge German concentrations in Poland—on the Russian frontier. They passed the news to London. Churchill

passed on the warning to Stalin—who, fortunately for us, took
no notice of it.

"Then, when the Warsaw rising began, Stalin refused to let
British aircraft land on Russian airfields to refuel. It was here,
though this was not recognized at the time, that the Cold War
began.

"If Germany is ever foolish enough to go to war again, we
should like to have the Poles on our side!"

VI

Marx advocated the abolition of private property. Lenin
agreed, and called private property "Robbery . . . as long as the
private ownership of the means of production persists . . . the
economic base of capitalism will be preserved."

This was the fundamental ideological idea of Marxism-
Leninism. But no Polish government has ever agreed with it. A
sizeable private sector has existed all through the twenty-two
years of Communist rule. And it is growing—with government
encouragement!

In 1961 privately owned workshops or small plants employed
158,000 workers. By 1966 the figure had increased to 188,700.
Under the present national plan, total employment in the private
sector is to reach 315,000 by 1970.

There are 147,000 craft workshops, 15,000 retail establishments,
and 7,000 small factories. In addition, during the past few years
about a thousand restaurants and bars, 5,000 retail stores and
hundreds of petrol stations and small garages have been leased to
private citizens. In effect, the state provides and owns the capital
while the individual manages the enterprise and runs any risk.

Real incentives have been offered to private business—tax
concessions, better and longer security of tenure, and the extension of social security benefits to cover owners and workers.

One reason for the government outlook is to create employment for the expanding population. Large factories need immense
capital which Poland cannot provide. Further, Gomulka was not
the only one to see the folly of subsidizing inefficient or un-
economical enterprises. They must either be closed, creating
unemployment, or handed over to private control.

True, the assumption that a private enterprise can make a profit where the State has had nothing but losses is a tacit admission of the greater efficiency of private enterprise.

In Britain we approach the same conclusion from a different angle. True, our nationalized industries never had a fair chance. We wait until coal is rapidly being replaced by oil and railways by road transport before the State takes over such enterprises: and then we wonder why they are a constant burden on the tax-payer.

It is a common claim that the Communists have abolished unemployment. But it is not true. Most have a percentage of unemployed. Some have deliberately provoked it by closing down factories which did not pay their way—surely a capitalist idea!

There is already some under-employment in Poland—over-staffed factories and State farms. Some Polish economists foresee the time when the country will have more workers than jobs.

The very high birth rate of the 1940s and 1950s was partly responsible: added to the new young generation of workers was the slow rate of capital investment. This in turn depended on imports of capital equipment—and the lack of hard currency in which to pay for it.

Some claimed that unemployment already exists in Poland—a figure of half a million has been quoted, but no official figures are available. Most are not wholly unemployed, but work only for a limited number of hours per week. It was even suggested that some emigration should be encouraged! Polish professional men and technicians are already working in East Germany—to replace those who have fled to the West—and in Africa.

VII

1956–7 witnessed a great revival in Polish intellectual life, so stilted during the long Stalinist phase. Literature especially flourished: it was no longer confined to the themes of "the gas chamber era", but sparkled with ideas. Gradually Gomulka applied a damper and then a brake: the ideas were not those of the party line.

Recalcitrant writers were not shot: their books were simply not published because of "shortage of paper". The censor does not confiscate books. He does not even tell authors that they will not be published. His anonymous actions are even more damping.

"We are not told what to write," a Polish author explained. "We are only told what we must not write."

Ideas are not dead in Poland, however. There are men who refuse to accept the loss of intellectual freedom. True, their voices are for the moment stilled, but their ideas are stirring in politico-literary groups and clubs. They will be heard of again.

They are not all anti-Communists. Jacek Kuron and Karol Modzelewski are party members. So far from wanting to destroy their creed, they wanted to make it better. They were tried, in effect, on the charge of being Trotskyists, though their principal complaint concerned bureaucratic incompetence in high quarters. They now languish in jail: but they too will be heard of again.

A much better known man, Professor Leszek Kolakowski, was expelled from the party for "taking a wrong view of the events which brought First Secretary Gomulka back to power in 1956". He had declared that there was still no genuine democratic freedom in Poland, so that there was no reason to celebrate the anniversary of the events. The action taken against him was not announced by the government, but it became known and provoked angry protests from the Warsaw intellectual community—including Communists.

They were already alarmed by the government policy of allowing "only constructive criticism" and clamping down on "propaganda hostile to socialism"—two phrases which can be widely interpreted. In 1964 the party's anti-intellectual line evoked a sharp letter of protest from thirty-four non-party intellectuals. Of these, ten were persuaded to withdraw their signatures.

"But the other twenty-four are still here, and still protesting. Their influence has spread. After all, there are twice as many as Jesus started off with!"

Polish journalists are experts at writing "double-talk" of a new type. And their readers can interpret it. "It is a matter of principle with us never to believe what we read. We have become experts at reading between the lines."

In Warsaw I met the niece of an old friend, Professor Dyboski, of Cracow University.

By a happy accident, he was away when the Nazis rounded up the entire staff of professors and lecturers, and deported them to Sachsenhausen concentration camp. Dyboski then established a remarkable one-man underground organization. He used his home as the university, gave lessons there, and even held secret examinations!

After the war the universities of Warsaw, Cracow and Poznan were revived. Lwow and Vilno had been incorporated into the Soviet Union, so most of their professors transferred to the new university at Wroclaw.

The Polish historians had an unhappy time. At a party conference in 1951 they were instructed by the Stalinist leaders that events hitherto regarded as important—the introduction of Christianity, the union with Lithuania, the loss of Poland's political existence and even her name, and the recovery of these in 1918—all these things were alleged to be of no importance.

Instead, all events to the east of the Curzon Line were to be omitted, as concerning Russia: the Partitions of Poland related only to Prussia and Austria—not Czarist Russia: in the conflicts with Russia, in fact, the czars were always right. This was indeed fantastic!

The report of the conference reminded me of a Russian history of England published a few years ago. This emphasized the most important event in England since the end of the war in 1945—the strike of waiters at the Savoy Hotel!

One distinguished Polish historian was not afraid to denounce the reason for the lack of initiative in historical research—"intimidation is still too strong".

Children in a Polish school

Children's playground

Wayside shrine in rural Poland

Newly-built peasants' cottages

18

CHURCH AND STATE

I

POLAND is as firmly a Catholic country as Italy, Spain or Ireland. For centuries it was the eastern outpost of the Catholic faith, which it always strongly held. It was as easy for a Polish king to raise an army to fight against the Protestant Prussians and the Orthodox Russians as against the Moslem Turks.

Even today something like nine-tenths of the Poles would describe themselves as Catholics. Many practise their religion regularly, others but seldom—they attend services only at Easter and Christmas, like some of ourselves—some have turned to the Church as the only opposition to Communism.

In the towns, it is estimated, 30 to 40 per cent of the people are regular churchgoers. In the villages "We all go," said one man: then added: "Except the militiaman (policeman), of course."

"And the teacher?"

"Oh, she goes."

This is remarkable. In most Communist countries a teacher who was a practising Christian would be promptly dismissed. In Poland she is honoured by the people she serves.

Any congregation will include a good proportion of young people, and it is estimated that 50 per cent of the students are regular churchgoers.

This does not please the Communists. A definition of a good Communist reads: "Maybe he lives in a house where some members of his family are religious believers. What has he, a person of advanced views, done to help the believer rid herself of such religious belief? Does he try? Or is he indifferent?

"Such a Communist, indifferent to religious problems, is greatly indebted to his parents. They brought him up—made a man of him, helped him to get education. It is his direct duty to use this education to help them to understand the falsity and harm of religious prejudice and to get rid of it."

When the Russians imposed a Communist government on Poland, it promptly declared war on religion. Catholic education was forbidden, and religious newspapers suppressed. Bishops and priests were imprisoned—even their leader, Cardinal Wyszynski. The Communist rulers believed that Christianity could be eliminated in a generation.

But the Catholic Church is resilient and patient. Atheist persecution drove not fewer, but more people to church. On a Sunday in August, 1956, Czestochowa was to celebrate the 300th anniversary of the appointment of the Black Virgin as Queen of Poland. The Stalinist government gave no aid to the pilgrims: on the other hand, it placed every obstacle in their way, but they came, from every corner of Poland. Regions classed as Communist sent large contingents—one of the largest was from the Socialist city, Nowa Huta.

No one could count the number of pilgrims who gathered at Czestochowa for the great occasion. The lowest estimate was a million, and tens of thousands had walked hundreds of miles.

The government was gravely concerned. But soon it was replaced by that of Gomulka, who was a realist. Like all Communist leaders, he was an atheist, but he had never taken part in the persecution of the Church—indeed, he had spent years in prison, like Cardinal Wyszynski.

(There is a good, but apochryphal story of an alleged conversation between Gomulka and the Cardinal.

"I'm not very popular with the Russians," said Gomulka. "Couldn't you help me to increase my influence—excommunicate me, for example?"

"Yes—if you will imprison me again, to increase mine.")

Gomulka released Cardinal Wyszynski unconditionally, and the popular reception of the prelate was a warning to opponents of the Church. The Cardinal was restrained: he realized quite clearly that the tragedy of Hungary might have happened in Poland, and that the alternative to Gomulka was not democracy but Stalinism.

He was as clever a negotiator as any politician, and Gomulka recognized his great influence. Religious education in the schools was restored—parents might decide this locally. Bishops and priests were released from prison. There was great enthusiasm among the ordinary people of Poland—especially among the villagers.

But the PAX organization was allowed to continue.

II

PAX was founded by a group of men, most of whom had been right-wingers, but had made the easy transformation from Fascism to Communism. They saw that the government needed an organization to rival the Catholic Church, and they provided it. They had emerged from a pre-war Student Fascist Movement, which never gained more than a thousand members. True, they fought against the German invaders in 1939. The Communists were prepared to use PAX, but not to collaborate with it. PAX was allowed to undertake its activities of "political realism" because it tended to divide the Catholics. It has had some success among the impatient young people, but to most Poles its leaders are some sort of quislings.

PAX claimed that it consisted of "progressive Catholics", but primarily it was a business concern. Government support secured it valuable commercial privileges. The State never gave it money, but, more fruitful, the monopoly of the sale of devotional objects. It owns fifteen newspapers and weeklies—the Catholic Church itself is allowed but one. PAX has shops, printing works and publishing businesses, and in all employs thousands of people. Its wealth is devoted to political purposes. It *has* done some useful work. For example, it publishes not only political tracts, but translations of English and French classics.

Needless to say, it is heartily disliked by the bishops, and its "progressive priests" are anathema to them. It has been useful to the government in foreign propaganda, for simple people may imagine that it is a genuine Catholic organization.

You can imagine its attraction for a country priest, working alone, and surrounded by opponents. Here, he thinks, are co-religionists who can take a strong line. And can he really oppose the government? Surely he would do better to follow the PAX line of collaboration with the Communists? After all, there is *something* to be said for their printed programme of ending poverty and seeking the good of all.

There are signs today that the PAX leaders are getting old, and are not as energetic as they used to be. They may be only tools of government policy—but they are rich, and not devoid of influence. Like the Communists, they are almost puritanical in their outlook.

III

Gomulka made a hesitant step towards democracy when he allowed more names on ballot papers than the number of members of parliament to be elected. But liberalism has *not* progressed farther. The Communists make out the lists, and try to ensure that even the "Independents" are in general favourable towards themselves.

The elections of 1965 showed that the three parties—all Communist controlled—had scarcely changed their representation. But the forty-nine non-party delegates included five pro-Vatican Catholics, and five PAX candidates.

Most of the non-party members follow the government line. The maximum opposition they allow themselves, or are allowed, is to abstain from a vote. The five Znap, or Catholics, are more active, but what can they do against 455 opponents? The PAX men always vote with the government, of course.

As the years passed, Gomulka began to drop his mantle of "liberality", and did not part company with his Stalinist colleagues. Inevitably this intensified the conflict between Church and State. And, perhaps also inevitably, Cardinal Wyszynski became somewhat less diplomatic. Scarcely disguising his true beliefs, he described Communism as "immoral and dishonest". In a sermon on Christmas Day, 1964, he said: "Respect for government will be brought about not by the police, the gendarmeries, the penal codes and prisons, but by respect for the rights of human beings." He quoted these rights from the government's own *Journal of Laws*, as "freedom of worship, freedom of conscience, freedom of religious belief, and the right to religious education of children". The Stalinists in the government were not restrained in their comments. And when the Cardinal attempted to address about 200,000 people after the usual Corpus

Christi procession, it was found that the loudspeakers had been cut off. But the Cardinal and twenty-seven bishops were allowed visas to take part in the Ecumenical Council in Rome.

The quarrel came to a head at the end of 1965. Both Cardinal and Church had firmly supported Poland's claim to the Oder-Neisse frontiers, and had welcomed a declaration by the Evangelical Church of West Germany: "A return to the previous status east of the Oder and the Neisse would be impossible today without threatening the existence of the Poles. As a result of the behaviour of the Germans towards their Polish neighbours during the war, the German nation is especially bound to respect the vital rights of the Poles."

Perhaps it was this which prompted the Polish episcopate to invite the German Catholic bishops to the 1966 celebrations of the Polish Millennium. The invitation was actually a lengthy document reviewing the thousand years of Polish-German relations, and granting (and asking) forgiveness for past wrongs. Then it dealt with current problems.

"The Polish Western border on the Oder-Neisse is for Germany, as we well understand, an extremely bitter fruit of the last war of mass extermination, confounded by the suffering of millions of refugees and expelled Germans (carried out in accordance with the inter-allied order of the victorious powers. Potsdam, 1945). Many of the population had left these territories out of fear of the Russian front and had fled westward.

"For our country, which did not emerge from the mass murders as a victorious power, but as one weakened to the extreme, it is a question of existence (not of more *Lebensraum*): unless one would want to concentrate a people of more than 30 million into the narrow corridor of the 'General Government' of 1939 to 1945, without the Western Territories but also without the Eastern Territories, from which millions of Polish people were forced to stream into the Potsdam Western Territories."

The Polish bishops concluded with an appeal to ease the burdens laid on by the past. "Let us try to forget. No more polemics, no more cold war."

The German episcopate replied in a similar spirit, making no effort to minimize German guilt.

"The Polish nation has suffered many horrors at the hands of the Germans and in the name of the German nation. We know that we must bear the results of the war, which are also grievous for our own country. We understand that the period of German occupation has left a burning wound which is healing only with difficulty, even despite good will. . . .

"We realize perfectly what these lands (i.e. the Oder-Neisse territories) mean to Poland today. Yet millions of Germans also had to leave their native land, where their fathers and fore-fathers had lived. . . . We must tell you, lovingly and truthfully, whenever these Germans speak of their homeland, there are—with some exceptions—no aggressive intentions in their words. . . . They are also aware of the new generation now growing up in the lands given to their fathers, and aware that this generation consider these lands its own."

The German response appealed to the principle of Christian love "to overcome hate, enmity and revenge", assured the Poles that they would support any discussion of the problem: they gladly accepted the Polish invitation to the 1,000th birthday of the Catholic Church.

The correspondence might be read as a moderate Christian exchange of views: but the Polish government was furious. How dare the bishops "wilfully enter the realm of foreign policy, which has nothing to do with the religious mission of the Church?" The Oder-Neisse territories were not "a problem", but a fact. And the bishops had made one error, fatal in Communist eyes—they had mentioned the Eastern Territories, seized by Russia.

The quarrel between Church and State was now intensified. Cardinal Wyszynski was refused a visa to visit the Vatican because of the invitation to the German bishops which contained "formulation harmful to the Polish *raison d'état*". What right had he to forgive the Germans? And to ask them to forgive the Poles? Why should they talk of the Potsdam Agreement as "an order of the victors" when it merely authorized the return of Polish lands?

Well-informed Polish sources declared that the onslaught was stimulated by Russia. "The Soviet leaders let it be known that they would appreciate it if the Polish government adopted an intransigent attitude."

The Church denied that it had encroached on the rights of the State—the letter was a Church document: and it had maintained the inviolability of the western frontiers. It complained that the

Press had distorted the invitation, and that it had been mis-interpreted and falsified.[1]

The Cardinal stoutly maintained his attitude. Preaching at Czestochowa early in 1966, he said: "We must stand up to the rulers, princes, and authorities and calmly and bravely proclaim the Gospel. . . . The people can be without kings, leaders, princes, and ministers, but they must never be without their shepherds. The bishop is the good shepherd who faces the wolves and, though wounded, defends the people against hatred, false-hood, and harm. Strike the shepherd and the sheep will dis-perse: often this has been tried and proved true, but whenever it was done in Poland it served only to draw the sheep closer together."

If the Cardinal's reception and the crowded churches were any criteria, it would seem that his last comment was justified. But the government's reply was to ban all foreign bishops. The Polish Church had invited those of over fifty countries, but no visas were granted. The Pope was advised that "a Papal visit to Poland at this time would be inopportune". And the Cardinal was forbidden to make a planned visit to U.S.A. and Canada. The official press denounced him as an anti-Communist, interfering in matters which were not his concern. It declared that his policy of "reconciliation and forgiveness" had encouraged revisionist circles in Germany, and might even lead to the loss of the Western Territories.

Then the conflict became a matter of pin-pricks. Cardinal Wyszynski was due to preach at a small town near Katowice. The local authorities did not interfere; instead, they arranged a double-header football match at the same time, followed by a motor-cycle rally. And TV stations rescheduled several popular programmes for the Sunday morning. In spite of these distrac-tions, the Cardinal attracted an audience of 200,000—to hear him warn the government, "If you respect our rights, we will respect yours," and to honour the Black Madonna of Czestochowa, which was being exhibited around Poland.

[1] For example, the German bishops had said that a new generation was growing up "there"—i.e. in the Oder-Neisse territories—which regarded these lands as their own. But in some press reports the word "there" was omitted, whereby the impression was created that the latter meant not young Poles but the younger generation of German expellees.

The Cardinal was determined that the 1,000th anniversary of the Church should not become part of the State celebrations. (In effect, both dated from the baptism of Mieszko I in 966.) The government propaganda had some success because millions of Poles were not yet prepared to "forgive and forget" the Nazi atrocities. At the same time it weakened the Polish position by creating the impression that the Poles were divided on the Oder–Neisse question, whereas on this point the nation was in fact united.

Gomulka withdrew the charge. He claimed instead that the Cardinal was seeking to break Poland's ties with Europe and to make the country once again a brickwall of Christianity—this time against atheistic Communism. But he seemed to be arguing a confused case. For years the Communists had claimed that there was no significant opposition in Poland. Now, by their unprecedented campaign, they were admitting that there was very serious opposition, for no one could underestimate the power of the Catholic Church in Poland.

They continued the policy of counter-celebrations and petty restrictions. When a copy of the picture of the Black Virgin was carried round the country as part of the Church anniversary, football matches and cycle races were organized at the same time: and the police tried to avoid the welcoming crowds by carrying the picture in their own cars by different routes "for safety".

There was an attempt to build up Archbishop Kominek of Wroclaw as a rival to Wyszynski—he had once spoken in favour of the possibility of co-existence between Church and State. But the archbishop denied that there was disunity in the Church. There were Communist "demonstrations" in the cities, with Catholic marches in reply. And it was noticed that exactly ten years had passed since the riots in Poznan.

The verbal warfare continued, with fantastic confusions. Organizations like PAX wished to erect a monument to Pope John XXIII, "who expressed his favourable attitude toward our Western territories, defining them as recovered after centuries". But the idea was opposed by the Catholic hierarchy—including the Archbishop of Wroclaw! At one celebration at Czestochowa 300,000 pilgrims overcame all the government obstacles, and arrived at the shrine. They carried posters: "We forgive!" The

Communists exhibited counter-propaganda: "We do *not* forgive!" Their slogan, of course, applied only to the West Germans, not to those in the East.

In the meantime, the Church flourishes. According to official estimates, in 1938 there were 22,919,000 Catholics in Poland, constituting 64·8 per cent of the population—of which 30 per cent consisted of Jews, Ukrainians, Bielo-Russians, and other non-Catholic minorities. There were 5,244 parishes and 7,257 churches in Poland before the war: these figures have now increased to 6,558 and 13,200 respectively. There has been a comparable increase in the number of priests. The Catholic University at Lublin has 1,600 students, and the Warsaw Academy of Theology 500. There are 30,000 nuns and 10,000 monks in convents and monasteries. There are no official statistics today, but of the population of nearly 32 million the Catholics claim 30 million as their adherents.

On the last day of the year representatives of Church and State met to discuss ways of ending the "unnecessary and harmful" conflict. No official report was issued, but the atmosphere eased. During the following month President Podgorny visited Pope Paul in the Vatican: while during the Corpus Christi celebrations the police went out of their way to remove obstacles to religious processions.

IV

There is a religious touch to many of the charming folk-tales of Poland.

God created Adam, and was sorry for his loneliness. "I need a helpmate," Adam declared, and God promised His aid. Since the feature of man is strength, then his helpmate should be beautiful, God argued. So He went out into the fields and gathered together the loveliest flowers He could find. He breathed upon them, and the warmth of His breath caused their beauty to exude from their petals. From this loveliness He made a woman glorious and radiant—He called her Mary. Taking her by the hand, He led her to Adam and stood back to enjoy His protégé's pleasure. But Adam looked at her and said: "She is very lovely, but she is too dainty for me; give me instead someone who will work by my side." So God created Eve and gave her to Adam for a helpmate;

and He took Mary back with Him to heaven till the time came for the birth of His own Son.

Christmas is the great day of the Polish year. On the afternoon before Christmas a great stillness falls over Poland: all shops and cafés close: even the streets and fields are deserted. The Poles are in their homes, preparing for the feast of the Christ Child. In every peasant cottage window are candles, to welcome any passing member of the Holy Family: there are no strangers, for everyone is welcome in any home. Every family fasts during the day, but a meal is eaten with the coming of the first star. There is an air of joyous expectancy, of overwhelming peace. Before midnight the bells of the church begin to toll. On foot and in sleighs peasants make their way to midnight Mass. When in the first hour of Christmas the priest elevates the Host, the congregation kneels in glad thanksgiving.

Then follow feasting and merrymaking. There is song and dance and laughter. Children play with their presents: everyone is happy. Yet the significance of the day is never lost in the gaiety. Hay is placed under the tablecloth, in commemoration of the Manger at Bethlehem: candles burn before representations of the Holy Family. Christmas in Poland still means what it should.

A Polish historian has argued that Polish religious conviction is not deep on the intellectual side. Had that been so, he points out, groups with strongly specialized convictions and differences of creed would have broken off from the parent body, as happened in the countries of western Europe. It is certainly true that creeds other than Roman Catholicism have practically no hold whatsoever in Poland. Thus, the historian argues, the Polish religious outlook is largely emotional rather than intellectual. This may be true, but even an emotional doctrine can be deeply held. Indeed, instinctive beliefs are sometimes more powerful in their influences than debated convictions.

The Reformation in the sixteenth century made scarcely any headway in Poland. What influence is left behind was cancelled, strangely enough, by the reactions following the Swedish invasions the following century. I have told how a Swedish Protestant army overran Poland, but was finally repulsed at Czestochowa, where a minute Polish force, assisted by the miracle-working "Black Virgin", forced the invaders to retreat. This was only an outward sign of the Polish faith in their religion. The great mistake the Swedes made was not that they tried to conquer Poland, but that they tried to impose their Protestant religion upon the people. The latter was resisted far more forcibly than the former.

19

CHARIVARIA

ODDMENTS from my notebooks which do not fit into my main theme.

In 1966 Poland celebrated its thousand years of history. A Polish comment was: "We have learned a lot in our first thousand years. The second will be better."

A Catholic priest: "Traditions count for a lot in Poland. The Communists have been here since 1945. We have been here for a thousand years."

B.E.A. and the Polish Airlines, LOT, share a daily service between London and Warsaw. As we learned during the last war, the Poles are good flyers, and their service is very efficient. They fly Russian turbo-jet Iliushin 18s, keep good times, and the refreshments are excellent. They have only one disability. London Airport is crowded, and LOT was rather late in the queue for time-space: so its London-bound service has to leave Warsaw at 6.50 a.m. This entails getting up before 5 a.m., which is not always convenient.

But, despite the daily air service, a letter from London to Poland, or vice versa, still takes a week, plus or minus two days.

"No, we don't look far ahead," said a Pole in a Warsaw department store, where his purchases were extensive. "With a war every twenty years, there is a great temptation to eat, drink and be merry—if we can."

As an English merchant, when I asked how he could do any business with such an unrealistic rate of exchange, explained:
"Oh, all trade is done in sterling or dollars. In effect, the Poles

reprice their goods at a proper value. It is almost like trade by barter.

"The Poles don't like this exchange business. It is so ridiculous that it makes them feel silly. But what can they do? They are tied to the rouble.

"They are good business men. Trade with Britain reaches a tidy sum—and the Poles would like a good deal more."

Polish purchases from Britain are mostly tractors, diesel engines, lorries and heavy machinery. Sales have recently increased considerably.

A very popular programme on Polish TV—the series, *Adventures of Robin Hood*.

Naturally, it attracts critical comment from Communist leaders. Said one: "Robin was obviously a Socialist. But he applied a crude method of equalizing wealth."

Other popular characters are Dr. Finlay, the Saint, and Perry Mason.

It was announced that in 1966 foreign visitors to Poland totalled 1,300,000. Of these 40,000 were from France, 30,000 from Britain, and 20,000 from U.S.A. More than 900,000 came from other Communist countries.

In the same year 800,000 Poles made visits abroad. Most went to other Communist countries, but 12,000 came to Britain.

Many times I was asked questions about Kuron and Modzelewski. I knew little about it, for their case was but little reported in the West. I might have missed it altogether, had not one of the men been a close relative of an old acquaintance.

The two men were lecturers at Warsaw University. In 1965 they were arrested on charges of "revisionism" and actions "harmful to the interests of the Polish state". They had denounced the present government as neither Socialist nor Communist, but merely a bureaucracy. And the revolution they proposed was a revolt against bureaucracy. This, from party members, was indeed a "crime". They were jailed. Disillusionment is a common disease of a revolutionary party: lest it develop into open opposition it must be suppressed.

The Polish theatre is not confined to plays with a Communist leaning. Shakespeare and Shaw are popular—and one of the most successful recent productions was *My Fair Lady*. Eighty per cent of the productions are Polish, including the classics.

There is no Communist Party in Poland: its title is the United Workers Party, which has less of a Russian tang.

But there *is* a Polish Communist Party—in Albania. It is very pro-Chinese, and claims underground adherents inside Poland. Its most remarkable achievement is the distribution of a map of the "New Poland". On this, the Oder-Neisse frontiers remain unchanged, but in the East Poland takes over Kiev and Minsk.

The Russian opinion on this has not been proclaimed, but it can be guessed.

In many Polish towns a new industry has arisen. A man stands beside bathroom scales, and weighs you for a penny.

Restaurant meals show not only the price but the weight of the items on the menu. Your steak is likely to be listed as 90 grammes. But no one could tell me if this applied to the meat before or after cooking: and I was not courageous enough to demand that the steak should be weighed in my presence. Doubtless there is some official regulation which covers this, but I never saw it applied.

Maybe this was because the helpings in Polish restaurants are ample, even generous.

"It now appears that the recent run on tooth powder in the stores was not caused by a sudden upsurge in personal hygiene, but by the heretofore hidden property of that powder—it is a successful substitute for white ceiling paint. From now on the tooth powder will be tinted pink: pink is not yet 'in' for ceilings" —Politzka, Warsaw.

"There was a broken window in a Kielu factory workshop. As the repair fund was already exhausted and the protective clothing fund not yet spent, the window pane was not replaced. Instead, all the workers received warm jackets"—Zycia Gospodarcze, Warsaw.

Despite the unfriendly relations between Poland and West Germany, trade does not languish. It amounts to about 350,000 million marks each way annually. The figure for East and West German trade is around 1,100,000 million marks.

In the last ten years, the number of privately owned cars increased from 21,000 to 181,000. The Warsaw *Slovo Powszechne* explained that many of the cars belonged to families of which two to five members were working, their combined earnings reaching 7,000 zloty or more a month.

But it warns readers that the upkeep of the car will cost at least 7,500 zloty a year. This means that even a rich family will have to think about it. The article declares that such families cut their food expenses by 37 per cent. Meat and culture were the principal victims.

Polish films have achieved a considerable reputation abroad. They are subjected to a political censorship which renders their historic background suspect. For example, the participation of non-Communists in the anti-Nazi resistance was almost negligible, but the party forbade any mention of the very active Home Army.

"After Gomulka" the censorship eased slightly, and the Andrzcj Wajda's films *Kanal* and *Ashes and diamonds* have a closer relationship to historical truth.

The post-war development of the Polish film industry was influenced by Aleksander Ford. It was his picture *Knights of the Teutonic Order* which we had seen at Grünwald—the first attempt at a Polish "spectacular". The censorship still affects the selection and treatment of modern subjects—most, but not all, producers prefer to play for safety. Perhaps because of this, recent Polish films have scarcely fulfilled their early promise. But the industry has some excellent young directors, who may one day come into their own.

In Cracow there was recently a free fight between fans of "beat groups" and young people who preferred Chopin. The Beatles' film in Warsaw provoked youth riots.

The government supports art, but only to its own taste. It commissions innumerable war memorials, and is prepared to use *avant garde* examples whose meaning is obscure—or non-existent.

An old friend, Antoni Slonimski, found himself involved in an argument with the government over the censorship's absurdities. But I was glad to find him well, active and free.

The Warsaw *Polityka* conducted its own poll. It found that the average housewife spent 6½ hours weekly in queues. If that time were spent on socially useful work, the paper concluded, the national income could rise 5 per cent in one year.

The marriage ages are peculiar, but logical. A girl may marry at the age of eighteen: a man must be twenty-one, i.e. after finishing his military service, eighteen to twenty.

In 1966 there were 6·3 marriages per 1,000 of the population. In the immediate post-war years there were 10: before the war 8·2.

When Richard Nixon, former vice-president of U.S.A., visited Warsaw in 1959 he was hailed by a crowd of a quarter of a million Poles. In 1967 he planned another visit on a "fact-finding" tour. The government refused him a visa.

In conversation with senior officers of the Polish Tourist Ministry, I pleaded for the abolition of visas—and visa fees. They have already been abolished for nationals of certain countries— why not for all? The visa is moreover not granted at the discretion of the local Consul; it has to be referred to Warsaw. This can occasion delay—our own journey was put off from day to day for five days because the authority for the visa had not arrived.

I quoted the finest speech made by Ernest Bevin when Foreign Minister: "My policy? It is simple—I want to go to Victoria Station and buy a ticket to anywhere I like without any of this damned foolery about passports and visas."

We pretend that the world is progressing. But, prior to 1914, a British citizen could travel in any country in Europe, except Russia and Turkey, not only without a visa, but *without a passport*!

I also recommended a realistic rate of exchange—I have already given details of the confusion between the different rates: and a wider range of shopping facilities—even picture postcards are

Peasant woman
with her calf

There is plenty of
up-to-date
mechanized farming
as well

Peasant market

Carts with fruit and vegetables wait outside a church on Sunday—as soon as the service is over the exchange of produce will begin

seldom obtainable. The result of all the restrictions officially applied means that the average tourist in Poland spends only one-half of what he does in Austria or one-third of what he does in France.

I was surprised to be told that my ideas received strong support from the PAX organization!

In spite of all petty difficulties, Poland is still more than worth a visit.

During the First World War I made the acquaintance of a fair-sized colony of Polish miners working in the French pits near Lens.

When Poland was re-established, many of these exiles returned. But when a Communist government was imposed on the country, more Poles fled to France, and were joined by others after the troubled upheaval of 1956. This time Paris was the chosen place of settlement.

Many of this fresh group of exiles were young and had technical qualifications, so they were welcomed by French industry. Their attitude towards work is unusual. In Poland they had to make ends meet by various stratagems, legal or otherwise. In France they are paid for work—so they are prepared to work hard and for long hours.

Most keep in touch with their families in Poland, but have no thought of returning: nor do the families resent this, for the exiles are generous with their gifts.

The first of the new batches of emigrés were usually old and very anti-Communist. The later ones are young and uninterested in politics. They represent Poland's "brain drain".

Just before our Polish visit, my wife and I had been touring in Turkey. There, over the Bosphorus from Istanbul, we found the Polish village of Polonescoy.

Over a hundred years ago Poles in the Russian army deserted to the Turks. The Sultan allowed them to stay, and they founded a village. There today the families speak archaic Polish as well as Turkish, and their village is an island of Catholicism in a Moslem sea. They are happy and prosperous, good citizens, and have no wish to change their way of life.

Poland exports mistletoe to England. The trade is growing, and according to one Polish newspaper this indicates "the increased sexuality of the Anglo-Saxons".

Could it be right?

In a Communist country all aspects of life are organized, and most activities need a licence.

Hitch-hiking, for example. To indulge in this activity you buy a licence for 50 zloty. This you wave as you stand by the roadside. A driver picks you up: at the end of the journey you give him coupons for the number of kilometres covered—your licence contains enough coupons for 2,500 kilometres.

The driver sends in his coupons to a central office, where they are included in a lottery. He may win a radio; or, if he is very, very lucky, even a car.

You may not hitch-hike without your Auto-Stop licence. There is one other restriction—you must have at least 300 zloty in your possession. If not, you lose your licence.

The hitch-hiking season is from June 1st to September 30th. Most of the exponents of the art of getting free lifts are students, of course. Girls form only about 10 per cent of the total—but can be useful.

One tendency is for groups to form at strategic points—to the dismay of drivers who could give a lift to one or two, but who boggle at an argument with thirty or forty. A favourite plan is to get the prettiest girl in a party to wave her card by the roadside. She should be appropriately dressed—tight jeans and a low-cut blouse or a sweater which emphasizes her figure. Few drivers can resist such a bait. Only at the last moment will she reveal her friends lurking in the background.

British students have successfully stopped cars by waving Union Jacks. Others have affixed cards printed with their destinations on hats or packs. In recent years the hobby has included whole families travelling together. There has been at least one example of a hitch-hiking honeymoon! And there are unconfirmed stories about parsimonious car-owners who lay up their vehicles for the summer and thumb lifts themselves!

I should say that the behaviour of Polish hitch-hikers has in general been admirable.

Tea is served in glasses—which are very hot.

Milk is usually available for breakfast, if specially requested. Later in the day lemon is substituted.

If you are interested in photography, take a supply of colour films with you to Poland. There are none on sale. The government, faithful to Comicon, uses an East German colour film for official purposes. It is not true to colour, but shows only brown tints. And the whole picture fades away in a couple of years.

The opera chosen for the gala performance on the occasion of President de Gaulle's visit was Gounod's *Faust*. "It suited him," the Poles commented. "The old man who wanted to be young again."

The Poles were chuckling over an incident first mentioned in Russian newspapers.

Old soldiers will remember the classic story of the colonel in the trenches who sent back a message: "Send reinforcements. Am going to advance." This was passed back by word of mouth at a dozen stages. By the time it reached headquarters it had become: "Send three and fourpence. Am going to a dance."

This after transmission in a single language. A Russian newspaper experimented with the fallibilities of translation. It took a paragraph from one of Gogol's short stories: "She used to gossip, eat boiled beets of a morning, and swear like a trooper; and which ever of these various occupations she was engaged in, the expression on her face never altered for a moment. That is something, generally speaking, of which only women are capable."

This was passed along a chain of twenty translators, including English, German, Japanese and Arabic. It emerged thus: "Having drunk the fruit-salad, she threw the old junk out of the hovel while he beat the tom-tom with rapture."

And then we bemoan the lack of understanding between nations!

I have mentioned the homely, friendly democracy of the Polish people. A new taxi was designed with a glass screen between driver and passengers. The drivers protested vigorously. The innovation would eliminate all the pleasures of driving, such as discussing taxes, pedestrians and militiamen (police) with the passengers.

"Revisionism" is a common failing in Communist countries, but sometimes it is applauded.

Prince Josef Poniatowski was killed while covering Napoleon's retreat from Leipzig with his Polish troops. A Danish sculptor made a statue of him in 1830, when Poland was under the Partitions. The statue was whisked off by the Czar of Russia, and languished on a rural estate. In 1923 it was ceremoniously installed in front of the tomb of the Unknown Warrior. And in 1944 it was blown up by the Nazis.

After the war, the city of Copenhagen made a copy of the statue, and presented it to Warsaw. The Danes did not know that Poniatowski was *persona non grata* to the Communist government, which hid his statue on an obscure site in Warsaw.

But in 1965 it was decided that this decision needed revision, and that Poniatowski deserved honour. So the statue has now been erected on a splendid site—in front of the building where the government ministers meet!

Statues of Pilsudski have *not* been reinstated in favour. But the Poles believe that many of them have been stored away against the time when the Communist outlook on him will be "revised".

In Spain Napoleon saw his soldiers ambushed and massacred by the Spanish in a great gorge. Suddenly the cavalry of the Polish Legion appeared, and attempted to gallop through the ambush. They were cut to pieces.

"Heroes!" Napoleon commented.

"Sire, they are mad," said one of his generals. (Some accounts read "drunk" instead of "mad".)

"I wish all my officers were as mad as the Poles," Napoleon declared.

Polish heroism is famous, but it has always included a touch of madness. In 1939, Polish cavalry charged German tanks: "*C'est magnifique but ce n'est pas la guerre.*"

My latest journey round Poland did not take me to Lublin, which I had previously visited.

It is an interesting old town, one of the oldest strongholds in the country. Battered more than once, it has always recovered, and is now the cultural and industrial centre of south-east Poland. To the visitor, its most fascinating corners are the old town, its richly decorated houses fully restored, and the castle—which has its own chapel, with Byzantine murals.

Lublin was for long the principal centre of Polish Jewry. Here gathered the scholars and rabbis: the town produced far more than its fair share of Jewish artists, musicians—a focus of Jewish culture.

The 45,000 Jews of Lublin were among Hitler's earliest victims —an uneducated man himself, he always struck first at the intelligentsia. They had not far to go. Two miles from the town was the extermination camp of Majdanek, where nearly half a million Jews and tens of thousands of Poles were slain. Conditions there were almost indescribable.

Just after the war I met a friend, one of the few who had escaped from Majdanek, and whose mind as well as his body still showed traces of his ordeal. He said: "What a task we face—to make the air of Europe fit for a free man to breathe."

Near Lublin is the delightful old town of Kazimierz Dolny, with arcaded houses and the ruined castle of Casimir the Great. Here there is a panoramic view of the Vistula and its wide valley.

It was here that Casimir fell in love with Esther, a beautiful Jewish girl: and hence he threw open the frontiers of Poland to Jewish refugees from Russia—to the economic advantage of his own land.

Lublin is also the home of a famous Catholic university—which has survived all misfortunes.

The reputation of Polish horses is international. Sales have been made to England, France, Germany, U.S.A., Mexico and Egypt, and Polish riders have acquitted themselves well at our horse shows—on Polish horses. One Polish stallion sold in America for 16,000 dollars—not a high figure in the international market, but *very* high for Poland.

"A truly elegant woman never wears the latest styles, but dresses according to the next-to-last collection so as to give herself time to adjust psychologically to the new models"—*Express Wieczorny*, Warsaw.

Hitler's megalomania included gypsies as well as Jews. By the end of the war, only a few hundred gypsies survived in Poland. Most of them belonged to the old gypsy "royal" family, the Kwiek. (The last "king" was murdered by his followers in 1950 because of his close ties with the secret police.)

A government commission attempted to organize gypsy "co-operatives" for kettle mending. It recommended that all aid should be given in the form of work, not money, "which might lead to sanction of begging". Gypsy children must go to school, where influences would counteract "a return to nomadic life". Gypsies should be "settled". They should be prohibited from fortune telling, "which gives them a good income but draws them away from constructive employment".

But the gypsies prefer their own way of life.

Three hundred gypsies "emigrated" from Poland to West Germany—without passports or visas. They caused so much trouble that they were not allowed to stay. And in 1960 German customs officers opened some large crates *en route* from Poland, duly sealed. Fifty gypsies sprang out, all carrying a reserve fund of gold!

It was an excellent idea to celebrate the 1,000th anniversary of Poland by building a thousand new schools. Actually, the figure was exceeded.

Eighty million zloty were collected from the people. Some workers gave a day's work—a "Miners' Sunday" raised sixty million zloty. School youth groups earned 170 million. And Poles abroad subscribed liberally.

"Before Gomulka" membership of the Socialist Youth Union was almost compulsory for young people, and its membership out-numbered two million. It collapsed completely in 1956 but was revived a year later. Official newspapers complained of the "passiveness and indifference of youth". Not until 1960 did the numbers of the revived organization begin to grow, and the membership has now reached three-quarters of a million. Of these, 48·3 per cent are young workers and 47·3 per cent pre-university students.

In 1962 I was very sorry to learn of the death of an old friend, Professor Adam Krzyzanowski, a famous historian, for long president of the Cracow Academy. He had made a firm stand against the "interpretation", or falsification, of history on Marxist lines. Among other fancies, all references to the minorities in Eastern Poland were excluded: they were Russian interests. Even Lithuania—for so long united with Poland—was omitted.

Krzyzanowski not only wrote history—he had lived it. He told me stories of the days when he was a Polish delegate to the Peace Conference of 1919: and of earlier times when he was appointed to a public office by the then ruler of Cracow—the Emperor Francis Joseph of Austria!

In 1955 a hundred senior students were asked to choose a great figure in history. Lenin got one vote, Stalin none: nor did the Communist leaders of Poland appear on the list. Easily leading the field, with forty-eight votes, was the Polish patriot, Kosciuszko.

In 1966 the students of Cracow Academy were asked to name their hero. The majority selected John F. Kennedy. He was followed by Yuri Gagarin, President de Gaulle, Pope John XXIII, and Karl Marx.

After Stalin's death in 1953 newspapers in Poland and its neighbours began to explain that Socialism did not mean sartorial shabbiness and uniformity. Polish women seized on this idea enthusiastically. Women's magazines promptly appeared: newspapers had their "women's pages". And happy the Polish lady who had access to a French fashion magazine.

At first only the wives of the new élite could afford good clothes. Gradually Polish factories began to copy "models". Today Polish women are smartly dressed—and we saw plenty of miniskirts.

We also visited Moda Polska, a leading Polish fashion house. It is government owned, but the manageress told us that the trade is left entirely to her discretion—with frequent visits to Paris and London to study their designs. Models paraded before us in the latest frocks. Helen was deeply impressed by some of the Polish materials—especially Polish silk, strong, and hand-painted in original and charming designs.

Polish men, like their fellows everywhere, were not so enterprising. Most of their suits were bought ready made, and often showed it.

Poles grumbled at the quality of their suits, and were not comforted when told that these were at least better than those in Russia and many of the other Communist countries.

And life is freer and happier in Poland than with her neighbours.

"Oh, yes. The others like to visit us—the Russians especially. They find the shops of Warsaw much better than those of Moscow. And they tell us that our hotels and dance bands are better, too."

"The industrialization of the Polish economy has been a Polish achievement," said a Warsaw acquaintance.

"With Russian help," I suggested.

"Very little. Russian loans and credits have amounted to less than 2 per cent of our capital investment."

20

NOT THE END OF THE POLISH STORY

I

LET us go back to Chapter 6, and take up the story of Poland from there.

Poland is a People's Republic. In theory it is not a Communist state: the dominant force is the P.Z.P.R., the United Workers' Party, formed by a shot-gun wedding between Communists and Socialists. This also controls parties purporting to represent the Peasants and the Intelligentsia.

There is much talk about "the Polish road to Socialism", but until the emergence of Gomulka there was little difference between Poland and the other Communist countries. It was Gomulka who earlier suggested "Communism by persuasion" (or, more colloquially, "Communism without tears"), and the Polish Stalinist government promptly jailed him for six years. He was a Pole, and realized that his people were Western in outlook—very different from those of Russia. Despite his Communist upbringing and opinions, he is remembered by the Poles as the man who stood up to the Russians in 1956—and who saved Poland from a tragedy like that of Hungary.

He shows no trace of the "personality cult". He lives quite austerely. ("He has no needs," say the Poles. "So how can he even appreciate the fact that *we* have?") There are no giant-sized posters of him in the streets. He has to keep up the appearance of democracy, and he knows it, for he is a highly intelligent man.

He has had more than one narrow escape. In 1937 the leaders of the Polish Communist Party gathered in Moscow, at Stalin's invitation. Stalin then accused them of "deviationism", which can mean anything; he had the whole lot murdered. But Gomulka escaped the holocaust—he was safe in Poland, in one of Pilsudski's prisons!

At first the 1945 government approved his plan for the gradual path to socialism. There would be no enforced collectivization, he declared, and only heavy industry would be nationalized—at first, it was understood. Everyone agreed with him. He was given the specific task of incorporating the Oder-Neisse provinces into Poland, and he succeeded brilliantly.

But four years later his Cabinet colleagues were cataloguing his "crimes". Bierut reported on "enemies who succeed in insinuating themselves into the ranks of the Party", with Gomulka as one of the "enemies". Fantastic rumours were circulated about "the accused"—Gomulka. There was no trial: he was simply flung into jail for six years.

His real "crime" was that he did not believe that Stalin was infallible. He had much sympathy with Tito of Yugoslavia. He protested against the power of Russian "advisers" in Poland, and its virtual rule from Moscow. He objected to the falsified statistics—the claims that the workers were breaking all records in production, while there was nothing in the shops. He objected even more strongly to the activities of the secret police: while he was in jail, his friend Marian Spychalski was being tortured in a neighbouring cell.

But, although a Stalinist government was in power, it consisted of Poles. Prisoners might be tortured, but they were not actually murdered. No immense statues of Stalin were scattered around Poland—these in the other Communist countries had to be hurriedly scrapped when Khrushchev revealed the true character of the Russian dictator.

It was this episode which changed the course of events in Poland. The Stalinists were revealed as the sycophants of a monster. Doubts appeared in the highest circles of Communism—and among the ordinary people there was a great discontent. Khrushchev made his peace with Tito, apologizing for his predecessor's "errors". The Stalin myth was exploded. Gomulka was released, but was kept under house arrest. His "crime" now looked different: he had been right!

Economic discontent led to the Poznan riots and the fall of the Stalinists. Many Poles would explain this differently. Not even the Stalinists had dared to close the Catholic churches—but they had arrested Cardinal Wyszynski. Hundreds of thousands of Poles made the pilgrimage to Czestochowa to pray for the

Cardinal's release and for the end of an oppressive government. In the autumn of 1956 both of these prayers were answered.

Confronted with the Poznan riots, the government had paused, and in its fear had turned to Gomulka—who had defied Khrushchev, and won!

In Poland Gomulka's popularity was overwhelming. He was cheered by Catholics as well as by the Communists. His first moves were liberal, and very promising. But then disappointment set in.

II

Khrushchev always was adept at adjusting his views to a fluid situation. He accepted his defeat—and promptly made friends with Gomulka.

He needed friends. Hungary was ablaze, and the Poles were intensely sympathetic with the Hungarian struggle for freedom. The government did nothing: but ordinary people began to send supplies to Budapest. Later they realized the fate from which they themselves had escaped. This was all to Gomulka's credit: evidently he had foreseen the possibility of this.

Gomulka soon changed his mind—maybe owing to the influence of Khrushchev. By May, 1957, he had adopted the Soviet line and had justified the Russian intervention in Hungary, "for the sake of preserving the peace and crushing the counter-revolution".

Counter-revolution! And Nagy, the Hungarian Gomulka, was executed by the Russians!

This was the beginning of the gradual decline of confidence in Gomulka. His first moves had been joyously received. He had abolished the secret police: he had allowed the collective farms to disband: he had lifted a corner of the Iron Curtain, and tens of thousands of Poles were now in contact with the West—through relatives, newspapers, radio and tourists. Private enterprise had been guaranteed its present limited rights: religious education was now permitted in the schools: industrial reforms were promised—as were many others.

Few of these materialized. Right from the start Gomulka had included Stalinists in his cabinet. Some were men who simply could neither believe in Stalin's crimes even now, nor accept his denigration. To them the whole episode was like a nightmare; in every way it contradicted their faith. As the nightmare receded, their faith revived. The democratization of the party was "deviationism": Lenin had never favoured it: Stalin was utterly against it. "The whole business was fantastic," a Polish Communist explained to me. "I simply could not believe what Khrushchev said. It was like telling a Christian that St. Peter was a wicked liar. I recalled the great things that Stalin had done. He may have made mistakes, but he had never strayed from the party line. I could not believe what I heard."

Nor could others of his kind. The new freedoms could be exploited—with the easing of censorship writers poured out their many and valid complaints. The Stalinists perceived that this sort of thing, this denunciation of Marxist discipline, if permitted indefinitely, would mean the end of their creed. They began to stiffen: inside the party, dogmatism again reared its head. Gomulka himself was criticized—although he had begun to sway in the direction of his critics. He was determined to keep on good terms with Russia, whatever the cost. His frequent contacts with the Soviet leaders may have affected his outlook.

Some of the new freedoms were retained. Others were lost. Gradually the censorship of words and ideas became stricter. At an interval of ten years I saw many signs of the return of Stalinism—not among the people, but in the party. Protests were forcibly repressed. Workers lost their right to strike. The contest with the Catholic Church had become more bitter. Economic ties with Russia were strengthened, but on fairer trade terms.

Gomulka's popularity slowly began to fade. This was scarcely his own fault. People had expected too much of him. In 1956 they thought that Communism was on its way out, and rejoiced. But Gomulka was a Communist, and emphasized that more clearly year after year.

Gomulka's liberalism may have been only skin-deep. A Stalinist pamphlet was published in Poland in 1965. It bitterly criticized the "revisionism" of the government: the party line had been distorted, it averred—it was moving away from Lenin, the dictatorship of the proletariat, the theory of the class struggle, and a planned economy. "Private enterprise is growing as in the best of capitalist times. The rich peasant flays the tenth skin from the worker. Corruption and speculation are spreading. Hooliganism is increasing: also demoralization and banditry." It declared that the working people had been disgracefully cheated by the demagogic slogans of the October Revolution of 1956. The only solution, of course, was a return to the basic principles of Stalinism.

Maybe one event had led to this pamphlet's production. The Communist government of Poland had made a deal with Krupps! The German firm would build factories in Poland, and supply equipment, managers and technicians. The Poles would make lorries, machinery and technical instruments, which would be sent to Germany for final processing and sale.

Krupps are no longer armament makers. But the Stalinists are years or even a generation behind the times in their outlook, and their outmoded prejudices led to furious criticism.

III

Our journey had emphasized that there was no doubt about the subject nearest to the Polish heart.

By the time we returned to Warsaw, President de Gaulle was there. He was to address the Seym, and I managed to secure a ticket—only one, but Helen was very understanding.

When I arrived in the press gallery, parliament was already in session. A deputy at the rostrum read interminably from a prepared script. The Press representatives ignored him, and chatted among themselves. A group of French and Swedish newsmen about me discussed the wooden seats we sat on. They were an advantage, it was agreed. A comfortable seat induced sleep; but, if you did fall asleep here, the seat would slide you on to the floor.

The deputies were as crowded in their seats as our own M.P.s. Not for them the luxury of Washington. One would have described them as a bourgeois-looking lot, in their best Sunday clothes.

The serious business began. De Gaulle received a very warm reception, the deputies standing to applaud him. In previous speeches he had emphasized Poland's position in Central Europe: he pointed out that France had got clear of the American power bloc, and suggested that Poland should pursue a similar policy with Russia.

De Gaulle had made it quite clear earlier that, though he agreed with Poland's frontiers, he thought nothing of Marxist ideology: he believes that eventually nationalism will prove to be more powerful. In one of his earlier Press conferences he said: "Doubtless the Communist régime recognizes that, while it may be ruling over Poland, Czechoslovakia and the other countries of Eastern Europe, it has not won the people over, and that there is no doubt that if the populations of these countries could express themselves freely, they would reject this régime by a tremendous majority."

But when, to the Polish parliament, de Gaulle advocated reconciliation with West Germany, Gomulka could hardly wait to set him straight. Poland's ties of friendship with Russia were fundamental, he said—and her treaty with the German Democratic Republic was a basic guarantee of Poland's security. He gratefully accepted the visitor's confirmation of the Oder-Neisse frontier, but rejected every other idea de Gaulle put forward.

Yet the French President had an enthusiastic welcome from the Polish people. "It was not his speeches," said a man in the street. "It was just his presence. We have always been close friends of the French, and de Gaulle's visit was a sign that Poland was not forgotten."

But now, facing the Seym, he kept to platitudes—the historic friendship between France and Poland, comments on Vietnam and the Middle East. He looked his age and was obviously tired—small wonder, for his programme was exacting. Yet he scarcely referred to his script. He spoke for only ten minutes, and his final paragraph was to the effect that if Poland wished to come closer to France, to contribute to European unity, then France was ready. On this note he concluded—not to a standing ovation, but to merely polite applause.

Only one sentence had aroused his audience to enthusiasm —and in that he referred to the irrevocability of Poland's frontier.

The Press looked and was disappointed. Nothing fresh, no fireworks. Some men declared that they had expected de Gaulle to shout *Vive la Pologne libre*, but his phrases were much more diplomatic.

Gomulka followed him. He is not a dramatic speaker. His

conventional reference to Poland's great ally, the Soviet Union, evoked no response. But when he declared that since 1944 de Gaulle had firmly supported Poland's western frontier, there was a frantic burst of applause.

He was very restrained in his thanks to Poland's guest. Two days earlier, after a dinner at Gdansk, de Gaulle had unloosed one of his minor indiscretions. He suggested that Poland should follow France in attempting to attain a much wider independence. This sentence was *not* reported in the Polish newspapers.

De Gaulle's theme throughout his visit was his emphasis on Western, Central and Eastern Europe, with the suggestion that the Central section—i.e. Poland—should move away from the East. Gomulka did not agree, but in his speech he was polite in that he did not raise awkward points for his visitor. For example, he did not mention France's attitude on nuclear weapons, which must surely provoke the demand for such things by the Germans. Nor had de Gaulle mentioned East Germany—except to suggest its reunification with West Germany! "The western frontier of the Socialist world is on the Elbe," Gomulka had said, but his visitor offered no confirmation.

The East German reaction was sour. Nor was that of Bonn very friendly. The official government spokesman accepted de Gaulle's remarks about the inviolability of the Polish frontiers as casual, but added: "History shows that the territories now under Polish administration have been for centuries German soil from which the German inhabitants were wrongly driven." This half-truth was doubtless spoken in deference to the feelings of the expellees. The latter were particularly upset. De Gaulle had visited Zabrze, once called Hindenburg, a town in the Oder-Neisse territories— he was the first Western leader to acknowledge their existence by a visit: it was of old German tradition, but he referred to it as "the most Polish of cities". But this was true—today.

"That was it—the Oder-Neisse stuff," murmured my neigh-bour in the Press gallery at the Seym. "But there's no news in it. We knew this before. Now, if only he had said, *Vive la Pologne libre!*"

That is one of the features of modern life—old news is no news. But this is not true in Poland. Any reference to the Oder-Neisse frontier is news.

IV

Let us recapitulate the outstanding points concerning the Oder-Neisse frontier, and add pieces of information not yet noted.

1. The Poles emphasize that the Oder-Neisse provinces were *recovered*. On all possible occasions they point out that the regions were once Polish. This is true. The reader will have remarked the frequent references to the Piast dynasty in our journey to the Oder.

But is the historic claim enough? If so, Mussolini might have been justified in claiming the boundaries of the Roman Empire—including England. Every frontier in Europe has known many changes, and to restore their "historic" boundaries would create a confusion infinitely worse than that of the present. It would be a stronger Polish argument to point out that there was nothing new in the present frontier—and that the beaten side in war has always lost territory.

East Prussia was part of Poland from 1466 to 1772. West Pomerania was ruled by Slavonic princes until 1637. Silesia passed under Bohemian rule in 1348. True, its princes belonged to the Polish royal family, but the province was no longer Polish territory. It was seized by Prussia in 1740.

Hence the historic claim is not strong. Probably the other term used in Poland, "the New Territories", is more real than "the Oder-Neisse provinces".

2. On the other hand, the lost territory still (in 1919) contained a considerable Polish population, despite the intense process of Germanization. The *German* census of 1910 showed 57 per cent of the people speaking Polish as their first language.

The First World War, and the re-birth of Poland, brought back three-quarters of these to Polish rule. The plebiscite in Masuria, we have seen, had confusing results.

3. The German lands east of the Oder were not especially important to the Reich—and for long people had been moving to the more prosperous West—the *Ostflucht* (flight from the East) totalled 4·6 million people between 1852 and 1939. The eastern lands were predominantly agricultural, farmed at a lower level than the rest of Germany. The lands east of the Oder supplied only 3 per cent of the food used by the rest of the country.

The eastern provinces had not kept pace with the economic development of Germany as a whole. They covered 24 per cent of the area, but had only 14 per cent of the population, and supplied only 10 per cent of the national income. So poor was their economy that the German parliament voted *Osthilfe*—financial aid and subsidies—in most years. There was a constant labour shortage—met by Polish transients seeking seasonal work.

British and American official opinion was not affected by "soft" feelings towards the Nazis, but by the problem of feeding the Germans. Britain, especially, very short of food herself, had over a million refugees in her battered and half-dead industrial zone of Germany. True, the Oder-Neisse provinces were not tremendously important for food supplies, but every little would help. Now they would supply nothing except millions of refugees as consumers!

4. The German surrender in 1945 was complete, and her territory was legally at the disposal of the Allies.

For what it is worth, the German Democratic Republic (East Germany) finally recognized the Oder-Neisse frontiers in 1950.

5. Britain, America and France delayed recognition on two grounds—the inter-Allied agreement at Yalta read that the question should be held over until the end of the war, and a democratic election should be held in Poland. This was not done.

The decision to withhold the final word on the Oder-Neisse frontiers until a peace treaty is signed has been seized by some German nationalists to claim that the frontier is illegal. But the German surrender was unconditional, and the Potsdam declaration said specifically that the territory to the east of the Oder and Neisse had ceased to be German land. The Potsdam Agreement placed the administration of these lands in Polish hands, including the evacuation of the German population and Polish resettlement.

Not all Germans expect the return of the Oder-Neisse provinces. Some are very frank—I have quoted examples elsewhere. The editor of the German magazine *Stern* wrote:

> The frontiers of our state have been fixed, and to a certain extent we ourselves are responsible for the fact that they are so restricted. Why should we harbour illusions for the return of settlers to the German fatherland in East Prussia, Silesia and the Sudetens? Without a war these territories will not be returned—and a war would certainly seal the final downfall of Germany.

16

This is indeed a crucial argument. He went on to point out that revisionist claims aroused suspicion both east and west, and thus postponed the reunification of West and East Germany.

Churchill and Roosevelt at Yalta would have handed over the frontiers to a democratic Poland, but jibbed at what looked like being a Russian satellite. Anthony Eden, the Foreign Secretary, said frankly: "We need not make the same concessions to the Lublin Poles which we were prepared to make to M. Mikolajczyk."

On the other hand, M. Arciszewski—the anti-Russian Socialist who succeeded Mikolajczyk as Polish leader-in-exile—said, while demanding Silesia and East Prussia, "We do not want to expand our frontier in the West to include eight or ten million Germans. That is, we do not want Breslau and Stettin. We claim just our ethnical and historic Polish territories which are under German domination."

Both Churchill and Roosevelt agreed to the Oder as a frontier, whatever the political future of Poland. They would certainly have agreed to the Eastern Neisse as the southern section of the frontier. Churchill said that if he had been re-elected in 1945 he would have risked a quarrel with Russia over the Neisse line.

In his famous "Iron Curtain" speech at Fulton (March, 1946), he said that "the Russian-dominated Polish government has been encouraged to make enormous and wrongful inroads upon Germany". This had an enormous impact in Poland. The British had been fooled, and once again were going to be "soft" with the Germans! Even non-Communist Poles swung towards Russia. Stalin had seized a slice of Poland, but at least he did hand over compensation at German expense. There was no dispute about East Germany and Danzig, which had asked for trouble—and got it.

6. When the Western leaders raised the question of the evacuation of Germans from the Oder and Masurian terrirories, Stalin asserted constantly that there was nothing required to be done, since the Germans had "all run away". He was completely misinformed. Many had indeed fled before the advancing Russians, and the male population of the provinces scarcely existed—men of sixty-five and boys of fifteen had been flung into battle.

The Nazis delayed the order for the civilians to evacuate—and thereby incurred hundreds of thousands of casualties. And many people *did* flee, without orders. The pre-war population of the provinces was 8·8 million. By the end of the war this had been reduced to 3·5 million.

The sufferings of the refugees was placed by the Germans on the Poles. The blame should have been placed on the Nazis.

"To a demagogue, refugees are what blood in the water is to a shark, and the refugee problem is large enough to create a revolutionary situation," wrote *The Times*. It did not prove as serious as that, but the demagogues had their day—and the moderate leaders could scarcely disagree with them in view of their popular support.

7. The territories acquired by Poland had been fought over, and were in a terrible condition. Forty per cent of all houses had been destroyed. Ninety per cent of the livestock had been looted. Of 9,255 industrial plants, two-thirds were in ruins. Fifty per cent of all bridges, 63 per cent of the railways, and 97 per cent of rolling stock were destroyed.

8. The Poles were instructed by the three Great Powers to transfer the Germans left in the "New Territories" "in an orderly and humane manner". This the Poles attempted to do. They were frustrated by the complete disruption of communications and by the severity of the weather. There *were* cases of Germans dying of cold in cattle trucks, though the figures were distorted by propaganda. The statistics reveal the true situation. Of 2,160,000 Germans officially expelled (others made their own way) a total of 1,136 died on the way.

In all, 1·8 million German "expellees and refugees" were resettled in the Soviet zone of Germany, and 1·2 million in the British zone before the end of 1947. Then the process was halted because of the intense cold, but 170,000 more travelled west in succeeding summers.

9. The Poles, save for their Communist leaders, did not accept the loss of their eastern provinces, including the ancient Polish university city of Lwow. But, brushing aside the claim that the Oder-Neisse territories had been "recovered" by Poland after centuries of escheatment, most regarded them as some compensation for their appalling sufferings at Nazi hands. A referendum showed 995,854 voters against the new western frontier—but 10,534,697 in favour of it.

10. The territories were occupied by Poles who

(a) had lived there under the Germans
(b) had been expelled by the Russians from Eastern Poland
(c) came from other and over-populated areas of Poland.

The government was naturally anxious to arouse the enthusiasm of (a)—the "autochones"—the Poles who had lived in Germany before the war. (The Germans called them *Wasser-Polacken*, suggesting that they were of watered-down stock, of mixed ancestry. Some of them were, and had to choose between Germany and Poland.) These already owned a total of 340,000 hectares. To these the government added 180,000 hectares, which made possible an allocation of 12 hectares per peasant. Once the ravages of the war had been cleared, and the disastrous "collective" experiment had collapsed, a farm of 12 hectares would yield a living.

In the early days there was a good deal of bad feeling between the autochones and the Polish newcomers, who had been accustomed to a different way of life. The latter regarded the natives as too German—and some of them did have an admixture of German blood. The autochones in their turn despised the immigrants for their rough manners, their poverty, and their ignorance of modern farming. The ill-feeling has now diminished, but still crops up in the rural areas.

The Oder-Neisse territories have a young population—42 per cent born since the war. The local birthrate is high. In 1950 it reached more than 40 per thousand. (The average for the whole of Poland was 30·7.) But with the general tendency to smaller families the rate is now only 22 (for all Poland, 19). A new surge in the natural increase is expected in the period 1970–5.

Despite the diminishing tendency in natural increase, Poland is still well to the fore. Estimates suggest that by 1970 Poland will be sixth in Europe in population—after Russia, West Germany, Britain, Italy and France.

The Germans stimulated rumours after the war that the Poles would never be able to populate the provinces. The pre-war population was 8·8 million (including 1·2 million Poles). The 1967 figure is 8·5 million, and demographers forecast the passing of the pre-war figure by 1970.

11. The development of industry has been considerable—more

than 500 per cent of pre-war. Wroclaw, Opole and Gdansk are
the principal centres. A few important figures are:

		1937	1964
Electricity	million K.w.h.	3,900	14,398
Coal, including			
brown	thousand tons	34,466	43,215
Cement	thousand tons	1,328	1,898
Machine tools	tons	1,320	17,473
Steel	thousand tons	520	1,575

Before the war, the shipbuilding industry produced only
coastal and fishing vessels. Now Poland is the ninth biggest
builder of ocean-going ships in the world.

Agriculture cannot change overnight. The mass flight of the
German population left considerable areas temporarily de-
populated and fields weed-choked. A plague of mice followed!
By 1950 agriculture had recovered and more: since then—and
especially since 1956—the advance has been impressive. In 1950
the New Territories produced 3,433,000 tons of the four main
grains. By 1965 it exceeded 4 million. The potato yield was even
more impressive, and the cattle population increased from 633,000
in 1946 to 3 million in 1965. Other branches of agriculture have
also progressed, and methods improved—the 18,000 tractors of
1950 had exceeded 50,000 by 1965. The Territories produce
considerably more than average quantities over Poland as a
whole—with 30 per cent of the farmland they produce 40 per
cent of the agricultural yields.

12. In all aspects of human life, the New Territories have been
fully integrated with Poland. Education and culture are well up
to local standards.

13. A suggestion put forward by Professor Henry Kissinger, of
Harvard, was scorned as likely to divide the Communist countries.
He proposed the withdrawal of Russian troops from East
Germany, free elections under neutral supervision, and thereafter
a neutral state on the Swiss or Austrian patterns. After fifteen
years a referendum should be held to determine the form of
unification with West Germany—maybe a confederation, or
perhaps East Germany as a federal state. In return, West Germany
should renounce nuclear arms and recognize the Oder-Neisse
frontiers as final.

Ten years earlier one of my own suggestions was under discussion. It was prompted by one detail I noticed—that in Lower Silesia the land on the left bank of the Oder sold for little more than half the price of that on the right bank. This suggested lack of local confidence that the district was firmly Polish.

I suggested that Lower Silesia between the Western and Eastern Neisse should be handed back to Germany as a final settlement, and that Poland should recover Lwow from the Soviet Union. I could foresee endless difficulties—especially in the latter part of the plan! But there was a time when Khrushchev was prepared to consider it.

Today, however, it would be impossible. Khrushchev has gone: and the land on the south bank is now almost as valuable as that on the right—a sure sign that the Poles believe that they have come to stay. Any new plan will have to be based on that premise.

V

The German outlook on the Oder-Neisse provinces is quite clear. Some years ago it was put to me very plainly by a German minister in Bonn.

"Suppose you had lost the war—after all, you might have done. Hitler says: 'Now, you English, I am going to detach the southern counties, from Kent to Cornwall. I don't want them myself—I shall give them to my friends the Vichy French. All the English must turn out of the southern counties at once—they can go to the Midlands and the North.'

"Well, you have lost the war, and have to comply. But, in your hearts, would you ever have admitted the loss of your southern counties? Of course not! You would have bided your time, and at an opportune moment you would have taken them back by fair means or foul. And if ever you got tired or reconciled to their loss, there would be plenty of refugees to remind you."

(Of the Federal German population of 50 million, more than 10 million are refugees, most of them from the Oder-Neisse provinces or from Czechoslovakia.)

The West German government established a Ministry of Refugees and Expellees. These still have local associations which organize events on all suitable occasions, and at one time sent a fair number of members to parliament—in 1953 they had 27 representatives. Gradually this number diminished, and today the associations have no parliamentary representation. But they still have a Minister!

There are still large numbers of Germans who lament the loss of their eastern provinces. Among the refugees, however, the yearning for their old homeland is much stronger among the older generation than the young. And the old people generally die off first.

Most of the young people have settled down willingly in Western Germany. To many, it is the attraction of the bright lights once again. The families of many came from Silesian or Pomeranian villages, and are now settled in German towns. There will always be a sentimental demand for the recovery of the lost territories, but it loses force year by year. And there *are* Germans who face the situation frankly. We have noted the comments of the German bishops. On the occasion of de Gaulle's visit to Poland and the angry comments on his speeches from Bonn, the *Neue Ruhr Zeitung*, a Socialist newspaper, wrote:

> Our Ministers should have regarded it as their duty to tell our people that Hitler's war has to be paid for. The General has done the Federal Government a service by insisting upon this truth. He has helped to open the eyes of dreamers in this country.

At the moment this is a minority outlook, but it is likely to intensify with the passage of time. But Hitler roused the Germans by waving a map of Danzig and the "Corridor". Any future Hitler could be just as dangerous with a map of the lost provinces.

At the moment protests are wordy: no one can suggest any useful action—for action involves the risk of war, wanted by no one.

The Poles seized upon the decline of the German Refugee Party eagerly, as a sign that German revisionism was waning. This could be true, but the contention assumes that only the refugees are interested in the recovery of the lost provinces. It is a universal German ambition to regain them, stimulated by every glance at a map. There are Germans who favour extreme methods, but the overwhelming majority favour revision by agreement, eschewing war. But no one can say for how long they will be in the majority.

In East Germany, of course, government pronouncements are very "correct". But opinions and comments among the ordinary people do not differ greatly from those in West Germany.

I met a group of East Germans in Wroclaw: they had fled in 1945, and were now visiting their old home town.

"We have no hope of coming back," said an elderly man. "Our government has recognized the Oder-Neisse frontiers as fair and just, as the Russians told them to do. Now my son lives in Western Germany. He tells me that the Silesian refugees are well organized there, and they are confident that one day they will return."

"They *want* to return?" I asked. "I have encountered a good many of the organizations you mention. They seem to consist largely of middle-aged and elderly people. The younger folk are doing well, and don't remember their old homes so vividly, so are not so eager to return."

"I suppose that is true," he admitted grudgingly. "But no true German will ever admit the justice of the Oder-Neisse frontier."

"How do you propose to amend it?"

"I don't know. We certainly don't want another war! It seems to me that the only hope is another pact between Germany and Russia, like the one Hitler and Stalin made in 1939."

The nervousness in Poland over the rise of neo-Nazi parties in West Germany can be understood. At the moment these are an unimportant minority, but Hitler started in the same way. The West German government can scarcely repress them by force: but it can point out to its people that extremist policies could lead to war. This would affect German viewpoints dramatically! I do not imply that every German has suffered a change of heart. But the final battles of the last war were fought on German soil. In a future war, Germany would be the scene of the *first* battles. No German wants that.

Is there any possibility of another pact on the Hitler-Stalin model? At the moment, none whatsoever. But in 1938 the idea of a Nazi-Communist agreement was derided: yet it happened.

There are occasional rumours in Poland and East Germany—sometimes mentioned in the Press—that one day Russia will decide after all to give Szczecin to East Germany. Another rumour suggests that Upper Silesia, with its industrial and mineral wealth, will be detached from Poland and become an autonomous state within the U.S.S.R. This could only be accomplished against fierce Polish opposition—led by the Communist leaders!

Political outlooks are changing in both Germany and Russia. No one can forecast the respective outlooks in either country in twenty or thirty years' time. History seldom repeats itself, but it does resemble itself. Hence the Polish nightmare.

The Poles have to put their trust in the Russian alliance—the only one available. Yet many of them are profoundly uneasy. We have seen that Poland was always in danger when Germany and Russia were friends.

The West Germans have already had plain hints from Russia. "You want to unite your country. Very well, you know our price. Germany must be completely neutralized. You can have a small army for internal security, but no more. You must leave the NATO pact and any other entangling alliances with the West—you can trade with Western countries, and play them at football, but you must not make military alliances with them. We want a neutralized Germany, on friendly terms with Russia.

"Those are our terms. If you are prepared to pay our price, we will allow you to unite with East Germany. We will even return your Oder-Neisse provinces. The Poles? Oh, we will clear them out for you. Maybe we will absorb Poland within the Soviet Union."

Such is the gist of the possible Russian idea. One day the hints could become open suggestions. The Western powers assume automatically that the German leaders would reject them. So they would, today, but what of their successors of tomorrow? The Russians are the only people who can offer precisely what the Germans want.

INDEX

A

Africa, 144, 206
Africa Corps, 167
America, 10ff, 27, 44, 59, 69ff, 79, 94, 111, 112, 120, 147, 150, 160, 180, 194, 198, 201, 207, 215, 224, 229, 237, 241
Arciszewski, M., 68, 242
Astrakhan, 11
Atlantic, 32
Atlantic Charter, 68
Attlee, Mr., 74
Auschwitz, *see* Oswiecym
Austria, 20, 22ff, 27, 29, 34, 37, 43, 93, 118, 119, 124, 180, 181, 187, 208, 225, 245

B

Balkans, 24
Baltic, 15, 17ff, 76, 97, 150, 151, 154, 155
Baria Giza, 91
Basques, 32
Beck, Colonel Josef, 48, 49, 50
Belgium, 55, 81, 180
Believers, the Old, 169
Belsen, 180
Bem, General Josef, 185
Berlin, 43, 82, 131, 150, 166ff
Berling, General, 197
Bevin, Ernest, 224
Bialowieza, 175, 176, 177
Bielo Russians, 29, 30, 31, 52, 217
Bierut (Krasnodebski), 73, 75
Bierutowice (Bruckenberg), 144
Biskupin, 149
Bismarck, 23, 53, 130
Bizezinka, 122
Black Market, 78, 103
Black Sea, 19
Blizna, 185, 187, 188
Bohemia, 15, 37, 130, 141, 143, 185, 240
Boleslas (Bolko), 128
Boleslas the Brave, 17, 24, 143, 148, 153
Boleslas Wry-mouth, 17, 134
Bolsheviks, 28, 29, 31, 36
Bonn, 181, 246, 247
Bor-Komorowski, General, 65, 67, 203, 204
Bo-Russians, 156, 157, 164
Bosphorus, 225

Brazil, 181
Breslau, *see* Wroclaw
Britain, 11ff, 28, 29, 37, 44ff, 51, 59, 62, 63, 65, 68ff, 74, 103, 166, 167, 180, 188, 189, 194, 202, 221, 224, 226, 241, 243, 244
  Battle of, 61, 94
Brown, George, 12
Brzeg-Lignica, 129
Budapest, 84, 86, 235
Bug, River, 187
Bulganin, Marshall, 83
Bulgaria, 180
Bursa, 155
Bydgoszcz, 53

C

Canada, 44, 113, 215
Capitalism, 11, 12
Carpathians, 15, 104, 184
Casimir the Great, 18, 229
Cassino, Monte, 94
Catalans, 32
Catherine the Great, 20
Catholic, 11, 23, 26, 87, 117, 118, 158, 164, 169, 201, 209ff, 220, 225, 229, 234ff
Cegielski Works, 82
Cepelia, 191
Chajnik, 143
Charlemagne, 16, 17
Charlie, Bonnie Prince, 20
Chicago, 93
China, 195, 196, 199, 222
Chopin, 92, 95, 223
Christianity, 16, 17, 19, 26, 57, 114, 150, 156, 167, 208, 210, 214, 216
Churchill, Winston, 55, 65, 68, 69, 72, 74, 75, 183, 204, 242
Clark Kerr, Sir A., 70
Code Napoleon, 22
Communism, 9ff, 29, 38, 60, 63, 66, 68, 72ff, 92, 95, 102, 107ff, 120, 126, 127, 135, 138, 146, 150, 155, 157, 160, 173, 196, 198ff, 220ff, 232ff, 243, 248ff
Constantinople, 17
Copenhagen, 228
Corpernicus, Nicolas, 115, 164
Corridor, Polish, 18, 20, 26, 28, 35, 36, 37, 49, 154, 155, 247

251